Practical Solutions to Practically Every Problem

The Early Childhood Teacher's Manual

by Steffen Saifer

Redleaf Press
St. Paul, Minnesota

Steffen Saifer has been a preschool teacher for nine years, the director of several early childhood programs, and a trainer for 12 years. He currently works as an Early Childhood Education Specialist with the Early Childhood Training Center at Portland State University, where he conducts research and trains staff for Head Start and other programs nationwide. He is also a doctoral candidate. Steffen lives with his son, Jonah, in Portland, Oregon where he enjoys running, biking, hiking, and skiing.

© 1990 by Steffen Saifer.

Cover photograph by Mike Fitzgerald.

ISBN: 0-934140-61-8

Published by: Redleaf Press
                 Formerly Toys 'n Things Press
                 a division of Resources for Child Caring
                 450 North Syndicate, Suite 5
                 St. Paul, Minnesota 55104

Distributed by: Gryphon House
                 PO Box 275
                 Mt. Rainier, Maryland 20712

Library of Congress Cataloging-in-Publication Data

Saifer, Steffen
   Practical solutions to practically every problem : the early childhood teacher's manual / by Steffen Saifer.
       p. cm.
   Includes bibliographical references and index.
   1. Education, Preschool--Handbooks, manuals, etc. 2. Preschool teaching--Handbooks, manuals, etc. 3. Preschool teachers--Handbooks, manuals, etc.
   LB1140.2.S235   1990
   372.21--dc20   90-42636 CIP

Printed in the United States of America.

Dedication

To Jonah Raphael Cohen Saifer and to early childhood teachers everywhere, who work so hard, care so much, and often get so little in return.

Acknowledgements

Dorothy Anker*
Alan Berlin*
Sue Bernt
Debra Blankenship
Kathy Bobula*
Claire Cavanaugh
Debora Cohen
Linda Crum

Ellen Galinsky
Stuart Gordin
Marilyn Harrison*
Rayko Hashimoto*
Janis Heigl
Jill Hix
Shelley Howard*
Karen Hyman
Nancy Jambor*

Jeannie Lybecker
Tammy McEnroe
Eileen Nelson
Cari Olmsted
Karen Ortiz
Mary Perkins*
Keith Stengel
David Wright*

I am particularly grateful to these people who reviewed the book offering great insight and assistance.

Foreword

Practical Solutions to Practically Every Problem: The Early Childhood Teacher's Manual, by Steffen Saifer, is one of those books that is so right that when you read it, you can't believe it hasn't existed forever. In fact, I found myself wondering why books like this haven't been written before. Perhaps it's because there has been an assumption that teaching young children is something that should come naturally. Perhaps that's why no one has written about the tricks of the trade—how to handle children who are disruptive at group time or children who are fussy at the beginning of the day, for example. This book was worth waiting for. It is comprehensive, solid, and easily accessible as a reference book.

I remember my very first day as a preschool teacher at Bank Street College's School for Children. Having settled the children for rest time, the woman with whom I was co-teaching left the room, with me in charge. The children took one look at me and rose up in unison, began jumping up and down, daring me to do something about it. Just at that moment, a group of observers stopped by my room to see the wonderful Bank Street teaching philosophy in action. Oh, if I had only had *Practical Solutions to Practically Every Problem* to turn to.

One thing that I particularly like about this book is that there are many solutions to problems. It is also a collaborative book, drawn from Steffen Saifer's extensive experience as well as from the wisdom of other teachers. In the introduction, he invites teachers to write in their best solutions so he can include them in subsequent editions of this book.

It would have been easy for a book that focuses on classroom management problems to stereotype children, parents, or directors. This book doesn't do so. It helps us understand other people's perspectives while dealing constructively with the issues.

All in all, this is an indispensible book. Its use will improve the quality of all of our teaching.

Ellen Galinsky
Co-President
Families and Work Institute

List of Illustrations

Table of Contents

Part IV — Children Who Must Cope with Major Changes (continued)

Part V — Children with Difficult Behaviors **109**

Introduction

The purpose of this book is to help make your job easier and to help you be more efficient and effective. This book will empower you to do what you know is necessary and right to make your classroom a fabulous place for children (and for you and your co-workers) to be nurtured, to learn, and to grow.

Know and follow the policies and procedures your program has in place. If some of those policies and procedures limit your ability to help your children and families thrive, work towards amending them in a helpful and positive way. Use this book as a resource and be open and clear to your supervisor and co-workers about what you want to change and why.

Also know your state's child care licensing requirements. If you work in a state licensed facility, you must abide by them. If they are more stringent than the recommendations in this book, the state's requirements must take precedence over this book's recommendations. If you work in a program that is not required to follow the state's regulations, you will still benefit from knowing them as they can provide helpful safety and health procedures.

This book approaches issues from the perspective of problems, but it also offers positive solutions. You will never eliminate all the problems in early childhood education. Instead, I hope to help you manage them so that, while working with young children and families, your experiences will be positive. When things are going well, no job on earth is more fun, more rewarding, and more important to society than teaching and caring for young children.

Carefully read the Preventing Problems section in each chapter. As you know, prevention is much easier than solving problems or coping with crises. If you didn't already believe in prevention, you would most likely be working with older children or in another field.

I have tried to make this book helpful to all early childhood educators. Although it focuses primarily on teachers of children between three and six years old, the book also offers numerous suggestions for working with younger children. Many of these ideas will work well with slightly older children. I make few distinctions between publicly funded and privately funded programs, between full-day and half-day programs, between public schools and Head Start, or between Montessori and developmental programs. In reality, excellent programs for young children have many more similarities than differences and the differences are exciting. They are ones of style and emphasis, which make for the diversity we need in education. Likewise, all good teachers essentially do the same things (see the preface) but with different styles, areas of strength, and talents. This book helps you solve problems while encouraging you to assert your own style.

I wrote this book for experienced and for new teachers, for teachers with formal educations and for teachers without. I assumed that all readers would be intelligent, capable, quick learners, and people who care deeply. For the new or not formally trained teacher I have strived to be clear, concise, and free of jargon. All teachers will find many new and useful ideas in this book.

By eliminating a great deal of theory, anecdotes, numerous examples, and detailed explanations, I have tried to provide you with direct, quick access to solutions. I have focused on the basic, most vital advice and information, which is based on current and revered theories. You can learn these theories through the resources listed at the end of most chapters.

Solving problems is hard. Rarely does one quick, easy answer suffice. Many times the cause of a problem is complex and multifaceted, or completely mysterious. Often problems are not what they appear to be on the surface. While I was in graduate school, an instructor told me a story about a four-year-old girl with whom she worked who had temper tantrums at seemingly random times. However, after close observation the instructor discovered that the child threw these fits every time she had to do a difficult fine-motor task, such as pouring juice from a pitcher and putting together a ten-piece puzzle. Rather than face the embarrassment of failing, she chose to create a distraction. After an outside observer saw this connection, the child's teacher was able to assist her with fine-motor tasks in ways that called little attention to her problem. The teacher gradually offered less and less help as the child matured and her skills improved.

The more severe the problem, the more complex, time-consuming, and difficult the solution. In most cases you will have to use many approaches, be persistent, and be very patient. However, I firmly believe that every problem has a solution.

One book cannot address all possible problems and many good solutions are undoubtedly missing in this book. I hope the suggestions included here will serve to stimulate your own ideas. Write to me in care of the publisher and let me know what you have come up with, what worked well, what didn't, and what is missing. Any future editions of this book will include the best ideas sent by contributors and will acknowledge them.

I mention classroom rules throughout the book. To get the most out of classroom rules, develop them with the children, explain the purpose of them clearly, have as few as possible, enforce them consistently, state them positively ("Walk inside the classroom" as opposed to "Don't run"), make them visual by posting a picture of the rule, follow them yourself, and include fun rules ("Run around a lot and yell loudly when you are outside" or "Always ask for a hug when you need one").

Keep this book handy in your classroom and use it often. Wear it out.

A favorite children's book of mine is *Miss Rumphius* (Clooney, B., New York: Viking, 1982). In this book, Miss Rumphius learns that the purpose of life is to leave the world a more beautiful place than it was when she came into it. This is a noble value to live by and to impart to children. Each day do something with or for your children that will make the world a little more beautiful. And have fun while you do it.

Steffen Saifer
Early Childhood Education Specialist
Divison of Continuing Education
Portland State University

The 20 Most Important Principles for Successful Preschool Teaching

1. Enjoy yourself! If you have fun, the children will have fun. Use humor generously.

2. Create an environment that has specific learning centers, many soft places, and child-sized furnishings. Make sure this environment is cheerful but not overly stimulating, clean but not overly tidy.

3. Base all your actions on a clear, easily stated philosophy of early childhood education. For example, "Young children learn and grow best when they are touching and interacting with real things and caring people around them."

4. Set your schedule so that children spend most of their time in active learning of their own choosing. Provide opportunities to learn through playing games, using building toys, exploring objects from nature, acting out roles, and using art materials.

5. Without being intrusive, involve yourself actively while children play. Observe their play and extend their play by adding materials and asking questions about it. Be available when needed.

6. Teach skills or give information individually or in very small groups, through active, playful and meaningful activities. Don't break down activities into isolated skills. For example, develop cutting skills by having children cut out their name tags to tape to their cubbies rather than by having them cut predrawn lines on a sheet of paper.

7. Match your curriculum to the needs and interests of the children. Note that the type of activities you use and their length will be different for a group of children who have short attention spans, lots of anger, many emotional needs, and little interest in academics, than for a group of children who have long attention spans, high self-esteem, and a great deal of interest in academics.

8. Teach children specific skills for getting along with others, solving conflicts, and acting cooperatively.

9. Give children many chances to make decisions, be leaders, make real choices, and be responsible. Set as your goal that children will be eager and interested in learning on their own in a class that almost runs itself. Encourage children to be in control of themselves rather than to be controlled by you. For example, place a kitchen timer where children can easily use it to set up a turn-taking system for themselves.

10. Tell children often and enthusiastically what they are doing well and how they are competent. Be specific.

11. Teach children correct behavior and give meaningful consequences, if needed, for continued misbehaviors. Avoid using rewards and punishment. Set as your goal that children will get self-satisfaction from their own achievements and actions.

12. Give children many opportunities to interact and to talk with each other in positive ways.

13. Treat all children equitably, but not identically. Recognize and meet individual needs and strengths.

14. Plan, review, plan. Prepare your activities and environment thoroughly and carefully in advance. Review what worked and what didn't. Based on your review, plan again.

15. Know your children and their families well. Do everything you can to communicate with parents and to receive information from parents. To establish rapport, increase your understanding of the child, and build trust, do home visits to willing families. Invite families to your home.

16. Share ideas and problems with other professionals in the field. Ask a respected colleague or supervisor to observe you teach and give you feedback. Benefit your classroom by using the insights you gain.

17. Take responsibility for your own growth and support the growth of other staff members. Don't wait to be sent to a class to learn a new

skill or to solve a problem; get the information from someone who knows it or from a book or magazine.

18. Use new ideas from reading, workshops, and training sessions to make changes in your classroom.

19. Know your limitations. Ask for help when you need it.

20. Accept responsibility for the quality of your program. Avoid excuses like "There isn't enough money" or "There's not enough time." Rather than create problems or complain about them, help solve them.

Part I
Daily Dilemmas

1. The Daily Schedule: An Active and Purposeful Program

The key to a successful daily schedule is alternating long, active periods with short, quiet periods and alternating short, teacher-directed activities with long, child-initiated activities. Young children are naturally active and learn best by exploring and discovering for themselves. Imposing long periods of quiet, sedentary activities on children will result in rebellious behaviors and will reduce vital learning opportunities.

The following samples will give you ideas for developing a workable schedule for your classroom. Make changes to fit your particular program's goals, equipment, meal schedule, space constraints, and the needs of your particular children.

Many half-day programs run less than four hours. Depending on whether you eliminate one or both meals, make adjustments to the following schedule. Keep about the same length of time for free choice and the outdoor/gym part of the schedule. Shorten other parts of the schedule if necessary.

Half-Day Toddler Program			
8:30 - 8:45	Limited Free Choice (table toys, puzzles playdough, and so on.)	10:35 - 10:40	Story
8:45 - 8:50	Circle Time	10:40 - 11:40	Outdoor/Gym (includes creative movement)
8:50 - 9:00	Wash Hands and Toileting	11:40 - 11:45	Book Browse
9:00 - 9:20	Breakfast	11:45 - 11:50	Music
9:20 - 10:25	Free Choice (includes teacher prepared art and individual attention)	11:50 - 12:00	Wash Hands and Toileting
		12:00 - 12:20	Lunch
10:25 - 10:35	Clean-up	12:20 - 12:25	Toothbrushing
		12:25 - 12:30	Closing Circle and Dismissal

Full-Day Toddler Program			
7:00 - 8:35	Free Choice (with some teacher-prepared activities and individual attention)	11:50 - 12:00	Wash Hands and Toileting
		12:00 - 12:20	Lunch
		12:20 - 12:25	Toothbrushing
8:35 - 8:45	Clean up	12:25 - 12:30	Story
8:45 - 8:50	Circle Time	12:30 - 2:30	Nap Time
8:50 - 9:00	Wash Hands and Toileting	2:30 - 2:50	Snack
9:00 - 9:20	Breakfast	2:50 - 4:00	Free Choice (includes teacher-prepared activities and individual attention)
9:20 - 10:25	Outdoor/Gym (includes creative movement)		
10:25 - 10:35	Story	4:00 - 4:05	Creative Drama or Story
10:35 - 11:40	Free Choice (includes teacher-prepared art and individual attention)	4:05 - 5:30	Outdoor/Gym (includes creative movement/ dance)
11:40 - 11:45	Music	5:30 - 5:35	Music/Rhythm
11:45 - 11:50	Book Browse	5:35 - 6:00	Art and Limited Free Choice

Half-Day Preschool Program

8:30 - 8:45	Limited Free Choice (table toys, puzzles, playdough, and so on.)		10:25 - 10:35	Clean-up
8:45 - 9:00	Circle Time		10:35 - 10:45	Story
9:00 - 9:05	Wash Hands		10:45 - 11:00	Small-Group Time
9:05 - 9:25	Breakfast		11:00 - 11:45	Outdoor/Gym (includes creative movement/ dance)
9:25 - 10:25	Free Choice (includes individual attention and teacher-prepared art and hands-on math activities). Breakfast is available to eat when individual children wish.		11:45 - 11:50	Silent Reading
			11:50 - 11:55	Wash Hands
			11:55 - 12:15	Lunch
			12:15 - 12:20	Toothbrushing
			12:20 - 12:30	Music and Dismissal

Full-Day Preschool Program

7:00 - 8:35	Free Choice (includes individual attention and teacher-prepared art and hands-on math activities)		11:50 - 12:00	Music/Movement/Rhythm
			12:00 - 12:05	Wash Hands
			12:05 - 12:25	Lunch
8:35 - 8:45	Clean-up		12:25 - 12:30	Toothbrushing
8:45 - 9:00	Circle Time		12:30 - 12:40	Silent Reading
9:00 - 9:05	Wash Hands		12:40 - 2:10	Nap Time
9:05 - 9:25	Breakfast		2:10 - 3:30	Free Choice (includes teacher prepared activities and individual attention). Snack is available to eat when individual children wish.
9:25 - 10:15	Outdoor/Gym (includes creative movement/ dance)			
10:15 - 10:25	Story		3:30 - 3:40	Story
10:25 - 10:40	Small-Group Time		3:40 - 5:00	Outdoor/Gym (includes creative movement/dance)
10:40 - 11:40	Free Choice (includes teacher prepared activities and individual attention)			
			5:00 - 5:15	Creative Drama
11:40 - 11:50	Clean-up		5:15 - 6:00	Art and Limited Free Choice

2. Starting the Day Off Right

The tone of the day for you and the children is often set in the first few minutes of the day. Children arrive at the center in many different moods and with very different early morning experiences. By respecting those differences and accommodating them whenever possible, the children will have a much better chance for a successful day.

Preventing Problems

➤ Greet each child and parent individually as they enter. Look them in the eye and use their names.

➤ If you and the child feel comfortable, make physical contact with her by hugging or by touching the child on the arm or shoulder. (This lets the child know that her presence is acknowledged and important.)

➤ Arrange for children (and adults) to wash their hands soon after arriving. Invite parents who bring their children to school to guide their handwashing. (This will help stop the spread of "germs" from home and greatly control disease in your program.)

➤ If children enter in a large group all at once, have them go to choose one of a variety of activities. If breakfast or a circle time comes early in the schedule, you may want to keep the children's choices limited to activities that can be cleaned up quickly. Use this time to greet each child individually, as described above.

➤ Set Free Choice Time early in your schedule. Note that children get anxious and restless waiting for the period of time they like the best. Being surrounded by enticing materials, activities, and friends, and not being able to interact with them is difficult for young children. They may refuse to comply, act silly, or misbehave. Scheduling free choice early in the day for at least forty-five minutes will prevent behavior problems from occurring.

➤ Time your first meal or snack to make it work for your own group of children. Experiment with the timing so that as many children as possible are getting the food when they are hungry, but not when they are too hungry. If they are eating the food quickly and voraciously, are irritable, or do not listen well before the meal, then you are scheduling the meal too late. If many children pick at their food and are sleepy during the meal, then the meal is coming too soon. Kitchen staff can usually be more flexible with breakfast. If necessary, make it yourself with the children. Hungry or overfed children will be difficult children.

Dealing with Existing Problems

Children Who Have a Hard Time Separating from Their Parents

➤ Encourage parents to spend five or ten relaxed minutes when dropping off and picking up their children. Invite parents to chat with staff and play with their children during this time. This helps ease the transition for the children. However, encourage parents to leave quickly and smoothly once they have given their child a goodbye kiss. Both rushing in and out or lingering too long can add to the anxiety of separation.

➤ If the child is still anxious when the parent needs to leave, hold the child's hand or put your arm around her shoulders and say: "I'm glad you're here. Now it's time for parents to go to work and children to go to school. You'll see Mom again when she comes to pick you up. Let's go see what there is to do today." Lead the child away as you

both wave goodbye.

➤ As a way to ease the transition, let the child bring in something comforting from home, such as a favorite stuffed animal. Or give the child something to hold on to that symbolizes the parent. This may be a picture of her parent(s) or an item from Mom's purse or Dad's pocket. Something like an (extra) house key works well because the child knows the parent must return to get it—which may be the cause of the separation fear.

Children Who Are Very Fussy at the Start of the Day

➤ You may have children in your class who are highly active, lethargic, very grouchy, or defiant in the morning—but they improve as the day progresses. Parents may know the cause, or the problem may be due to one or more of the following reasons:

Allergies: A child who is sensitive to particular fabrics may be grouchy in the morning because of sleeping on synthetic bedding. If this type of allergy runs in the child's family, she is probably affected also. Using only cotton and other natural fibers for bedding and clothing should relieve the symptoms. Food allergies can also cause behavior problems. Many children are allergic to typical breakfast foods, such as milk, eggs, and wheat. Suggest to parents that they eliminate one category of food at a time to determine if the removal of this food improves the way their child feels. This is best done with the guidance of an understanding doctor. (See "Active and Distracted," on pages 119 to 120, for more information.)

Lack of Food: Some children may arrive at school having had little or no dinner the previous night and little or no breakfast that morning. Securing food is your first priority, if the parents cannot. Teaching young children means meeting all their basic needs. Children who are hungry will learn little. In one public school, a kindergarten teacher was able to give a midmorning snack to the children from funds for children with special needs. Because the children made the snack themselves, it became a learning experience

Lack of Sleep: Ask the child which TV show she watched the previous night to determine the time the child went to bed. Discuss with parents the importance of an early, consistent bedtime. Make a cot available for any tired child to take a short nap at any time during the class.

Chaos: Too Much Going On at Once

Parents want to talk to you, several children are demanding your attention, the director needs you, your assistant has a question, and two children are chasing each other through the room! This probably sounds familiar, because all teachers have had mornings like this.

➤ Remember that children must always come first. Adults can wait. Greet and talk with parents each day, but if you are concerned about the children's behavior or well-being, ask an assistant to help the children or excuse yourself from the adult conversation.

➤ Keep a clipboard or note pad on a bulletin board posted near the door for parents, visitors, or other staff to write messages to you.

➤ To reduce attention-getting behaviors, greet children warmly and individually when they enter, as described earlier in this chapter. Make sure the children can get settled into the first routine of the day without much help. If the children cannot read their names, tape a picture of them in their cubbies. Have children help each other in the morning. ("Ask three before you ask me" is a great classroom rule. The three refers to three other children. This will also foster independence and communication between children.)

➤ Assign each adult, including yourself, some tasks to do each morning before the children arrive. Keep the written task-list posted. To provide variety and the opportunity to learn new skills, swap the set of tasks once a month. The lists, prepared ahead of time, might look like this:

Adult #1

a) Mix paints and set up easel.

b) Take trikes and wagons out.

c) Set out the following activities on tables:

Activity:	Cherry Picker board game
Located:	red storage shelf
Place it:	round table

Activity:	five puzzles
Located:	puzzle rack on wood shelves
Place it:	rectangular table by window

Adult #2

a) Take chairs down from tables.

b) Wipe off tables.

c) Set out the following gross-motor equipment:

Equipment:	large ball, frisbee, bat and ball
Located:	in classroom closet near front door
Place it:	on bench next to porch

Equipment:	plastic climber
Located:	storage shed behind building
Place it:	grassy area in center of field

➤ Write your task-list daily on paper forms or on a reusable writing surface like a chalkboard or markerboard. Organize clean-up tasks in a similar way.

Resources

Alger, H.A. "Transitions: Alternatives to Manipulative Management." *Young Children* 39(6) (September 1984): 16-25.

3. Circle Time: Meeting Individual Needs in a Group

Circle time, also called group time, refers to any time that a group of children are sitting together for an activity involving everyone. Typically this might include reading a story, sharing events from the weekend, playing rhythm instruments, or singing songs.

Preventing Problems

➤ Keep your circle time short! (Most groups of toddlers have a maximum attention span of five to ten minutes. For most groups of preschoolers the maximum is ten to fifteen minutes.) Start the year with the circle time lasting a few minutes and gradually increase the the time throughout the year.

➤ Several short circle times with part of the group is better than one long one with the whole group. These can take place during the course of the day or simultaneously, if enough staff is available. Short circle times with small groups allow you to give more individual attention, increase children's chances for participation, and have fewer distractions for children.

➤ As a guideline for children to sit on, place tape in the shape of a circle on the floor. If more defined guides are needed, put six-inch-long pieces of tape on the floor for each child to sit in back of. (This provides individual spaces so children will not conflict with each other. Some groups of children, particularly older preschoolers, attend better when sitting on chairs placed around the circle.)

➤ Hold circle activities away from toy shelves and other attractive places in the room. Make the circle big enough to seat all the children comfortably.

➤ Establish one or two simple circle time rules and remind children of them at the start of the circle. They might be the following:
  "Keep your hands next to your own body."
  "Talk only when no one else is talking."

➤ Avoid using circle time for teaching specific skills. Circle time is most successful when you use it for singing together, playing movement games (like "Hokey Pokey"), listening to stories, partici- pating in active group games that involve handling things or moving, watching films, planning activities for the day, making classroom rules, or assigning "jobs" for the day.

➤ Plan circle activities that are not too difficult nor too easy to follow, and are highly interesting to your particular group. Prepare well. Know your material well enough that you can stray from your plans, answer unexpected questions, and easily get back on track.

➤ Start off your circle time with an active but not boisterous game that requires the children to focus and attend, but not sit still and quiet. You might use the game "Follow the Rhythm." With everyone sitting around the circle, tap out a simple rhythm and then invite the children to repeat it. Make the rhythm a little harder each time you tap. Give some children a chance to lead the game. After playing for a minute or two, begin your circle activity. (This type of activity will draw children to the circle who have not yet made the transition.)

➤ If your planned activity does not hold the children's interest, have alternative activities to use or move on to the next activity.

➤ Place another adult (teacher, assistant, or volunteer) behind the children in the circle. There she or he can see the whole group and move quickly to an area where children are having a hard time. Sometimes just sitting behind them or gently touching their backs will settle them.

➤ If possible, involve all adults in the group activity. An assistant or volunteer who is doing other things within sight or sound of the circle will be distracting. Adults who participate can act as role models for the children.

Dealing with Existing Problems

Hitting, Arguing, or Talking with Each Other

Boredom during circle time is the most common cause of hitting, arguing, or talking with others. Follow the suggestions in "Preventing Problems" to make the circle time short and stimulating.

➤ Keep the children who "set each other off" away from each other in the circle. If necessary, assign seats.

➤ Focus your attention and encouragement on the children who are behaving well. Say things like the following, "Thank you, Sam, for looking right at me. It lets me know you're listening well." Give minimal attention to misbehavior.

➤ Remind the children of the circle time rules you have established.

➤ Begin your activity without waiting for everyone to join or be entirely quiet. Start with a louder voice to get the children's attention and quickly tone down your voice when the talking or moving has stopped.

➤ At the start of your activity, remind the children that they will have an opportunity to talk right after you have finished.

➤ During group games, give children opportunities to be the "Teacher" and decide what the group should do.

➤ Use a nonverbal cue to get the children's attention, such as placing your thumb and index finger in the shape of an *L* and putting it by your ear (American Sign Language for *listen*). Use this cue to remind children that this is a time to listen. Quickly go back to your activity.

➤ Whenever possible, give children opportunities to talk and move in appropriate ways. Involve them actively during the circle. For example, invite the children to take turns holding the book being read. For well-known stories, leave off the ends of some sentences for the children to finish. Ask questions occasionally to give children opportunities to talk.

Can't Sit Still

➤ For a variety of reasons, some children cannot sit still for more than a few seconds. For these children, provide an alternative quiet activity, such as doing puzzles or drawing at a nearby table, where they will not distract the circle. (This is not a punishment or a reward, but a recognition of the different needs of the children. If they were able to exercise control, they would.) If other children want to do this additional activity also, explain that the children are choosing another activity because sitting quietly is difficult for them at this time, although they will get better at it. Tell the children who *can* sit still that they are able to sit and listen well and that you appreciate their participation in circle.

➤ For some active children, sitting on an adult's lap during circle will provide the soothing stimulation to keep them calm.

➤ Let the children who cannot sit still start the circle with the others, but when they are close to reaching their limit, give them a choice of alternative quiet activities or listening a little longer. Note that the time they are able to stay in the circle should gradually increase if you are also working on the root cause of the problem. (See "Helping Children with Difficult Behaviors," pages 110 to 112, for more information.)

➤ If a child is still disruptive to the group, even after given the opportunity to do another activity, another adult (who is not leading the circle) should calmly guide him to a place where the child can be involved in a solitary activity but cannot be seen or heard. The adult should keep an eye on the child but give as little attention as possible, as the goal of disruptive behavior is usually to get attention. Tell the child that he can return to the activity (or the circle) when he is ready to work quietly. Give the child lots of encouragement when he does return and is quiet for a few seconds. Say something like the following: "I can tell that you're really listening because you're quiet. That's very polite because now everyone can hear."

Interruptions Directed to the Teacher

➤ Ignore the first interruption (unless the child needs to use the bathroom or has some other emergency). If the child interrupts again, he will likely keep interrupting until you will have to respond. Act on the second interruption. (Usually it will be a request like "Tie my shoe" or "Can I get a drink of water?" Or, the child may ask a question about the activity.) Tell the child that you are very interested in what he has to say but that he must wait until the end of circle time. If the child interrupts again, signal by nodding your head to another adult to help the child with his needs. Go back to the activity quickly.

➤ Keep a mental note of the nature of the distraction. At a later time, talk with the child about what he may be able do differently the next time so as not to interrupt.

Bored Children during "Show and Tell"

➤ Limit the number of children who share during "Show and Tell" by assigning some to share only on Monday, others on Tuesday, and so on. Consider doing "Show and Tell" in small groups as this will keep the time appropriately short.

➤ Involve all the children in this activity by making sure the child who is talking speaks to the other children, not just to you. Encourage the other children to ask questions of the child who is sharing. Place yourself behind the child to facilitate this.

➤ Have children share family experiences, a picture they made, or what they did earlier in the day at school. Sharing themselves rather than things, helps children who have no item to share; develops the children's ability to review; and makes for more personal, meaningful sharing.

(For additional ideas on getting children to circle and to the next activity after circle, read "Transitions: Structuring Unplanned Time" on pages 31 to 33.)

Resources

McAfee, O. "Circle Time: Getting Past 'Two Little Pumpkins.' " In *Reducing Stress in Young Children's Lives*, edited by J.B. McCracken. Washington DC: NAEYC, 1986.

McAfee, O. "Group Time in Early Education: An Exploratory Study." Paper presented at NAEYC, Los Angeles, 1984. (Eric Doc. #251 243).

4. Successful Small-Group Learning

If you are not already doing so, schedule a time during the day for fifteen to twenty minutes of small-group learning. Plan to have at least three small groups of children in three areas of the room (or at three tables) working on activities at the same time. If you have enough staff, plan on each group doing a different activity with an adult. Rotate the groups to a different activity each day, so by the third day, every child will have done all three activities. For the remaining two days of the week, repeat the more popular activities, introduce new activities, or do a combination of both. For the activities, include art or craft projects, dictating or writing stories, simple science activities, lotto games, simple board games, manipulating objects to learn counting and math, memory games, or cooking projects. By doing this, you individualize more than you can in a large group. You can provide direct information, answer questions, encourage problem solving, and give more feedback to individual children. Also, you can provide more challenging activities than children can do on their own during Free Choice. Finally, with these small groups you are able to observe children better. You can more readily determine how they think, act, and feel and what their strengths and weaknesses are. You can then plan and adjust activities accordingly.

Preventing Problems

➤ To get children to their places easily, name each group. Place a picture of that name on the table or the area where the children are to go. For example, the six children who are in the "Tiger" group will go to the table with the picture of the tiger placed in the center. Similarly, the children in the "Bear" group and those in the "Elephant" group will go to their tables. Give each child a picture tag that corresponds to her group. Attach this tag to the child's clothing. Within a few weeks, each child should know her group.

➤ Prepare all your materials and written instructions for the other adults ahead of time. Discuss the activities with the adults beforehand so your expectations are clear. Tell them why the children are doing the activity and what you want the children to gain from it.

➤ Develop activities that involve the children in handling real objects and that do *not* consist of children using only pencil and paper or adults demonstrating something or lecturing.

➤ Divide children into mixed groups. Include within each group some slow learners and some quick learners, some compliant children as well as difficult children. (This allows children to learn from each other and to help each other.)

➤ As the activity is taking place, individualize when you see the need. If a child is having difficulty, ask her to do only part of the activity, give extra help in accomplishing it, or offer a different way of doing it.

➤ Individualize according to abilities. For example, if your activity is making playdough, invite the child with poor small-motor coordination to pour liquids from the measuring cup into a large bowl. Encourage the child with good small-motor coordination to pour and measure a tablespoon of oil. Invite the child with reading skills to read the recipe for the group. Encourage the child with poor counting skills to count along with another child the number of tablespoons of salt needed. Plan for this before the activity.

Dealing with Existing Problems

Not Enough Staff

➤ Small-group time requires a capable adult for each group. If only two are available, you can have two groups with the third involved in an activity they can do well on their own, with some occasional checking. In any case, include no more than six children in a small group.

➤ As an alternative to this or if you are the only adult, extend your free choice time and involve five or six children in a small group activity while the others are in free choice. When the first group is done, choose a different group of children to do the same activity, until all the children have participated. Unless you are doing a long project that will take several days to complete, select a different small-group activity each day. (The drawbacks to this system are that pulling children away from free choice activities is difficult, the continuity of their play is broken, and you cannot be actively involved in free choice while working with small groups.)

➤ To minimize the drawbacks, allow children to save whatever they have constructed during Free Choice Time by making themselves a "Do Not Touch" sign or placing their project in a special "saving" place. (They can then pick up where they left off and not worry about others ruining their work.) Also make free choice long enough so that children have time to play after they are done with small group, and you can have time to be with children during free choice.

Bored or Resistant Children

If your children clearly indicate that they would rather be doing something else, try some of these ideas:

➤ Plan activities that involve the children actively in movement or in handling real objects. Provide many chances for each child to talk and to do.

➤ Use more activities that are creative, that allow children to express themselves, and that do not require one right answer. (Using three wood scraps to build and glue a sculpture is more satisfying than circling the picture of three balloons on a ditto sheet. Yet the same information—the concept of three—is being taught in both activities.)

➤ Shorten each small-group activity so that children have to sit for only a few minutes.

➤ Schedule very physical activities, such as outdoor play, gym play, or movement games, before and after your small-group time.

➤ Lead a short stretching game (e.g., "Shake Your Sillies Out" or "Head, Shoulders, Knees, and Toes") just before small-group time and/or between each small-group activity.

Resources

Activity Ideas

Baratta-Lorton. *Math Their Way*. Menlo Park, CA: Addison-Wesley, 1976.

Baratta-Lorton. *Workjobs*. Menlo Park, CA: Addison-Wesley, 1972.

Baratta-Lorton. *Workjobs II*. Menlo Park, CA: Addison-Wesley, 1978.

Gilbert, La Britta. *I Can Do It! I Can Do It!* Mt. Rainier, MD: Gryphon House, 1984.

Graves, M. *The Idea Book*. Ypsilanti, MI: High/Scope Press, 1989.

Jorde-Bloom, Paula. *Living and Learning with Children*. Washington, DC: Acropolis, 1981.

Kamii, C. and DeVries, R. *Group Games in Early Education: Implications of Piaget's Theory.* Washington, DC: NAEYC, 1980.

Karnes, Merle B. *Creative Games For Learning.* Reston, VA: The Council For Exceptional Children, 1977.

Madras, Lynda. *Child's Play.* Culver City, CA: Peace Press, 1977.

Marzollo, Jean, and Lloyd, Janice. *Learning Through Play.* New York: Harper & Row, 1972.

Movement Ideas

Cherry, Clare. *Creative Movement for the Developing Child.* Belmont, CA: Fearon, 1971.

Sullivan, M. *Feeling Strong, Feeling Free: Movement Exploration For Young Children.* Washington, DC: NAEYC, 1982.

Torbert, Marianne. *Follow Me: A Handbook of Movement Activities for Children.* New York: Prentice Hall, 1980.

Valeri, Michele, and McKelvey, Janice. *Wiggle Your Waggles Away.* Washington, DC: Wolf Trap Foundation, 1985.

Weikart, P. *Movement Plus Rhymes, Songs, & Singing Games.* Ypsilanti, MI: High/Scope Press, 1988.

Videos

Small Group Time Video Series. High/Scope, Dept. 10, 600 N. River Street, Ypsilanti, MI 48198.
1. *Counting with Bears.* 17 minutes.
2. *Plan-Do-Review with Found Materials.* 25 minutes.
3. *Working with Staplers.* 12 minutes.
4. *Representing with Sticks and Balls.* 14 minutes.
5. *Exploring with Paint & Corks.* 12 minutes.

5. Free Choice: Making Learning Fun

Since young children learn best through play (which is set up and guided by skilled teachers), free choice time provides the greatest opportunity for learning. Free choice is the time children love the most. They get to decide what they want to do, how to do it, and for how long.

Preventing Problems

➤ Schedule the first free choice time early in the day and for at least forty-five minutes.

➤ Involve yourself with your children's play and move around the room. Don't control the play or tell them what to do. Ask questions. Add supplies and equipment to expand their play.

➤ Rotate equipment. Keep some in storage and then bring out this equipment after several months. When you do this, put some other equipment away to reduce the boredom caused when children use the same toys every day.

➤ Change the dramatic play area fairly often. Have the children help you set up a post office for three or four weeks, then a restaurant for several weeks, then a campground. Have the children come up with other ideas. If space is available, have a permanent "house" area but change the materials and supplies on a regular basis.

➤ Set out a variety of activities to choose from, such as art materials, paint and easels, board games, puzzles, water play and clay.

➤ Use free choice time to interact with some children one to one. Make special time with the teacher one of the choices.

➤ Establish a system where children place cards with their names on them at the area they choose to use. This will help them plan and think ahead. You can limit the number of children in each area by having a set number of hooks to place their name cards on.

➤ Set up projects for children to pursue playfully and help guide them when necessary. Invite them to help decide the subject of the projects. (This might include designing and building a school bus, creating a large "sculpture" of a dinosaur, creating a model of the school or the neighborhood, or developing an elaborate hospital area.) To help them learn through play, ask questions about what they need and how they can obtain or make it; read information about the subject of their projects; and help them use tools and skills to measure, count, write, diagram, graph, and negotiate. (See "Project Work" in "Selecting and Using a Curriculum," on page 44, for further information.)

Dealing with Existing Problems

The Child Who Spends Most of His Time in One Area

This is not necessarily a problem. A child who is three years old or under or who is a slow learner needs to spend time using materials over and over. This is particularly true early in the year when equipment and games are new to the child.

➤ If you are concerned about this, add some variety to the child's play. Introduce new materials or suggest different ways to play with the same materials.

➤ Entice the child into other areas by providing challenging and fun art projects, cooking projects, water or sand play, woodworking or a new dramatic play center.

➤ If a child uses an area too much, close it to all children for one or two days per week. (This will give the child a chance to try new areas.)

➤ If enticements do not work and closing the area brings shrieks of protest, consider that the child is getting something from playing in that area that is vitally important to him emotionally or physically. Back down. Be patient. Let the child continue using that area for another month or two before trying again to promote a change.

The Child Who Spends Very Little Time in Any One Area

Free choice can be over-stimulating to some children. They are so excited by all the activities and choices that they can't settle down. So, you see them move quickly from area to area.

➤ Cut down on the number of choices offered if this does not adversely effect your program too much. Gradually add more, one at a time. Start the year off with a limited number of choices and then add more as the year progresses.

➤ For the child who is over-stimulated, create a small, quiet area that is blocked off from most of the room, although make sure that you can easily see into the area. Typically this is a library corner. But if you have enough room, create another private place, containing a small table with one or two chairs. Encourage the child to play with building toys or other games in this area, perhaps with one friend. Stay with the child for a short time to help him focus on the activity. Ask questions, talk about what the child is doing, or do the activity yourself at the same time.

➤ Use a refrigerator box to make a private space for one child. Encourage the child to use this space when she feels over-stimulated.

➤ Make free-standing cardboard dividers (one-and-a-half feet high) that can be placed on the sides and in front of the child while he works at the table on a project. (This will cut down on the visual distractions around him.)

➤ Another reason a child may not stay in any area of the room very long is that the activities there are not challenging. Provide different levels of complexity for different activities and within an activity. For example, make available a wide variety of art supplies and collage materials so that a child can create a simple or very detailed project according to his interest and ability.

➤ Before free choice time, ask the child to tell you what he will do and in which areas he will play. Encourage the child to stick to his plans. (This will help the child who flits from one area to another to become organized. As most preschool children are developing self-organizing skills, doing this with all your children is a good idea.)

Too Noisy, Too Boisterous

If fights break out and the noise level rises to an intolerable level, try some of the following ideas.

➤ Establish a classroom rule that only quiet voices can be used inside the classroom. Demonstrate what a quiet voice sounds like. Remind the children of the rule just before free choice. Let them know that they will be able to use loud voices when they are outside.

➤ Provide more activities with more challenges to keep the children's interest high.

➤ Put number limits on the noisiest areas, at least temporarily.

➤ Encourage children who are playing appropriately by saying something like the following: "Thank you for using a quiet voice. It helps make the room a pleasant place for everyone to work."

➤ Provide enough supplies to prevent arguments over toys. Purchase duplicates of popular toys, especially for toddlers.

➤ Provide supplies and activities that are fun and of high interest to the children—not too easy and not too difficult.

➤ If one or two children are responsible for the high noise level or most of the fights, remind them of the quiet voice rule. Tell them that if the incident happens again, they will have to choose a quiet activity to do by themselves. Follow through on the consequence if necessary. If this happens, tell them they can return to play anywhere when they feel ready. Every five to ten minutes, tell them that they are playing well: "When you play well we can all hear each other, nobody gets a headache, and everyone stays safe. Thank you."

Too Messy

➤ Children may misuse the blocks, table games, the dramatic play area, or other areas, so that materials are left in a mess or are damaged. If this happens, remind children of rules like the following:

"Take blocks from the shelf as you need them to build."

"Put items back in their place when you are finished using them."

"Pick up anything from the floor that belongs on a table or shelf."

"Use all materials so that they don't break or hurt anyone."

➤ Remind the children of these rules before they use the area and make sure each item has a specific place that is clearly labeled for the children. Lead children back to an area they have left messy and have them straighten it up.

➤ Observe the children's play carefully. If it starts to get out of control (which will lead to misuse of materials), help them by suggesting a different direction for the play, adding new materials, taking a role in the play, or redirecting them to different activities.

➤ Briefly demonstrate and discuss the various ways different materials can be used appropriately. Ask the children for ideas and help them determine if their ideas make safe and constructive use of the materials. (This is especially important to do when a new dramatic play area is set up.)

Resources

Bredekamp, S., ed. *Developmentally Appropriate Practice in Early Childhood Programs Serving Children from Birth through Age 8.* Washington, DC: NAEYC, 1987.

Katz, L., and Chard, S. *Engaging Children's Minds: The Project Approach.* Norwood, NJ: Ablex, 1989.

Rogers, C.S., and Sawyers, J.K. *Play in the Lives of Children.* Washington, DC: NAEYC, 1988.

Wardle, F. "Guest Editorial: Getting Back to the Basics of Children's Play." *Exchange* 57 (September 1987): 27-30.

Watts, D.W. "Extraterrestrial Children and Techno-Professional Society: Why 'Learning Through Play' Has Not Caught On." *Early Childhood Education* 21(1) (Winter 1987-1988): 26-31.

6. Mealtimes Can Be Pleasant

Mealtimes are opportunities to teach children healthy eating habits, a positive attitude toward food, and pleasant manners. it can be a time for quiet reflection and conversation. However, some children use mealtimes to engage you in a power struggle or to assert themselves in a negative way. Some children have already developed very poor eating habits. The ideas in this chapter will help you make mealtimes relaxing and enjoyable for all.

Preventing Problems

➤ Arrange tables for eating so that they are not close together. (This will help keep the noise level down.) To avoid the need for you or the children to get up and down often, set the tables so that all food, utensils, and supplies are close at hand.

➤ Avoid making children wait at the table to start

eating or wait for others to finish at the end of the meal. This causes boredom, which leads to acting out. If they must sit for a short time, lead the children in a song, finger play, or simple riddle game to engage their interest.

➤ If everyone can begin the meal together without waiting, start with a short ritual, such as a grace (if you work in a religious-affiliated program); a poem about friendship; a song of thanks; or a "secular grace," such as "Thank you, Earth. Thank you, Sun. We won't forget what you have done" or "I like the moon. I like the trees. I like the food the earth brings me." (This sets a quiet, contemplative tone to start the meal and gets all the children settled down and focused.)

➤ To teach responsibility, manners, promote language skills, and reduce behavior problems, actively involve children during mealtimes. Before the meal, assign children to jobs as "Waiters" (set the tables) and as "Custodians" (wipe the tables, sweep the floor). Unless you are not permitted to do so for health reasons, serve food family-style in bowls for children to pass around and

serve themselves. When finished, allow all the children to clear their own places, scrape their plates, throw away paper trash, and put dirty silverware in a container.

➤ To prevent children from licking serving spoons during family-style service, put bright red tape or another marker that can be felt as well as seen on the handle of the spoon. Remind children at the start of the meal that red-taped spoons are for serving and passing only. Explain to them that keeping the spoons away from their mouths keeps them clean and that using clean spoons helps everyone get fewer colds. Note that the greater the difference in size, look, and shape of the serving spoons from their own spoons, the easier it will be for the children to remember not to lick them.

➤ Because you are an important role model for good eating habits and manners, eat with the children and eat what they do.

➤ Offer food to children but do not force it on them. ("Please take one bite of each item to be polite" is a good rule.) If a sweet dessert is served, offer it to those children who have eaten all of the protein on their plates and at least one bite of everything else. This is not a reward but a way to make sure that children eat more than just dessert. (A child who refuses to take even one bite should be allowed to refuse. With no pressure or tension the child will likely come around to eating. A relaxed attitude about food is conducive to good eating habits for everyone.)

➤ Engage the children in low-keyed conversation during meals. Ask them about their families and about activities they did at home and school earlier in the day, discuss the food being eaten and where it came from, and share some things about yourself. (This will set a calm tone which is important for good digestion.)

➤ Do cooking projects with the children often. To increase their knowledge and appreciation of the food they eat, serve the food you cooked with meals.

➤ Avoid using food for art projects. Pudding paintings and vegetable prints teach children that playing with and wasting food is okay. You will find that using food as art makes reinforcing proper eating habits during meals difficult. Finger paint and sponges work just as well as food for art projects.

➤ Visit the cook in the kitchen often. Ask her or him to demonstrate and explain to the children how to make some of their favorite dishes. Invite the cook to eat with your class so that he or she can see how the children respond to the food. Help the children send "thank-you" cards for especially good meals. (This creates a positive attitude about the food served and the person cooking it.)

Dealing with Existing Problems

The Overly Zealous Eater

This child grabs the food from the table, takes too much, eats very fast, or stuffs too much food in her mouth. The child may have to do this at home to get her share of food, she may be very hungry, or this may be how she has learned to eat.

➤ To start with, develop a clear system of serving the same amount of food to each child—one spoonful of vegetables, one slice of pizza, two ladles of soup, and so on. If leftovers remain for seconds, divide them up in equal portions for each child. If everyone does not want seconds, give thirds to the children who want them, although for overweight children, you may want to limit food to seconds. Before each meal, remind the overly zealous eater of your system for equal sharing of food. (After a few weeks of this routine, scarcity should not be an issue for any child.)

➤ Sit across the table from the overly zealous eater so you can help her slow down. Because she probably does the behavior out of habit, you will need to stop the child, show her how to chew slowly, talk her through the meal, and model good eating habits for several weeks. Tell the child that chewing food well is important. Explain to the child that chewing helps her body take in all the food's goodness and makes her grow tall and strong.

The Sloppy Eater

The child who is a sloppy eater is usually a child with some coordination difficulties or problems organizing herself. This child probably also has trouble with puzzles, writes or draws messily, and is a disheveled dresser. Getting slippery food from the plate to the mouth is not an easy task for any preschooler, but it is an exasperating one for the child with poor small-motor control.

➤ Help the child organize herself before she starts to eat. Help her place her milk glass where it won't be easily knocked over by a stray elbow or unruly arm. Make sure she has pulled her chair close to the table and is sitting straight. Help her put her plate directly in front and near to her body.

➤ Because spoons usually provide more control than forks, provide the child with a spoon for most foods. A fork and a spoon together may provide even more control since the child can push the food onto her fork with the spoon. Because plates with high edges prevent food from easily falling off, use them if possible.

➤ Help the child who is a sloppy eater to fill her glass and soup bowl less than half way and then provide additional servings when she is done. Point out that smaller amounts are easier to handle, and if spills do occur, there is less waste, less to clean, and less frustration.

➤ Do not focus too much attention on the problem, as this may humiliate the child and make it worse. Accept the child as having physical difficulties. Provide her with many nonthreatening, playful opportunities to improve her small-motor skills through such activities as cutting with scissors, doing simple puzzles, building with Legos™ and unit blocks, and painting at an easel.

The Picky Eater

➤ To begin with, provide the picky eater with small servings. Note that several small servings can feel less intimidating than one large serving of food.

➤ Do not force any child to eat. Set a pleasant and relaxing tone, model good eating habits, give children control wherever possible (serving themselves, starting and finishing when they are ready), and follow the other suggestions in *Preventing Problems*. Allow the child who is a picky eater the time and autonomy to develop better eating habits without pressure.

➤ As you know, some children have acute taste buds and are very sensitive to foods. Other children have allergies to certain foods and are lucky enough that their bodies tell them not to eat those foods. These children may gag or vomit if forced to eat certain foods. If offered only the offending foods, they will go hungry for long periods rather than eat. Allow parents to provide meals from home, if they are able, with the condition that the meals will meet the nutritional requirements of the program. Allowing one child to eat potato chips and cake while insisting all others eat nutritious food is hypocritical. If the child has a note from a doctor stating that she is on a special diet, provide alternative foods.

Unappealing Food

Some children are picky eaters for good reason. They know, as well as adults do, that the food is not good. Child-care centers and schools have a reputation for serving substandard food, and in many cases the reputation is warranted. Understandably, food is a big budget item. Much money can be saved by serving low-quality food and good cooks are hard to find at the wages most early childhood programs can afford to pay. But some experts in the administration of programs for young children believe that the single most important reflection of quality in a program is good food.* A great curriculum is severely marred when laced with bad food. A hungry child will be difficult to manage. She will have a hard time sitting still and concentrating and may become aggressive. Serving high quality food makes an important statement about your respect for and care of children. This will not go unnoticed by parents. When children are enthusiastic about the food, problems at mealtimes are reduced.

➤ Educate the powers-that-be in your program about the importance of good food. Explain why the amount expended on good food is money well spent. Invite the director or principal to eat with the children often so she can see the impact of the food on the children. Ask to have a food specialist consult with the program to improve the menu. (This specialist can often provide ways of improving the food without adding much or any cost.) To educate yourself about the issues, read about nutrition and cooking for children. Ask your director, cook or nutritionist if you can suggest different meals or snacks.

Wasted Food

➤ If many children leave a great deal of food on their plates, which then gets scraped into the trash, serve much smaller portions. If the children serve themselves, set clear limits on the amounts they can take to start with. Explain that they can have additional portions if they wish.

➤ Give feedback to the cook about how much food is actually consumed. (The cook may be able to prepare much less and save the program a great deal of money, which can then be used for equipment, supplies, or salaries.)

➤ Follow the suggestions provided previously in this chapter on food not being eaten because it is unappealing or because the atmosphere during meals is not calm.

Losing Silverware in the Trash

This is a surprisingly common problem in preschool programs. Giving children the responsibility of clearing their own places is an excellent idea, but it is unrealistic to expect them to do this perfectly every time. The consequence in this case is the expense of losing silverware.

➤ A simple solution is to assign a child the job of "Environmentalist." Have this child stand by the trash and watch for any silverware that may accidentally get put in. Most children enjoy this job because it makes them feel important, and they do it well. In programs where organic trash is separated from litter, the "Environmentalist" can watch for correct separation of trash as well.

Too Much Noise

➤ To aid in eating slowly, enjoying the food, and digesting it well, make mealtimes calm and relatively quiet. If the noise level rises too high, shut off the main lights. (Dim lights are easily associated with hushed tones for young children.) In a very quiet voice, explain why you have turned down the lights. Tell the children that you expect quiet voices during mealtimes.

➤ Use one signal consistently to get children to stop and be quiet. For example, you might use a special bell or the flashing of the lights. Or, you might raise your hand or place the thumb and forefinger of your right hand to make an *L* and put it next to your ear. (This is American Sign Language for *listen* and makes a good cue for quiet. It is instructive at the same time.)

➤ To demonstrate acceptable behavior, converse with the children in quiet, pleasant tones. Have an adult strategically placed at each table to assist the children. Separate children who tend to be loud and boisterous when near each other.

---

*Dora Fowler. In a speech given to the Oregon Association of Day Care Directors, April 1986.

Resources

Alger, H.A. "Transitions: Alternatives to Manipulative Management." *Young Children* 39(6) (September 1984): 16-25.

Endres, Jeannette B., and Rockwell, Robert E. *Food, Nutrition, and the Young Child*. St. Louis, MO: Times Mirror/Mosby College, 1985.

Goodwin, Mary T., and Pollen, Gerry. *Creative Food Experiences for Children*. Washington, DC: Center For Science In The Public Interest, 1974.

Harms, Thelma, et al. *Cook and Learn*. Menlo Park, CA: Addison-Wesley, 1981.

Harms, Thelma. *Learning From Cooking Experiences*. Menlo Park, CA: Addison-Wesley, 1981.

Holt, B. "Food As Art?" *Young Children* 40(4) (May 1985): 18-19.

Lansky, Vicki. *Feed Me I'm Yours*. Wayzata, MN: Meadowbrook Press, 1974.

Luksus, Elaine R., et al. *SWITCH to Good Nutrition*. Morgan Hill, CA: Growth & Opportunity, Inc., 1981. (Developed by a grant from NETP California State Dept. of Education, 721 Capitol Mall, Sacramento, CA 95814.)

McAfee, Oralie, et al. *Cooking and Eating with Children*. Washington, DC: Association for Childhood International, 1974.

Wanamaker, N., et al. *More Than Graham Crackers: Nutrition Education and Food Preparation with Young Children*. Washington, DC: NAEYC, 1979.

Warren, Jean. *Super Snacks*. New York: St. Martin's Press, 1985.

Whitener, Carol B., and Keeling, Marie H. *Nutrition Education for Young Children*. Englewood Cliffs, NJ: Prentice Hall: 1984.

7. Transitions: Structuring Unplanned Times

Transitions are those periods of time when the children are moving from one activity to the next. Because waiting, with no directions from the teacher, is difficult for young children, transitions can be a problem. Even a few minutes seems like a long time to children. The usual result is that children will wander, run around, or do things they are not supposed to do. Dealing with those behaviors further delays the next activity. Even if you experience no behavior problems, having short, smooth transitions means that more time will be spent in meaningful activities.

Preventing Problems

➤ Develop a consistent daily schedule with as few transitions as possible built into it. Plan in advance what each adult will do during transition times.

➤ Tell the children when a transition is about to occur and explain exactly what they are to do: "When you go inside the classroom, hang up your coat and then sit on the rug for a story."

➤ Structure staff time and duties so that as children move from one activity to another, something engaging is already happening at the next place.

➤ Have materials ready for the next activity so the transition will be short.

➤ Begin the next activity as soon as even one child is ready. (The other children will be attracted by what is going on and will join quickly.)

➤ Keep a list handy of favorite finger plays, short songs and simple activities to use during transitions. Because the following simple games require no materials, consider using them for transition: 1) Describe what a child is wearing and have the children guess whom you are describing; 2) Have one child mime an action (playing the piano, sweeping, making a pizza) and the other children guess; 3) Name a list of objects and have the children guess what category they belong to, (e.g., bracelets, necklaces, and earrings are jewelry.) After leading the activity once or twice, give the children opportunities to be the leader.

Dealing with Existing Problems

Transition from Eating

➤ As children finish, have them clear their places and move immediately to the next activity, if possible. Avoid making everyone wait until all are finished eating. If the next activity is not quite ready, let them get a paper and some pens to draw, or let them browse through books while waiting.* Provide a place where unfinished pictures can be stored to work on later.

➤ If more than a few minutes will pass before the next activity begins, provide children with table toys so picking up will not take very long.

➤ If there is more than one teacher, one should begin the next activity while another helps the children who are still eating. If appropriate, invite the children to set up the next activity.

➤ To eliminate several transitions, consider having a snack or a meal take place during free choice time. Put the food out and let children eat when they are hungry (over a limited time period) with adult supervision. Make expectations for washing hands and cleaning up after eating very clear.

Transition to Outdoor Time

➤ Dismiss children from the previous activity a few at a time. (This can be done by dismissing children by kinds of shoes, colors of shirts, first letters of their names, and so on.) If coats are needed, invite the children to help one another put them on, zipper, and button before asking for help from an adult.

➤ If at all possible, avoid lining up. This produces only boredom and tension, which lead to pushing and hitting. Ideally, one teacher will go outside with the first children who are ready, and the others will follow when they are ready. Another teacher or adult can bring out the children who move a little slower.

➤ If there is only one teacher, involve the children in a song while helping to get them ready. A teacher on her own can also bring out all the children when they are close to being done with coats. Zipping and helping with mittens and hats can be done outside so the children can begin to play as they are ready.

*Book browsing should be more than a short transition activity. At least once a day, provide a period when the children have plenty of time to look through books and/or when adults read to small groups or individuals on laps.

➤ To avoid a rush for coveted pieces of play equipment, arrange a schedule ahead of time. Write a list of all children who want to use a piece of equipment so names are visible and can be crossed off. Rotate who gets the toy first from day to day. Use a kitchen timer to time the length of turns.

Transition from Outdoors or from Free Choice

➤ Give a five-minute warning before the children have to finish playing. Use a clock for a visual cue for them to gauge five minutes. Say something like the following: "The long hand is on the five; when it reaches the six, it will be time to stop." Or, use a kitchen timer. Give the warning or have a child give the warning quietly and calmly to each small group of children or individual children as they are playing. Note that this is usually more effective than shouting to the whole group.

➤ When the five minute period ends, have a child tell the others that it is time to put equipment away, ring a bell, or flash lights to focus the children's attention. Following these procedures makes the children feel like this transition is an aspect of the daily schedule, not an arbitrary directive from you. This results in less disappointment at having to end play. Also, you maintain your proper authority as the teacher by guiding the children to follow the daily schedule without being overly controlling.

Clean-Up

➤ Label all shelves for all materials for quick clean-ups that require little adult assistance. Provide mops, brooms, dustpans, sponges, and other clean-up materials available where children can get them easily. Teach them how to use these materials.

➤ To make the work fun, make a game out of clean-up. Pretend that everyone is a robot or a clean-up monster from space. Or, encourage the children to be the quietest clean-up crew in the world. Singing a song while picking up can also be an effective way to gain cooperation from the children.

➤ Give generous encouragement to the children who are conscientious about cleaning up: "Thank you for working so hard to make our room pleasant for everyone."

Transition from Nap

➤ Let children get up off their cots or mats when they awaken. Guide them to quiet activities (playdough, puzzles, and so on.), while you are getting others up and helping them with shoes.

➤ Move gradually and quietly from nap time into another activity. Cuddle with the children and talk with them. Ask them about their dreams. Turn on lights a few at a time if possible. If children are able to carry their own cots or mats, have them bring them to where they are stacked. (For transition to nap, see "Peaceful Nap Times," on pages 37 to 38.)

Transition to Going Home

➤ Many programs end the day in free choice time or outdoor play, and parents pick children up during this time. This makes for a smooth transition and makes chatting with parents a little easier. Encourage children to put away what they have been using, before going home. Enlist parent support in this clean-up effort.

➤ If children leave as a group, invite them to end the day by looking at books, listening to music, or drawing pictures. Dismiss them a few at a time when the bus is ready or when parents arrive. As they leave, encourage children to get their papers and art work to take home from cubbies or from a teacher. End the day by giving a hug or a handshake to each child as the child leaves to get on the bus, or in the family car.

➤ Allow time to talk with parents about the day's events and to share any concerns or comments you or they may have.

Resources

Alger, H.A. "Transitions: Alternatives to Manipulative Management." *Young Children* 39(6) (September 1984): 16-25.

8. Art: Mess without Stress

A mess during art time may mean that children are working hard and having fun. Too much mess, however, results in valuable time being wasted while cleaning up, in ruined equipment, in soiled clothes (that make parents unhappy), and in frustration. The following suggestions will help you keep messes to a minimum, while promoting creativity.

Preventing Problems

➤ Establish a policy that children should wear to school clothes that can get messy. Children may still wear good clothes occasionally (often because they insist on it), but at least parents have been forewarned and are aware that clothes may become soiled.

➤ Keep a bottle or a stick of prewash stain remover handy to use on clothes (yours and the children's) in case of spills.

➤ Have a classroom rule that children will clean up their own area before moving on to another activity.

➤ Before the start of a project, give a few clear, specific directions for using materials. Include a visual reminder. For example, if you want finger paints limited to four tablespoons to avoid too much paint flowing, say so, demonstrate it putting four tablespoons of paint on the paper, and put up a picture sign with four tablespoons drawn on it.

➤ Gather together all the materials you will need for an art project. Make the task easier by using a cart on wheels to hold and transport the materials.

➤ Do art activities in small groups while most of the children are outside, in another room, or engaged in other activities during free choice. To avoid a big clean-up job at the end, clean up some of the mess after each small group.

➤ Keep art project items (cotton balls, buttons, paper scraps of the same texture and color) in separate, labeled containers. Do this to avoid the

from messy art projects, part of the aesthetic of your classroom. Note that an old table used only for art will look attractive with drips and spatters of colorful paint left on it. This allows children to be free from worrying about being neat and from spending time cleaning.

➤ Keep a trash can next to the art area. Both children and adults are more likely to use it.

➤ Provide a small size broom and a large dustpan. Many children enjoy sweeping, especially when two can do the activity together—one sweeps while the other holds the dustpan.

➤ Keep a basin of soapy water with sponges and some towels nearby. Children can help themselves and clean up on their own. Use large auto or boat sponges because they make clean-up quick and easy. You can purchase these sponges cheaply from janitorial supply companies.

mess created by children rummaging through large boxes filled with a variety of collage materials and to encourage a more thoughtful approach by giving the children clearer choices.

➤ Lay newspaper down across the whole table and tape the edges. Roll up the whole mess at the end of the project.

➤ Lay plastic or newspaper down on the floor beneath your easel or below the table where art work will be done.

➤ To avoid paint dripping on the floor, place the art table and easels close to a sink. Add a small amount of liquid soap to paint. (The quality of the paint will not change, and removing spots from clothes will be easier.

➤ Consider making "abstract art," which results

➤ Have at least one apron or smock for each child in the room. (Although you may never use that many, there will be an extra if one gets too soiled or gets torn. Old adult-sized shirts with short sleeves or long sleeves cut off halfway make excellent smocks and can cost nothing if donated.)

➤ Put Contact™ paper over easels so that paint will wipe off easily.

➤ If the bathroom is far away, have a basin of soapy water and/or damp towels so that children can rinse their hands.

Dealing with Existing Problems

Drippy Paint

➤ Mix powdered tempera with nontoxic liquid cornstarch to keep it thick. (This causes less dripping and makes painting more satisfying to children by giving them more control over the paint.)

➤ Give children specific directions, individually at the easel, on wiping both sides of the brush on the edge of the container before painting with it. (Many reminders may be needed.)

Paint Spills and Waste

➤ Paint containers that are short and wide are less likely to tip over. Use frozen juice containers that you have cut down, half-pint milk cartons, and commercially produced plastic no-spill containers.

➤ Use paint brushes with short handles (about six inches). This gives children more control over the brush and eliminates the problem of the brush flipping out of the container or tipping it over. To eliminate the danger of one poking a child in the eye, consider cutting off the ends of brush handles if they are pointy.

➤ To avoid wasting paint due to drying up, pour unused paint back into a storage jar or cover the individual containers at the end of each day. Wash brushes thoroughly each day to make them last.

Gluing

White glue squeezed from a bottle is often a cause of conflict between teachers and children. Teachers admonish children to "just use a little," and children feel frustrated because either nothing comes out or too much does. Too often there are not enough bottles for each child to have one, the tops glue shut, and children become too involved in the fun of pouring, squirting, and smearing. (Pouring, squeezing, and smearing are very important physical needs that young children have, but they can be better and more cheaply met through water or sand play.)

➤ As an alternative to the squeeze bottle, put a small amount of glue in a cup for each child and provide an ice-cream stick, small brush, or plastic eyedropper (with the hole widened) as an applicator. To save money, purchase the glue in a large, gallon size.

➤ An alternative to white glue is paste, which is less messy but will not work as well with certain materials such as wood. A few small containers of paste could be passed around or children can have individual squares of paper with some paste on them. Each child can use a stick, brush, or their fingers to apply the paste.

Resources

Bos, B. *Don't Move the Muffin Tins*. Roseville, CA: Turn-The-Page Press, 1978.

Jenkins, P.D. *Art for the Fun of It*. New York: Prentice Hall, 1980.

Kohl, M.A. *Scribble Cookies*. Bellingham, WA: Bright Ring Publishing, 1985.

Lasky, L., and Mukerji, R. *Art: Basic for Young Children*. Washington, DC: NAEYC, 1980.

Mayesky, M.; Neuman, D.; and Wlodkowski, R.J. *Creative Activities For Young Children*. Albany, NY: Delmar, 1975.

Warren, J. *1-2-3-Art*. Everett, WA: Warren Publishing, 1985.

9. Safe Fun Outdoors or in the Gym

Large-motor (or gross-motor) play is another name for outdoor or gym play. In this type of play, young children learn to coordinate their large muscles and increase their strength, agility, and understanding of how their bodies move. Developing these large-motor skills is as important to their overall healthy growth as practicing cognitive skills (learning colors, shapes) or small-motor skills (writing letters, doing puzzles). Your task is to provide children with many different and safe activities that allow them to practice balancing, jumping, running, climbing, hopping, ball handling, aiming, and more.

Preventing Problems

➤ Schedule outdoor/gym time for at least thirty minutes each morning and thirty minutes each afternoon (for full-day or double-shift programs).

➤ Post outside or in the gym a list of activities that the children enjoy. Consider including the following on the list: "Duck-Duck-Goose," "Red Light Green Light," hopscotch, and hide-and-seek; playing gas station with tricycles; jumping rope; playing with a parachute; tossing beanbags into a box; dancing to taped music; painting with water and big brushes; pretending to be firefighters; and walking through an obstacle course.

➤ Use your list of activities to provide different things for the children to do each day. (A limited number of choices or the same choices every day does not provide enough large-muscle growth and also leads to boredom. Accidents on the playground are often caused by bored children taking dangerous chances.)

➤ Most accidents in child-care settings are caused by swings. If you have a swing set, create a visible marker around the outside of the swing area to signal children not to move too close so they won't be hit by a child swinging. (Railroad ties work well as they are big enough that children will not trip on them, but not so big that they take up a great deal of space. They can usually be obtained inexpensively.) A teacher should always be watching the swing area.

➤ Set a few firm playground/gym rules, relating to your particular equipment. You might use the following:

"Go down the slide on your bottom."

"Swing only while seated and stop swinging before jumping off."

"Climb using two hands."

➤ Before going outside, assign each staff person a different part of the playground to supervise. Make sure all children can be seen easily and reached quickly by an adult.

Dealing with Existing Problems

Limited or Unsafe Play Equipment

If you have very little in the way of usable play equipment such as swings, slides, and climbers, and there is not a park nearby you can walk to, you can still provide a good large-motor program.

➤ Hang a tire swing from a tree.

➤ Bring with you boxes of equipment that include balls, hoops, jump ropes, bubble blowing supplies, a parachute, balance beams, beanbags, shovels, pails, and frisbees.

➤ Fill boxes with props that relate to particular themes. For example, in a beach theme box, put shells, towels, sunglasses, empty plastic suntan lotion bottles, swim goggles, swim fins, inflatable pool toys, and so on. Use a wagon to haul the boxes.

➤ Use foam rubber sports equipment (tennis balls, baseballs, soccer balls). Note that these are inexpensive, safe, easy for young children to use, easy to haul, and can be used indoors or out.

➤ Supply dress-up clothes and art activities for variety.

➤ Use large cardboard boxes for a variety of creative play activities. Invite the children to make forts, cars, stages, and more, from wooden boxes, boards, and old sheets.

➤ Put wheels on your water table so you can bring it outside on warm days.

➤ Use your list of fun activities (as described in *Preventing Problems*) often. You will need to provide more structure if you have little usable equipment.

➤ Make a large sandbox with wooden boards. (Supplied with shovels, funnels and other creative sand toys, the sandbox will be a well-used and loved area of the playground.) To keep out neigh-borhood pets, cover the sandbox with an inexpensive plastic tarp.

➤ If you have access to a gym but the equipment is designed for older children (high basketball hoops, tall volleyball nets), adapt to that equipment by using a large beach ball for a volleyball and a small rubber ball for a basketball.

➤ Check equipment at least weekly to determine if there are loose pieces, sharp edges or nails, splintered wood, or other problems. (Children can help you find these problems and usually become aware of them before you do.) At the first sign of an unsafe condition, keep children off equipment until it can be fixed or replaced. Rope off the equipment or have a similar highly visible marker to prevent children from using it. The children can help fix equipment in some cases by sanding wood surfaces, hammering protruding nails, and painting rusted areas. Close adult supervision will be needed.

Wood, Concrete or Paved Play Areas

➤ A hard surface under play equipment or where children run is extremely dangerous. Put mats, mattresses or similar cushioning under and around any climbing equipment used in a gym. Surround outdoor structures with bark dust, pea gravel, sand, tire shreds, or similar loose materials. If possible, cover the entire play area, except where wheeled toys are used, with a cushioning material. Some programs have been able to get these donated from suppliers, as they can be quite expensive. In the long run, bark dust and sand can be more expensive than the more permanent materials, as they have to be replaced regularly. (The cost to a program of one serious accident makes the cost of essential safety equipment worth the expense.)

No Indoor Gym Space for When the Weather Is Bad

If you live in a part of the country where children cannot go outside for very long for many months of the year, how can you provide your children with an adequate large-motor program?

➤ Unless the weather is severe, take your children outside for a short time every day. Start collecting a supply of extra boots, mittens, hats, and so on for children who do not come properly dressed. If heat is the problem, keep a supply of sunscreen and sun hats. Some fresh air and only ten minutes of running and playing will provide children with a satisfying experience. Afterwards, they will be better able and more willing to be involved in more structured indoor play.

➤ If at all possible, move tables and shelves to provide room for children to move around within your room. Use records, tapes, or your own voice for movement games and exercises. Make sure the children have plenty of time to move on their own to music (creative dance), move freely to their own ideas ("Let's move like giraffes in outer space"), and be physical with each other by exercising with partners. Creative expression with their whole bodies provides a great emotional release for any strong feelings or anxiety children may have. The hassle of moving furniture out of the way and then back will be worthwhile, as you will prevent behavior problems and meet children's large-motor needs. Invite the children to help with moving.

Resources

Baker, K.R. *Let's Play Outdoors*. Washington, DC: NAEYC, 1977.

"Outdoor Play." *Beginnings* (Summer, 1985), Exchange Press, Redmond, WA.

Frost, J.L., and Klein, B. *Children's Play and Playgrounds*. Austin: Playgrounds International, 1983.

Frost, J.L., and Wortham, S. "The Evolution of American Playgrounds." *Young Children* 43(5) (July 1988): 19-28.

Greenman, J. *Caring Spaces, Learning Places: Children's Environments That Work*. (Redmond, WA): Exchange Press, 1988.

Kritchevsky, S., et al. *Planning Environments for Young Children: Physical Space* Washington, DC: NAEYC, 1969.

Miller, K. *The Outside Play and Learning Book*. Mt. Rainier, MD: Gryphon House, 1989.

Travis, N. *Planning Playgrounds for Day Care*. Atlanta, GA: Southeastern Day Care Project, Southern Regional Education Board, 1973.

U.S. Consumer Product Safety Commission. *A Handbook for Public Playground Safety. Volume I: General Guidelines for New and Existing Playgrounds. Volume II: Technical Guidelines for Equipment and Surfacing*. Washington, DC: U.S. Government Printing Office, 1981.

Werner, P. "Playscapes: Children's Needs and Safety Standards." *Dimensions* 1 (January 1983): 11-14.

10. Peaceful Nap Times

Naptime can be a stressful time of day or a warm and relaxing time for both you and the children. Careful attention to the environment, to comforting routines, and to individual needs for rest and activity will help make naptime peaceful.

Preventing Problems

➤ Schedule the nap time late enough so that most children are tired.

➤ Establish a routine such as reading a book or singing a song just before each nap time.

➤ Remind children of nap time rules (no more than two) that you have established, such as "Stay on your cot and use a whisper voice only."

➤ Have a transition period when children can lie down and look quietly at books for fifteen minutes.

➤ Reassure new children that they are not going to sleep for the night but just for a few hours and they will be picked up by their parents later in the day.

➤ Leave at least three feet of space between each

cot and place children who are near to each other, head to toe. This prevents the spread of colds as well as minimizes talking.

➤ Darken the room and play soothing music throughout nap time.

➤ Ask parents to bring in blankets, teddy bears, and other sleeping aids used at home.

➤ Gently rub backs or foreheads.

➤ As children want to do what adults do, lie down yourself for awhile.

Dealing with Existing Problems

Infants/Young Toddlers

Different Schedules: As most programs allow children under two to fall asleep when they are tired, you have the problem of almost always having some children sleeping while others are awake. In a week or two, most children will get used to sleeping through the noise. Create a separate sleeping room (ideally with a large glass window between it and the main room for easy viewing). If this is not possible, use a curtain to section off a portion of the room for sleeping.

Older Toddlers/Preschoolers

Squirmers: Some children need to squirm for about a half hour before they can relax enough to sleep. These are the children who do not settle down or relax when you rub their backs or foreheads. Let them get their wiggles out before trying to help them sleep.

Non-nappers: Some children are just not nappers. However, they still need a rest period in full-day programs. After they have rested for about forty-five minutes, arrange for these children to play in another place or allow them to do quiet activities in the room.

Noisemakers: Children who are deliberately loud and wake others up are usually either bored or enjoy the attention their disturbance brings. Try the prevention ideas and non-napper ideas listed above to prevent boredom and to encourage good behavior. If the problem persists, calmly place the child, with her cot or mat, just outside the room in the hallway or in an adjoining room (assuming the area is safe, not too hot or cold, and the child can be seen by an adult). Show no anger or frustration. Tell the child she can come back to the room when she can lie quietly. Repeat this procedure until the behavior stops.

Socializers: Some children have a difficult time not talking and playing with their friends who are lying nearby. Place the cots or mats of such chil-

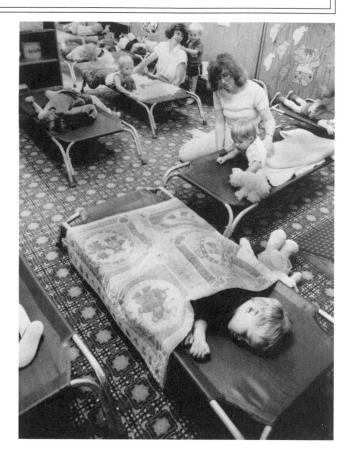

dren behind shelves or other furniture so they can't see their buddies. Strategically place room dividers and rearrange the room to create as many private sleeping areas as necessary.

No Rewards: Tell the children who have followed the rules that they have done well: "Because you were quiet, naptime was peaceful, and all the children who wanted to sleep were able to." Do not reward children for sleeping, as it is not something most children can control.

Resources

Alger, H.A. "Transitions: Alternatives to Manipulative Management." *Young Children* 39(6) (September 1984): 16-25

Part II
Classroom Concerns

1. Making the Classroom Environment Work for You

2. Selecting and Using a Curriculum

3. Individualizing

4. Field Trips Are Supposed to Be Fun

5. Toys from Home

6. Lost or Missing

7. Coping with Accidents and Emergencies

8. Children Who Are Ill and Other Health Concerns

1. Making the Classroom Environment Work for You

How you organize the classroom environment and what equipment you place in it affect children's behavior. Children who are bored, overstimulated, or confused by the environment will react by developing behavior problems. An appropriate environment will help reduce overactive, aggressive, and disruptive behaviors. It will also provide many fun learning opportunities for children.

Preventing Problems

➤ To avoid arguments, have several duplicates of toys for toddlers. Include both push and pull toys, items that can be put in and taken out of containers, trucks to fill up and low vehicles to ride on. Make sure that all the toys are too big for the children to put in their mouths.

➤ For all children, provide toys and games with a wide skill range so more able children will be challenged but less able or younger children will not be frustrated. For example, have four-piece, ten-piece, and 25-piece puzzles.

➤ Arrange the furniture so that you have no long corridors that may invite running in the room. Place quiet areas (library, table toys) away from noisy areas (blocks, dramatic play).

➤ Rotate supplies and toys to avoid boredom. Provide many toys and activities that children can use without help from adults. To create calm, paint walls pastel colors and display posters that are soothing to look at. Consider reproductions of famous works of art or scenes from nature. (These can be obtained inexpensively by purchasing art or nature calendars when they go on sale in about March of each year.) Avoid very busy, brightly colored rooms, which please adults but overstimulate children.

➤ Change the dramatic play area fairly often. Set up a post office for three or four weeks, then a restaurant for several weeks, then a campground. Have the children come up with other ideas.

➤ Label all shelves and counters with words and pictures so that children will be able to put materials in their proper places without adult help.

➤ To avoid arguments due to overcrowding and to provide for safety, limit the number of children allowed in certain small areas of the room. To indicate the allowed number, put up picture signs that children can understand. (A small water-play basin or a woodworking table may need to be limited to two to four.)

➤ Make popular areas of the room, such as dramatic play and blocks, as large as possible to accommodate many children. Avoid putting number limits in these areas (unless the areas are very small) because children will feel frustrated if they are kept out. (Setting number limits in these areas may cause more problems than it will solve.)

➤ Balance the hardness in the room (chairs, tables, floors, walls) with things that are soft. For example, use beanbag chairs, large floor pillows, rugs (which can be easily cleaned), wall hangings, and fabric draped from the ceiling.

➤ Create at least one private space where a child can choose to be away from others. For example, use a large, painted refrigerator box with pillows inside.

➤ Establish a place to store unfinished art work and other projects to be completed later. Provide individual, personal storage areas where children can keep projects, notes, extra clothes, and stuffed animals from home.

Dealing with Existing Problems

Small Spaces

➤ One way of dealing with small rooms is to designate each room for certain activities. All groups of children then share all rooms on a rotating basis. One room can be for art and games, another for dramatic play and group times.

➤ To increase usable space and make a creative and fun room, install a loft. (Caution: Ceilings must be high enough and there should be enough money allocated to build a sturdy and safe loft, which can be easily removed and rebuilt in another room.)

Not Enough Storage Space

➤ Build shelves high up on the walls to provide valuable extra storage space. If closed cabinets are too expensive, consider covering open shelves with fabric to make the room look neater. (This also helps solve the problem of children being attracted to the items on the shelves.)

➤ Store large items that will not be used for a period of several months with a mini-storage company or perhaps, for less money (or free), with a local business or agency that has some extra space and is willing to help you out.

➤ See if a staff member with a good deal of extra storage room at home might be willing to store items there. In this case, post a list of every stored item at the center where the list will be accessible to everyone. When items are brought back to school, cross them off the list. Add newly stored items to the list. Consider having the staff member who is providing the storage space sign a statement agreeing to the arrangement and agreeing to return all items at the request of the director, board president, or other supervisor.

A High Ceiling

➤ Lower the ceiling by draping fabric or a parachute or by hanging umbrellas or other items. Be cautious: hang these securely. To avoid any fire danger, make sure the objects are not near light fixtures or heat sources. Before doing this, ask your local fire official if hanging material violates regulations.

A Big Open Space

➤ Because large spaces tend to make children feel overwhelmed and small, partition them. (An inexpensive partition can be made using a 4' x 6' sheet of particle board and four metal brackets to hold it upright. Stringing fabric for a curtain can also work. Perhaps the unused area can be set aside for an indoor gym.)

Little Money for Supplies or Equipment

➤ Teacher-made games are often the most used and best liked materials in the classroom. Look in equipment catalogues for many items that you can make without much difficulty and for much less money than if purchased. Cover them with a clear adhesive paper or laminate them to make them last for years.

➤ Ask parents and staff to help you collect free materials, such as cardboard, cereal boxes, paper towel tubes, egg cartons, juice containers, Styrofoam™ meat trays, and so on, that can be used to make different games.

➤ Host a party for parents during which they help make these games. Serve snacks and allow plenty of time to chat. Allow parents to make a game or two for home use.

➤ Check with manufacturers in your area. Often they can give you useful scrap materials, such as paper, wood pieces, plastic containers, and cloth.

➤ You can save hundreds of dollars a year on paper supplies by using paper scraps donated by local printers and by using old computer paper from a company such as your electric utility.

➤ A local carpenter, skilled parent, or friend can make classroom furniture and shelves for much less money than the equipment sold in catalogs.

➤ Check garage sales, used-furniture stores, and Salvation Army or Goodwill-type stores for usable items. Note that these used items often need only some paint or a few screws.

Sharing Your Classroom

➤ To avoid problems, meet at least monthly with the teachers who share your room. Discuss expectations for use of materials and cleanliness. Define exactly what materials can be shared; what needs to be put away; and what, if anything, needs to be locked up. (Having a supervisor at your meeting to mediate can help avoid an impasse and help determine what constitutes reasonable expectations.) When you find the room left in good condition, leave notes thanking the other teachers.

➤ If you have to move furniture and put away supplies at the end of each day or each week, make your job easier by putting wheels on the bottom of all your furniture. (Hinged shelving units which fold together and can be locked are very handy.)

➤ As the end of the day approaches, enlist the help of the other staff and the children in putting things away gradually. Close up areas of the room one by one so that at the end the day you are in a space that is easy to clear. (This avoids putting in extra hours of hard work after class, when you are already tired and anxious to leave.)

Resources

"Designing Indoor Spaces." *Beginnings,* Redmond, WA: Exchange Press, (Summer 1984).

Dodge, D.T. "Strategies for Achieving a Quality Program," *Exchange,* (June 1989): 67, 43-47,

Greenman, J. *Caring Spaces, Learning Places: Children's Environments That Work,* Redmond, WA: Exchange Press, 1988.

Greenman, J. "Living in the Real World: 'Learning Environments for the 1990's - Part One,'" *Exchange* 67, (June 1989): 49-50.

Jones, E. *Dimensions of Teaching-Learning Environments: A Handbook for Teachers,* Pasadena, CA: Pacific Oaks College, 1973.

Kritchevsky, S.; Prescott, E.; Walling, L. *Planning Environments for Young Children: Physical Space,* Washington D.C.: NAEYC, 1969.

Prescott, E. "The Physical Setting in Day Care." In *Making Day Care Better,* edited by Greenman, J.T. and Fuqua, R.W. New York: Teachers College Press, 1984.

Weinstein, C., and David, T. *Spaces for Children: The Built Environment and Child Development,* New York: Plenum Press, 1987.

2. Selecting and Using a Curriculum

There are basically two types of curriculums. One consists of prescribed-activity ideas to use with children and the other consists of an approach to teaching (including a philosophy, general principles, and specific ideas for structuring your schedule and environment). In the teaching-approach curriculum, the teacher develops the actual activities or obtains them from resource books.

Purchasing a curriculum with prescribed activities is like purchasing a closet full of clothes. You may save a great deal of time and effort by not having to buy clothes, but many in the closet will not suit you and will not fit. Of course no one does this, yet many programs *do* purchase prescribed activity curriculums. A teaching-approach curriculum is like an empty closet with hangers, storage, shoe racks, and shelves. On these structures you can properly and conveniently place clothes of your own choosing. You will have to make decisions about what to buy and take the time and energy to do the purchasing, but the result will be more satisfying. Without question,

teaching-approach curriculums are better for children. The activities you develop can come out of the children's interests, immediate needs, and culture. There is also no question that these activities require more planning time, work, energy, knowledge, and thought on your part.

If you are a beginning teacher and will not be provided with thorough training for using a teaching-approach curriculum, you might choose (or have been required to use) a curriculum with prescribed activities. When you feel comfortable enough with your knowledge of how young children (and your group in particular) learn and which activities work well and which do not, you can switch to a teaching-approach curriculum. Be prepared, however, to change many of the prescribed activities and to drop some that do not work for your group.

The greatest benefit of a teaching-approach curriculum is that it will provide you with a sound theory or philosophy on which to base all your activities and interactions with children. This curriculum will give you a *reason* for doing what you do with children and help you determine how to do it most effectively.

Themes

Themes or units are probably the most common curriculum approach found in preschool classrooms. Almost all prescribed-activities curriculums use themes such as the following: community helpers, transportation, our neighborhood, fire safety, nutrition, Spring, Halloween, and so on. You can also use themes with many teaching-approach curriculums, but you don't have to. A theme typically lasts for one or two weeks and provides the basis for art, math, science, literature, language, field trips, and other activities.

A shortcoming of a theme-based curriculum is that it does not come from your important theory base (unless it is used with a teaching-approach curriculum). Therefore, you may not know how to carry out the themes effectively. Also, themes may lead you towards using activities that you control and direct rather than toward using activities that children choose and direct themselves.

Being able to implement a particular theme as the interest or need arises is important. For example, if two children in your class will be having new siblings in their families, you will want to do a theme about babies. Themes, like the activities themselves, should come from the needs, interests, and culture of the children. Some of the best themes are those that affect all children and are deeply important to them. Consider using the following themes, which include a few activity ideas as examples:

Separations

To grow, all people must separate from others and from situations. Children deal with separations everyday and will deal with them for the rest of their lives. To develop a theme on separation, provide concrete activities that show children the difficulty and pain of separating, but also show the positive things that usually result from the separation, especially when proper nurturing and support is provided.

Science: Transplant shoots from a mature spider fern to show how they separate. Focus on the special care needed to help the shoot survive and grow. Chart the growth of the new shoots. Transplant one without fertilizer and water. Observe and chart what happens to it.

Cooking: Separate eggs and make something with the whites and a different dish with the yolks. Point out how one thing separated into parts can result in each part having very different but very wonderful qualities.

Literature: Read books about separation. ("Hansel and Gretel" and many other fairy tales deal with separation.) Create books about events that happened to you or to the children involving separation, such as getting lost but making a new friend in the process.

Fairness

Almost all children feel strongly that everyone should be treated equitably. They feel deeply hurt if they do not get their "fair share."

Math: Strengthen counting skills by counting votes. Have children stand, at the same time, in one area of the room to have their vote counted for a particular choice, another area for the other choice, and a third area for undecided voters. (This "forced choice" method eliminates the common problem of children voting for both choices.) Use graphing to compare how many children voted for a particular choice or were undecided. Show fractions when food is divided up and simple division when toys are divided up.

Science: To determine that each child will get the same amount of an item, demonstrate weighing and measuring with a scale, ruler, unifix cubes, or a length of string.

Social/Cognitive: Discuss various ways of creating a list for the order in which children will take turns using a popular toy. Use some of the following ideas: alphabetical by first initial, picking names out of a hat, youngest first, tallest first, or rolling a die with the highest number going first. Ask children for their ideas. Vote on which idea is fairest and use the one that gets the most votes.

Try the other ideas during the course of the next few days. Vote again after the children have seen all ideas in action.

Changes

Change is part of living and growing. Although often painful, changing means growing up. Examples of change are everywhere.

Cooking: List the qualities of uncooked eggs. Ask children to predict what they will look like when cooked various ways (fried, boiled). Cook them and observe changes as a result of heating. Eat them. Cook other foods that change when heated and compare them. Note that although eggs get harder when heated, vegetables get softer.

Find out why.

Science: View the metamorphosis of a caterpillar into a butterfly and a tadpole into a frog. Observe which types of paper absorb water and which do not. Discuss the reasons why.

Literature: Read *The Very Hungry Caterpillar* by Eric Carle, *Changes, Changes* by Pat Hutchins, *Love You Forever* by Robert Munsch, and *Lifetimes* by Bryan Mellonie.

Art: Let children experiment with mixing and changing colors. Provide a small plastic pitcher of water, clear plastic cups, eyedroppers, food coloring, and a basin to dump out cloudy water. Make available paper towels or watercolor paper to see how the colors change when dripped on the paper.

Consider other themes such as the following: Losing/Winning/Cooperating, Choosing and Making Decisions, Feeling Scared/Feeling Safe, and Angry Feelings and What To Do with Them.

Repeat or review the themes at various times during the year as issues arise in children's lives. Cut short, delay, or run concurrently one theme with another to focus on a more important issue to the children, such as a sudden snowstorm or a child entering the hospital. Once the ideas and activities in a theme have become familiar to the children, integrate and use them throughout the year and at various times during the day. For example, have the children use the skills gained during the "Fairness" theme to solve daily conflicts.

Drawbacks of a theme-based curriculum are the following: It sets up a structure that can be artificial and arbitrary if not directly related to the needs and interests of the children; it may overload the children with more information than they can take in; the themes are never referred to again after they have been used; and it does not readily facilitate individualizing.

Teaching-Approach Curriculums

Project Work[1] involves focusing at length on a specific topic or object that is well known and important to the children. Activities are developed based on discovering as much as possible about that topic or item. For example, in one school, the school bus was chosen as the focus. The children spent many weeks (unlike themes, *Project Work* units often last as long as six to seven weeks) discussing how to build a detailed school bus in the

classroom, gathering materials, and building it. They used cardboard boxes, tin foil, Styrofoam™, paint, and so on. They interviewed the bus driver to obtain all the information they needed. When the bus started falling apart, repair crews fixed it. During this process, the teacher encouraged the development of reading (she read all the words that were found on a real school bus), writing (the children made signs for the bus), social skills (the children took turns using popular tools), and problem-solving skills (the children decided on who would work on what part).

Although *Project Work* does not directly address some of the important themes discussed previously (fairness, change, and so on), the potential is there for these issues to emerge while working on a project. These themes can also be addressed during other parts of the day.

The **High/Scope**[2] curriculum is also called the *Cognitively Oriented Curriculum*. Extensive research has shown that it is a very effective curriculum approach.[3] Central to the *High/Scope* curriculum is that children need to be repeatedly exposed to fifty different key experiences. Some of these experiences are the following: classifying (separating jungle animal toys from forest animal toys), seriation (putting objects in order of shortest to tallest), spatial relationships (moving in a direction and describing if the movement was to, from, into, toward, over, under, or away), and time (drawing a picture of a past event and talking about it).

This curriculum places a heavy emphasis on setting up an appropriate classroom environment, scheduling, and planning because most of the learning takes place through children choosing activities and doing them. The teacher assists children in their own learning but usually does not give direct instruction.

Another important part of the *High/Scope* curriculum is the idea of "Plan/Do/Review." This means that children are helped to plan what they will do, they do it, and then, at some point afterwards, they review what they have done. For example, a child might decide she will play in the block area after circle time. When excused from circle, she will place her name tag on a hook below a picture of blocks. Later in the morning, in a small group, she will draw a picture of the block structure she made and tell the teacher and the other children about it.

Emergent Curriculum[4] is a teaching approach that encourages teachers to build curriculum ideas based on the emerging interests or needs of the children and sometimes the interests of the teacher (if appropriate). Other sources for curriculum ideas are "hot topics" in your community (pollution, a new animal at the zoo, a new building in town, and so on); other teachers or early childhood specialists; new or newly found books, tapes, or records; observations of people or places in the community; and unexpected events (the devastating earthquake in Armenia in December 1988 could have generated many activities about earthquakes, emergencies, hospitals, separation, death and loss, orphans, and more). Curriculum ideas can change rapidly or last a long time, depending on the children's needs and interests.

Being keenly tuned in to the children's interests and concerns, being flexible, and being responsive so you can act on those interests and concerns are all important elements of *Emergent Curriculum*.

The Creative Curriculum[5] is another teaching-approach curriculum, although activity ideas are also suggested. This curriculum revolves around the classroom environment. The curriculum is divided by learning centers such as the block area, table toys, the art area, and so on. For each learning center, there are guidelines for selecting and arranging equipment, examples of ways to interact with children to encourage meaningful play and learning, suggestions for setting reasonable limits, and many activity ideas. Themes can be used with this curriculum, or it can stand alone.

Prescribed-Activity Curriculums

The Crayola Creative Program[6] consists of information on designing learning centers, skills for preschoolers, and themes. It includes 260 activities, a director's manual, a teacher's guide, assessment folders, and a videotape. The themes discussed are the following: colors, shapes, animals, seasons and weather, numbers, growing things, letters, foods, where things go, and symbols and signs. The learning centers discussed are arts and crafts, block play, language and listening, manipulatives, science and nature, and dramatic play.

Crossties[7] utilizes learning centers and sets of books to build a month-by-month theme-based curriculum. Themes for the month of November are the Farm, Fall Harvest, Farm to Market, the Grocery Store, the First Thanksgiving, Forest Resources, and Water Pollution. Also included are sample parent letters, pupil record forms, and a teacher manual.

PEEK: Peabody Early Experiences Kit[8] provides 1,000 activities for three- and four-year-olds. It includes lesson manuals, a teacher's guide, four puppets, 335 photographs, story cards and picture stories, song cards, cassettes or records, posters, various sizes of beads, cloth balls, a magnetic fishing pole, and more.

***The Portage Classroom Curriculum*[9]** provides specific activities arranged in the following themes: School; Animals; Friends; Transportation; I, Me; Safety; Family; Jobs. Also included are family activity letters, a checklist, and an administrative manual.

***Small Wonder*[10]** is a curriculum for children birth to 18 months (Level I) or 18 to 36 months (Level II). Each level includes 150 activity cards, a user's guide, picture cards, a progress chart, hand puppets, and more.

Multicultural/Bilingual Curriculum

The ***ALERTA*[11]** curriculum uses a theme approach to help you structure a program for a multicultural, bilingual (Hispanic) group of children. This curriculum combines a teaching approach (theory) with specific ideas, such as making maracas, ways to incorporate cultural items or themes into typical preschool activities, planning forms, and observation methods.

3. Individualizing

Individualizing means your schedule suits each child's needs for action and rest. It means that the equipment, materials, and layout of your classroom enhance the growth of every child and that the activities you choose are good ones for each child. It also means that the way you present the activities makes each child feel successful but challenged. Is this possible? Well, probably not for every child at all times, but you can do a great deal to ensure that success happens almost all of the time. You can ensure this by thorough planning, and by observing children carefully during an activity so you can change and adapt your curriculum.

Individualizing is an important goal to work towards because the more you individualize the smoother your classroom will run. Behavior problems will decrease and the amount of learning and growth will increase.

Preventing Problems

➤ Know your children well through assessing them, talking with parents, and observing children in action. Jot down notes about your children's strengths and weaknesses and keep your observations on file. Refer to the file at least weekly to refresh your memory about particular children, especially when you are planning. (This will help you maintain realistic expectations about what each child can and cannot do.)

➤ Prepare for the unexpected. Assume that any activity might not be successful, at least with some children, and plan for alternative ways of doing it or an alternative activity.

➤ Do all you can to get good volunteer help from the community, from parents, or wherever possible. Note that individualizing can be done much more effectively in small groups or one on one. Spend time informing your volunteers of what they can expect from particular children and train these volunteers to work effectively with those children.

➤ If you cannot get extra help, do activities in small groups while the rest of the children are doing free choice activities. If you have only one aide, divide the large group of children into two smaller groups. (Each child can have much more individual attention and many more chances to talk in a small group.)

➤ Individualize during free choice, which should last at least 45 minutes. Move around the classroom and observe each child at play. Ask questions or begin a converstion that will extend the child's thinking or creativity, if it will not interfere with his play. You might say, "Tell me about the picture you are painting."

➤ Add new equipment or materials to make the child's play more challenging or more fun. For instance, you might put out pieces of garden hose when the children start playing firefighter.

➤ Help the children solve any problems they may be having by asking questions and by having them generate solutions: "How can you get Sara to give you a turn with the puzzle without hurting her?"

➤ Provide a wide variety of equipment and materials. Have some simple three-piece puzzles as well as more difficult ones. Have some lightweight, easy-to-ride trikes as well as two-wheeled scooters or small bikes (some with training wheels).

Planning for Individual Needs

➤ When you are planning, meet with as many of your teaching team as possible, including volunteers. (By doing this, everyone will have a good sense of what you hope to achieve through your activities and how you hope to achieve your expectations for each child. They also can provide additional ideas for ways to individualize.)

➤ Review the previous week's activities before you plan. Determine what was successful, what was not, and why. Pay particular attention to the children who have special needs and review what worked well for them and what did not. Use what you know to plan for successful experiences for those children.

➤ Consider that a great deal of important individualizing can happen only when you make it part of your planning. For example, you decide to plan an activity with small groups of children during which they will take turns following verbal directions, such as, "Please put the red block underneath the chair." During your planning you realize that several children will find this direction easy and can be given more complicated directions, such as "Please put the blue block on the chair and the yellow block behind the chair." But some children will need simpler directions, such as "Please put a block on the chair."

➤ As you plan this verbal-direction activity, go through your list of children and pay particular attention to those with special needs. (This will help you get a good idea of how to individualize this activity.) For example, you may realize that one or two children will have trouble waiting for a turn. Several options to deal with this are possible:

• Allow these children to have their turns early and then to move on to another activity shortly after their turn.

• Do the activity with half the group while another adult does the activity with the other half in another room.

• Actively involve the children more, especially the ones you are concerned about. Let them take turns being the "Teacher" and giving out the directions.

• Make the activity more physically active. You might say, "Hop to the chair and put the red block on it."

• Do the verbal-direction activity with children during a time other than group time, especially if it can be done as part of a real activity. For example, during free choice ask individual children to help set the table for a snack. Give them commands related to setting up the snack: "Please put the blue bowl on the table."

• Plan this activity so that it will relate directly to your particular children. Note that the result, written on an index card or planning form, might look something like the following:

Small Group: Directions Game with Blocks and Chair

Me—Tiger group

Aide—Lion group in room 2

Mike and Jessica—Do puzzles if restless and help set snack later.

Celia—Harder (three directions)

Debbie and Anthony—Easier

Individualizing on the Spot

➤ Because you will not be able to think of all the possible needs for all your children, you will have to observe them carefully during an activity. If many of the children are restless or bored, change your activity. Do something else or change the way you are doing the activity. Make it simpler, quicker, or involve the children more actively. If one or two children are restless or bored, give them something specific to do or to hold. If that is not successful, let them do a different activity that will not be disruptive.

➤ If a child is having a difficult time accomplishing the activity you planned, modify it for him or give extra help, unless this will cause embarrassment. Ask the child first if he wants help: "Pouring juice is difficult. Would you like to pour from a smaller pitcher, wait until there is a smaller amount left, or ask a friend to do it for you?" Give encouragement to the child for what he can do. If he decides to wait, you might say, "You really have a lot of patience waiting for the juice pitcher to come back to you."

➤ Avoid highlighting a child's problem. If a child with gross-motor difficulties cannot do jumping jacks as well as the other children, ignore the differences, tell him about the abilities he does have, and provide help at a later time when you can be with the child privately. (This will prevent him from feeling different and less able than other children. It will also enable you to provide direct and effective help.)

➤ If a child can do your planned activity quickly and easily, add a little challenge to the activity. For example, you discover during a cooking project that a child knows how to measure half a cup. For the next ingredient have her measure out one-fourth of a cup. If he has some trouble, talk him through this process. "One quarter is a half of a half. Can you find the line on the cup that is halfway between the bottom and the one-half line?"

Individualizing the Physical Environment

The way you set up the classroom last year might have worked well for that group, but several children in your group this year wander about the room, are easily distracted, and do not settle into an activity. Use some of the following ideas to alter the physical environment to help those children and to benefit the other children as well.

➤ Provide a private, quiet space such as a refrigerator box with soft cushions inside.

➤ Define the learning centers and other areas in your room clearly. Put up dividers or tape on the floor around the areas.

➤ Make a planning board for each area, where children can place their name tags after they have decided where they will play. Ask them to tell you their plans.

➤ Limit the busy-ness of the room. Cover storage areas; have a few large, soothing posters rather than many small, brightly colored pictures; take down mobiles; organize and label all shelves and counters.

Individualizing Your Daily Schedule

➤ You may also need to revise your schedule for your group of children this year. Several children may tire easily or have short attention spans. You will have to shorten group times; lengthen free choice time; and perhaps add an additional, short rest time.

➤ Several children in the same group, however, may have high cognitive abilities. Use the increased free choice time to provide challenging activities for these children. Invite them to do silent reading or writing (to the best of their ability) during the additional rest time, if they are not tired.

➤ You will probably need to revise your schedule one or more times during the year as the children change and grow.

Resources

Bredekamp, Sue, ed. *Developmentally Appropriate Practice in Early Childhood Programs Serving Children From Birth Through Age 8*. Washington, D.C.: NAEYC, 1987.

Schickedanz, J., et al. *Toward Understanding Children*. Boston: Little Brown, 1982.

4. Field Trips Are Supposed to Be Fun

Field trips are an extremely important part of a program for young children. Although they can be costly and are often stressful, they are worth the effort because children get to see, smell, and touch firsthand the world around them (which is the way they learn best). After a field trip, children enjoy recreating what they experienced when they return to the classroom. After a field trip to a city harbor, the children in one class made elaborate ships and docks with blocks, drew pictures of boats, and acted out riding on a ship for several weeks. Providing opportunities for children to see and experience something new, followed by time to recreate it through play and art, is a powerful way to help children learn and grow.

If at all possible, plan one or more field trips a month. A field trip does not have to be very elaborate or be to an unusual place. You can show the children a new aspect of something familiar. A trip to a popular local restaurant where the children can see how the food is prepared and ask questions of the cook can be very rewarding. This can then provide the basis for some great play situations back in the dramatic play area, especially if some playdough is provided to "cook" with.

Preventing Problems

➤ Before a field trip, get parent permission forms signed and place large notices to remind parents of the trip.

➤ To allow time for preparation, arrange the field trip early in the week, but not the first day back after a weekend. Note that children are often more attentive early in the week, so take your field trip then. During the rest of the week you can provide activities in which the children play, talk about, and draw what they have experienced on their trip.

➤ Carefully scout out and plan your trip. Visit the place yourself before the trip so you will experience no unpleasant surprises. Make sure there are things to see and do that will hold the children's attention and interest. (Places such as museums which do not allow touching will be frustrating for them.) Request that the guide be someone who is experienced with young children. If no one is available, gather some basic information and do the tour yourself.

➤ Keep the trip short and simple. Avoid the temptation to visit several different places on the

same day because they are close by. Visit only two or three rooms of a large museum or only two sections of the zoo. (Overstimulation caused by doing and seeing too much will make the children crabby and tired.) If the field trip will be a long one, plan for at least one unstructured time when the children can freely play at a nearby park, playground, or gym.

➤ Before going, tell the children a little of what they can expect to see on the field trip. If possible, show some pictures of the place. Read a book and sing songs related to the trip. For example, you might sing "Johnny Works with One Hammer" and read *In Christina's Tool Box* (Dianne Homan, Lollipop Power, 1981) before a trip to a hardware store.

➤ Set one or two rules for safety, such as "Walk at all times" and "Stay with the class." Ask the children to repeat the rules. If necessary, practice them by taking a short walk before the field trip. Set any special rules needed for a particular field trip, such as "Stay back from the water."

➤ Put a name tag on each child with the name and phone number of your center/school on it in case a child gets lost. Consider dividing the class into two smaller groups for a field trip. Line up extra help from responsible adults such as parents, your supervisor, or volunteers. Assign several children to each adult. (The adult will then be responsible for those children throughout the trip.) Ask for a "head count" from each adult about once an hour to make sure all the children are accounted for. Make sure each child has a partner whom she will stay with during the entire field trip.

➤ Consider using a long loop of rope with knots tied along it when walking on a field trip. Have each child hold onto a knot and one adult hold the front while another adult holds the back. Control the length of the rope, the spacing of the knots (so that children don't step on another's heels), and the walking pace. (This provides the group control you need for safety while giving children some responsibility and autonomy.)

➤ Bring along snacks and plenty of water, especially on hot days. Build slack time into your field trip schedule to allow for stopping for food or drinks. (When children are hungry or thirsty, they learn little from a trip and may misbehave.)

➤ Take along a first-aid kit and emergency numbers for each child, as well as tissues and some extra clothes.

Dealing with Existing Problems

Active, Overly Excited, Unruly Group

➤ Start the year out with short, simple, nearby field trips. Get as many adults as possible to help. As the children gain skills and learn rules for field trips, increase the length and complexity of the trips.

➤ If the children become difficult to manage during a trip, consider cutting the trip short, if possible. If transportation problems do not allow this, change your plans and walk to a nearby park or playground.

➤ If only one child typically makes your trips unpleasant and difficult, assign an adult to be with just that one child during the trip. As a last resort, consider leaving this child with another class for the day or making a similar arrangement. In any case, don't deprive the majority of your children the value of field trips because of one difficult child.

No Transportation or Budget for Field Trips

➤ Provide the valuable experiences gained from field trips by visiting nearby stores, businesses, services, and agencies. The special attention the children can get from an owner or worker and the "behind the scenes" look provide a very different experience from the one they get when they go to these same places with their parents as consumers. Visit some of the following places on your neighborhood trips: library, post office, fire station, police station, telephone company, newspaper publisher, office building, hospital, doctor, veterinarian, dentist, optometrist, other schools, lumber yard, florist, hardware store, auto dealership, repair shop, photographer's studio, radio station, recycling center, teachers' homes, motel, restaurant, construction site, bank, supermarket, service station, pet store, scrap yard, and carpenter's shop.

➤ Prepare children to look for certain items by giving them a set of pictures to match to things they will see on the trip. Encourage them to check off the picture when they see it. (They will feel very grown up carrying clipboards,* pencils, and checklists, and you will provide a focus and a sense of purpose for them.) Challenge them cognitively by asking them to look for some things they might not usually notice. Enhance their social and language skills by having two children work together on one list. (This is a good way to make a familiar trip a unique experience.)

➤ Take a walk around the neighborhood or to a nearby park as another alternative to an elaborate trip. A walk can have a particular theme or purpose and a great deal of spontaneous learning can happen. On your neighborhood walk, look for or collect (if appropriate) items like the following: leaves of various kinds, grasses and weeds, wildflowers, insects, animals, trees, colors, shapes, litter to recycle, simple architectural features (columns, steps, gargoyles), working people, and smells. Note that the clipboard idea can work well for neighborhood walks when looking for items that cannot be collected. With this activity you will enhance the important cognitive skill of classification, especially if you are creating unique categories such as smells: sweet smells (candy store), polluting smells (cigarette smoke), food smells (deli), strong smells (gasoline). Remember that the younger the children, the simpler and more concrete the categories should be. When you are back in the classroom, discuss, sort, and graph what the children saw or collected.

Resources

Redleaf, Rhoda. *Open The Door Let's Explore: Neighborhood Field Trips for Young Children.* St. Paul, MN: Toys 'n Things Press, 1983

Russell, Helen Ross. *Ten Minute Field Trips*, Chicago: Ferguson, Chicago, 1973

5. Toys from Home

Although most teachers have a rule that toys from home are not allowed in school, children still bring them in. They crave the security of a link from home and they may have a need to show off what they own. Children also use toys from home as a way to make friends. Accommodate these needs in your classroom. Stifling them will only lead to frustration and frustration will lead to misbehavior. Consider some of the following ways to allow toys from home in the classroom while preventing the problems caused by them.

➤ At least once a week, give children an opportunity to share their toys during the day. You might do this through a "Show and Tell" session. To prevent "Show and Tell" from lasting too long, have some children share every Monday, others on Tuesday, and so on.

➤ Allow children to play with their toys from home during the first fifteen minutes of free choice.

➤ Provide a special shelf where toys from home are kept. Set up a procedure whereby during free choice, children who want to play with the toy must ask the owner. The owner can refuse or agree to the request. This promotes language and social development, although it takes more work on your part to remind children to ask and to help them find the right words. Several months may pass before this routine works smoothly. It will work better with four- and five-year-old children than with younger children.

Resources

Oken-Wright, Pamela. "Show and Tell Grows Up," *Young Children* 43(2) (January 1988): 52-57.

---

*Make inexpensive clip boards by stapling paper to a stiff piece of cardboard and attaching a string with a pencil on the end of it. Store the pencil on the cardboard by gluing a small piece of Velcro™ on the pencil and by stapling the corresponding Velcro™ piece to the top of the board.

6. Lost or Missing

Clothing and toys (or parts of toys) are the two most common items lost or missing in early childhood programs. In either case, the loss is very frustrating because clothing and toys are expensive and time consuming to replace, and the loss was probably preventable. When there are many lost items it is usually symptomatic of a disorganized program. Although lost or missing items will always be a reality for groups of busy adults and active young children, losses can be minimized by using some of the ideas in this chapter.

Preventing Problems

Clothing

➤ In your parent handbook and during new parent orientation, include a statement that requests that all clothing be labeled with the child's name. Also include a statement that says that in spite of all the care you take, clothing will occasionally get lost or be taken home by another child, never to be seen again. (This creates a realistic expectation that if the child is in the preschool for more than a few months there is a chance that some item will get lost.) Ask the parents to please check all clothing their child brings home to make sure it indeed belongs to their child. Note that many children have clothing that looks similar to those belonging to another child.

➤ Include in your parent handbook a statement making clear that the program either will or will not reimburse parents for lost clothing. If the program will reimburse parents, state how the rates are determined.

➤ Encourage parents to purchase a laundry marker pen and put their child's initials on the inside label of her clothing. Ask parents to do this at school if they are not able to do it at home. Only do this marking yourself as a last resort.

➤ Bring a box outside or have a very specific place designated where children are required to put any clothing that they remove when they're outside.

➤ Make sure each child has her own cubby or box where she can keep her personal belongings. Be very consistent about requiring the child to put in her cubby any clothing she removes when inside.

➤ Give a quick check of cubbies before the children go home each day and before leaving any area (field trip site, playground) where children may have removed jackets or sweaters.

➤ Keep a "Lost and Found Box" in a place where it can not be ransacked too easily. Keep a supply of clothing that has been donated or purchased cheaply from secondhand stores. If you can replace an item of lost clothing, with a reasonable facsimile, you may be able to reduce the parents' unhappiness.

Toys or Toy Parts

➤ Put the name of your class on any item that may be used in another classroom, but that belongs in your room. Put the name of your school on any item that is shared by various classrooms. Make an inventory. List every item in your class on a sheet of paper so that you will know if anything is missing. Update this list at least once a year. Add any new toys or equipment to the list. Remove from the list any item that has been discarded.

➤ Keep a file of addresses of toy companies listed on the boxes or wrappers of items you purchased. Most companies will replace missing pieces of games or toys for a small fee. You may have to wait a number of weeks, however, before you receive the part. Many companies also have toll-free numbers for you to call to find out if the part can be replaced and the cost.

➤ Most cardboard toy boxes will not hold up very long under constant use in a preschool classroom.

Start to build a collection of sturdy plastic containers (the clear ones are best as they make it easier for a child to find the one he is looking for). Transfer the toy or game into the container when you bring it to the classroom. (These regularly go on sale at discount department stores. Pieces of a toy are much less likely to be lost in one of these than in a dilapidated box.)

➤ Label all your shelves and containers. Always require that toys and games be put back where they belong when each child is finished playing with them.

➤ Code your puzzles and all the pieces. For example, on the back of a puzzle, write the number *1* with a permanent marker and write the same number on the back of each of the pieces of that puzzle. Code your next puzzle number *2*, the next *3*, and so on. If pieces from various puzzles get mixed together (not uncommon in preschools), you can separate them easily using this method.

Dealing with Existing Problems

When Clothing Is Missing

➤ Enlist the help of the children and other staff in tracking down the item. Form a search party and make a game out of it.

➤ As you know, clothing is a major expense to parents, and so the loss of any clothing is upsetting. Explain to the parents the program's policy about missing clothing. Show them the policy in writing. Explain what you have done to locate the item. Assure them that you will continue to look for it. Send a note home to all parents in case the missing item mistakenly went home with another child. Place a note on your parent bulletin board about the missing item. Knowing that you are concerned, that you take the problem seriously, that you tried your best to find it, and that you will continue to do so will usually satisfy most parents.

(For ideas on dealing with parents who are irate about lost clothing, see the chapter "Complaining Parents" on pages 144 to 146.)

When a Toy or Part Is Missing

➤ Check your shelves at the end of free choice time to make sure all items are back where they belong. Check puzzles and games to make sure all the pieces are still there. If any pieces are missing, take the time to have every child look for the missing piece before the class does anything else.

In looking for the piece, move shelves, tables, chairs, rugs, and other furnishings as necessary. Check in the trash cans and sort through all the toy containers. Ask all the children to check their pockets and cubbies.

Do this all-out search for a number of reasons: First, the longer you wait, the less likely you are to find a missing piece. Second, you are teaching the children that the supplies are valuable and must be taken care of. Note that they will be much more diligent about not losing pieces after one or two such searches.

➤ If the piece is still not found, ask the janitor (if you have one) to look for the piece when cleaning. If it does not show up in a day or two, write to the company for a replacement as described previously. Have the children help you write the letter so they can appreciate the process necessary to obtain a new piece.

➤ If a replacement can be made, do so. If the missing item or piece is something the children can make themselves or help make, then involve them. Puzzle pieces can be made from wood scraps with a band saw or jig saw, from "plastic wood," or from cardboard. Layer cardboard pieces or use cardboard from packing boxes to make them thicker. Laminate the pieces with clear Contact™ paper for durability.

7 . Coping with Accidents and Emergencies

Nothing is more frightening than a hurt child. Not only are you concerned about the health of the child, but you are worried about appeasing anxious parents and perhaps an upset boss. Although you can do many things to prevent problems, an accident will occasionally happen even in the best program. Any time large numbers of children are in one place along with climbing equipment and room to move, accidents will occur. Although preventing and avoiding injuries is one of your most important tasks, allowing children to take some risks is a vital part of helping them learn and grow. Making risk taking as safe as possible is a difficult balancing act. Every insurance company would love a center or school without a playground, but the need children have to develop themselves physically far outweighs the risks.

Most injuries happen on playgrounds or gym equipment. Swings are the cause of most serious playground accidents. (For safety ideas, see the chapter "Safe Fun Outdoors or in the Gym" on pages 35 to 37.)

Preventing Problems

➤ Before a child enrolls in your classroom, obtain from her parents the name of their doctor to call and permission (an emergency release form) to take their child to the nearest hospital in case of an emergency. Update the form every six months and make a copy of it. Put the original in the child's file, and keep all the copies together to take on field trips.

➤ In your classroom, post an escape plan, which consists of written instructions and a map with red arrows showing the quickest way out, as well as alternative exits. Use different colored arrows on your map.

➤ Keep emergency phone numbers clearly posted by each phone. Include fire, police, ambulance, and poison control (unless you have a centralized system accessed by dialing 911). Also keep a sign with your address on it near the phone so it can be quickly recited in an emergency.

➤ Role play with the children what you will do and what they should do when a child gets hurt outside, on a field trip, or inside.

➤ Set a few inside and a few outside rules related to safety. Among your inside rules, you might include the following:
"Always walk inside the classroom."
"Throw only soft things and throw them away from people."

"Build blocks only as high as your nose."
"Pick toys up from the floor after you have finished playing."
"Touch other people only after you have their permission."

For your outside rules you might include:
"Swing only when seated."
"Go down the slide on your bottom."
"Climb using two hands."

➤ Enforce these rules consistently. Focus your energy and attention on the children when they are following the rules. Give them information about their behavior: "When you build the blocks lower than your nose, they can't fall on your head. You're keeping yourself safe and healthy." Practice the rules by role-playing in small groups.

➤ Keep your first-aid and CPR cards current. (First-aid training is available through most Red Cross chapters. However, it is important to request and receive first-aid training that directly relates to young children and to medical emergencies typically seen in preschools.)

➤ Have a first-aid kit available where you can get to it quickly. Have in it at least the following: adhesive strip bandages (various sizes), adhesive tape, sterile gauze bandages and pads (various sizes), disposable and sterile plastic gloves, syrup of ipecac, a thermometer, and tweezers. Check with your local health department for additions to your kit. On field trips take a first-aid kit as well as emergency release forms for each child. Check expiration dates on items such as syrup of ipecac periodically.

➤ Keep several ice packs in the kitchen freezer. (Bags of frozen peas work well because they are pliable. Make sure, however, that they will not be used for food.) Keep a bee sting kit on hand and learn how to use it. (Some children are highly allergic to bee stings and require an injection to keep them breathing if they are stung.) Ask each parent when they enroll if their child is allergic to bee stings. Take the kit on any outings or field trips if you have an allergic child in your class.

➤ To prevent choking, do not give popcorn, peanuts or whole grapes to children under three years old, or peanuts to children under four years old. Do not give balloons to any child.

➤ Keep any poisonous or dangerous substance in a locked cabinet with a "Mr. Yuk" sticker on it. Tell the children what the sticker means. Keep your poison control phone number posted by the telephone and keep a bottle of syrup of ipecac available (in a locked cabinet) in case you need to induce vomiting. (All drugstores sell this syrup. Be sure to check the expiration date monthly.)

➤ Cover all electrical outlets with childproof safety covers. Check with your local child-care licensing agency to determine which type of outlet covers are best to use.

➤ Remove from outside the building as well as from inside the classroom any plants and shrubs that are toxic. Replace them with nontoxic plants.

➤ Provide plenty of water for the children to drink, particularly outside on hot days. If there is no water fountain outside, take a thermos of water and paper cups outside with you. On hot days, put sun block on children to prevent sunburn. Obtain parent permission first, and ask them to supply the lotion.

How to Make Risk-Taking Reasonably Safe

➤ After you have established safety rules and the children understand them well, provide opportunities for the children to take physical risks while minimizing the possibility of injury. Most children love to take risks, which is one reason they disobey safety rules. If they know they will have many opportunities to take risks, they are more likely to obey the established rules.

➤ The following is one example of structuring safe risk-taking: Bring out mats to put under a climbing structure. One at a time, allow children to hang from their knees, do flips, swing with one hand, or do something similar, depending on each child's ability. Be the "Spotter" to make sure the children do not fall too hard. Teach the children to break their falls with their arms. If needed, add additional safety equipment such as more mats, kneepads, and a bike helmet. If the bars are not too high, teach the children to be spotters for each other. Allow only one child on the equipment at a time and put a short time limit on each turn, as accidents are more likely to happen when the children are tired. By structuring and monitoring a risky activity, as just described, you will help children learn that risks can be taken, that they are fun, but that there are sensible ways to take a risk.

➤ Using a similar structure, try other activities such as the following: tumbling games and hand stands, wrestling, jumping from reasonable heights, and swinging on a rope.

➤ Invite an older child to the class who is a good skateboarder. Before this older child demonstrates tricks, have her talk about all the safety equipment she wears and why she wears it. Encourage her to talk about the hours of training she did before she could do tricks and about the cautions she takes.

Successful Fire Drills

➤ At least monthly, check your smoke detectors and sprinkler system (if you are lucky enough to have one) to make sure they are in good working order.

➤ Invite to your classroom a fire safety specialist from your local fire bureau to give you help on establishing safe classroom procedures and equipment use. If she talks to the children, make sure she can speak at their level without being condescending.

➤ Practice a fire drill at least once a month with your class. Early in the year, before the first actual fire drill, slowly walk through a fire drill several times. Talk to the children about what they are doing and why. Tell them about the loud bell and what to expect. Make sure each adult knows her specific duties for fire drills. Time your fire drills with a stopwatch. Set a goal with the children for reducing the time they need to evacuate the room and work together towards this goal.

➤ Remind the children periodically of the fire drill rules:
   "Be silent."
   "Walk quickly."
   "Follow the teacher's directions."
Also make sure they know and can find the specific destination where the class will meet outside, such as "Along the fence behind the big climber."

➤ Take your class attendance list with you and account for each child once you all arrive at the outside destination.

➤ Shut off the lights and close the doors when leaving the room. (This will slow the spread of a fire if one actually happens.)

➤ When the children and adults are safely outside, briefly discuss how much time the evacuation took, what went well, and what can be improved.

➤ If you do not have a formal fire alarm bell, use a special whistle or hand bell that is loud and is used for no other purpose. (In order for the children to respond quickly, they must associate this sound with a fire alarm and with nothing else.)

➤ Hold fire drills at various times of the day, including when children are outside. Invest in smoke detectors.

➤ When the children are proficient at fire drills, change a part of the drill. Block one of the exits or doorways and use another way to go outside. (In a real fire, your quickest exits may be blocked by heat or smoke.)

➤ Also have children practice "Stop, Drop, and Roll" in case their clothes catch on fire. Tape a large cloth or paper "flame" to their clothes to make the experience more concrete.

Keep Track of Injuries

➤ After an injury has occurred, write a note (or fill in a preprinted form) to give to parents, explaining what happened and describing the treatment you gave. Sign the note yourself and have the parent sign it. Keep a copy for your own records. (This will keep all information clear and straight and will protect you and the parents from liability.)

➤ At the end of every month and every year, look back over the records to determine the most common injuries. Set a goal to reduce those injuries by making specific changes such as fixing or removing certain equipment, setting some new classroom rules, rearranging furniture or materials, or starting a fund-raising campaign for a new playground surface.

Resources

Big Bird Earthquake Kit. FEMA, PO Box 7024, Washington, DC 20024. (Free material from Federal Emergency Management Agency includes safety information, activity ideas, a board game, information about what causes earthquakes, a cassette called "Beatin' the Quake," and a story called "Elmo and the Earthquake.")

Bosque, Elena, and Watson, Sheila. *Safe & Sound: How to Prevent and Treat Most Common Childhood Emergencies*, New York: St Martin's Press, 1988.

Channing, Emily Blair. *Emergency First-aid for Children*. Reading, MA: Addison-Wesley, 1984.

Dworkin, G.M. *CPR for Infants and Children: A Guide to Cardiopulmonary Resuscitation*. Washington, DC: Child Welfare League of America, 1989

Esbensen, Steen B. *An Outdoor Classroom*. Ypsilanti, MI: High/Scope Press, 1987.

Green, Martin I. *A Sigh of Relief: The first-aid handbook for childhood emergencies*. New York: Bantam Books, 1977

Health in Day Care. Developed by Georgetown University Child Development Center, 3800 Reservoir Road NW, Washington, DC 20007, with grants from ACYF and Maternal and Child Health, 1986. Includes, in looseleaf format, *A Manual for Day Care Providers* and *A Training Guide for Day Care Providers*.

Kendrick, A.S.; Kaufmann, R.; and Messenger, K.P., eds. *Healthy Young Children: A Manual for Programs*. Washington, DC: NAEYC, 1988.

Maraty, L.; Puse, J.; and Cross, M. *Health, Safety, and Nutrition for the Young Child*. Albany, NY: Delmar, 1985.

Pantell, Fries, Vickerery. *Taking Care of Your Child: A Parents' Guide to Medical Care*, Reading, MA: Addison-Wesley, 1977.

Agencies

Consumer Product Safety Commission (1-800-638-2772). To report an unsafe toy or product, or to get safety information about a particular toy or product.

Environmental Protection Agency (1-800-424-9065). To report hazardous/toxic materials or to get information about particular materials.

8. Children Who Are Ill and Other Health Concerns

There is a great deal of concern about children in early childhood programs becoming sick more frequently and with more serious illnesses than other children. Although some evidence indicates that this may be generally true, in programs where reasonable health precautions are taken and where teachers are aware of the causes of and ways to prevent common illnesses, the threat to children's health should be no greater than anywhere else.

Preventing Problems

➤ Stay home when you are sick. Because you may get little sick leave and substitutes are hard to find, you probably feel obligated to be at work unless you are practically dying! If you do this, however, you may infect some children, who will infect other children, who will then infect you again. (This cycle of sickness is not uncommon in preschools.)

➤ Make sure all children are fully immunized. You can obtain information about immunization schedules from your local health department.

➤ Before children enroll in your program, require that they receive a physical examination from a physician clearing them to participate fully in all preschool activities or explaining any limitations.

➤ Require parents to fill out a health and medical history form. This can be very helpful if, for example, you notice spots on a child which look like chickenpox. The form will tell you if the child has already had the chickenpox. Thus, you can determine the nature of the spots more easily. If the program keeps these files in a central location, make sure you know how to find them for the

children in your class and that you see the form for each new child.

➤ Wash your hands thoroughly with warm water and disinfectant soap. Note that this is the single most important thing a teacher can do to prevent a wide variety of illnesses and diseases. Wash your hands after diapering, using the toilet yourself, helping a child with toileting, helping a child blow his nose, blowing your own nose, and before serving and/or eating food.

➤ Supervise children's handwashing carefully. Make sure they thoroughly wash when arriving at school from home; after toileting; after blowing their noses; before meals and snacks; and after playing with dirt, sand, paint, and so on.

➤ Keep handy spray bottles of bleach water (one tablespoon of bleach to one quart of water; one part bleach to ten parts water for blood spills). Keep this out of children's reach. Use bleach water to wipe off surfaces (especially changing tables after diapering), toilets and sinks once during the day, and classroom tables before and after meals and snacks.

➤ Wash toys regularly and spray plastic toys with a bleach solution. Put toys through the kitchen sanitizer/dishwasher twice a week, especially infant and toddler toys that are often "mouthed." Many infant and toddler toys need to be cleaned on an ongoing, daily basis. Sanitize only those toys that will not be ruined by high heat or bleach. Or, wash toys in the water-play table with warm, soapy water. (Most children enjoy doing this.)

➤ To prevent the possible spread of AIDS (Acquired Immune Deficiency Syndrome), use sterile, disposable plastic gloves to avoid direct skin contact with blood from cuts or wounds. To prevent the spread of Hepatitis and other diseases, use these gloves when serving food.

➤ Exclude children from attending your program if they show signs of any infectious disease (caused by a virus, bacterium, fungus, or parasite), communicable disease (easily spread), diarrhea, or if they feel too sick to participate in activities. (Fever is not a good indicator of a child's condition or contagiousness, so judge by the child's behavior, actions, and symptoms.) If a child becomes ill while in school, notify parents (or the emergency contact person the parents have designated if they cannot be reached) to pick him up. Make sure your program has a written policy, which parents receive upon enrollment, stating that this will happen. Notify the parents of all children who came in contact with a child who has an infectious or communicable illness. Notify your local health department and find out what actions need to be taken.

➤ For the most common illnesses, have preprinted forms that list the symptoms, suggested treatment (if confirmed by a physician), and when the child can return to preschool. Give this form to the parent when he comes to pick up his child. Make clear that you do not know definitely what the child has but that based on the symptoms, you are stating what you suspect.

➤ Keep trash, especially soiled diapers and used tissues, in a container with a secure lid. Keep the container covered. Empty the trash daily in half-day programs and at least twice a day in full-day programs.

➤ Provide at least three feet of space between cribs, cots or mats. Place children "head to toe" so that their faces are not close to each other during naptime. (These measures will prevent colds from spreading.)

➤ See that each child has his own toothbrush. Store the brushes in such a way that the bristles of one brush never touch another brush. Do not let children touch any brush but their own. Use some of the following ways to accomplish this: plastic travel covers, hooks in individual cubbies, a rack with separators between each brush. Sterilize toothbrushes frequently with bleach water or in the dishwasher.

➤ Provide a "get well" space where a child can lie down on a cot if he is not feeling well. Set up this space away from other children, but within eyesight of an adult. Have the children who are waiting to be picked up by parents because of illness use this area.

➤ Contact your local health department for information and charts on common contagious illnesses and suggested policies for your center.

Lyme Disease

Although not contagious, Lyme disease is relatively new and spreading rapidly, but it can be prevented by preschool teachers who are aware.

Lyme disease is caused by a small "deer tick." In most cases, symptoms start with large red ring-shaped welts, one to three weeks after the bite. Flu-like symptoms often appear next. If not treated early with antibiotics, serious complications can develop including painful, swollen joints, partial paralysis, or heart problems. If treated early, the illness remains mild.

➤ To prevent Lyme disease, make sure all the children wear long sleeves and long pants when walking in or near tall grass and woods, especially during the warm months.

➤ If a child is bitten by a tick, remove it by grasping it firmly with tweezers or with a tissue and by pulling straight out. Wash the area around the bite and your own hands. Save the dead tick and refer the child to a doctor.

➤ Keep up to date on the latest information on Lyme disease through newspapers and your local health department.

AIDS

AIDS (Acquired Immune Deficiency Syndrome) and ARC (AIDS-related complex) are very serious, usually deadly, viruses. They fall under the category of HIV infections (Human Immunodeficiency Virus). The virus attacks the immune system and breaks down a person's ability to fight off illness and disease.

HIV (AIDS) spreads exclusively through sexual contact and blood-to-blood contact. Most children who are HIV positive can attend a preschool program. No direct evidence indicates that AIDS can be transmitted from a bite or from an open cut, although this is theoretically possible if blood-to-blood contact is made. The decision to enroll a child who is HIV positive must be made on a case by case basis by a team of people consisting of the child's parents, the teacher, the director/principal, the child's doctor, and any others directly involved in the care of the child.

➤ A child whose immune system is weak should be given extra protection from infectious and communicable diseases (send him home at the first sign of these illnesses in the program) and should have his right to privacy protected. Give medical information only to those who absolutely need to know. Remember that other parents do not need to know.

➤ When treating cuts or dealing with blood in any way, take precautions at all times with all the children in your program. Use disposable, sterile gloves, clean spilled blood with bleach water, and wash your hands thoroughtly. (You may have a child who is HIV positive in your class and not know it.)

➤ Information about AIDS is changing rapidly. Stay informed through newspapers and your health department.

Giving Medication

This often causes problems for teachers as they sometimes have to remember to give medication to several different children at various times during the day. A missed dose may harm the child and will undoubtedly irritate parents.

➤ Use an electronic "pill reminder" alarm. (They are very small and relatively cheap. A parent may be willing to purchase or lend you one if it means not missing a dose of medicine.)

➤ Administer only prescription medications with written orders from the doctor and the parent's signature. (This will limit the number of medicines given out.) Don't give over-the-counter medications to children at the request of parents. Insist on permission from the doctor.

➤ Ask if the parents will provide the same medication or a similar one that requires two or fewer daily doses so it can be given at home. (This can be done with many drugs and usually can be arranged over the phone with the doctor and/or pharmacist.)

➤ If a parent works or lives nearby, request that he come to the class and administer the medicine.

➤ Ask the parents to have the pharmacist provide a small, extra, labeled bottle to use at preschool. (This will eliminate the hassle for parents of pick-ing up and bringing in the medicine daily and relieve you from having to return it to them at the end of each day.)

➤ Post a log sheet near where the medicine is locked and write down each dose of medication you give. (This will help you remember if and when you gave it.) Provide a separate sheet for each child.

Children Who Come to School Dirty

Cleanliness can be a personal or cultural issue. Some people and some cultures accept body odor and have different standards of cleanliness. In many cases those standards are related to the limited availability of water, soap, towels, washing machines, dryers, and so on, because of poverty or circumstances. A reasonable amount of cleanliness is necessary, however, for children to stay healthy and to be pleasing enough for other children to want to play with them. If the lack of cleanliness creates a real problem for a child in your class, consider the following:

➤ Meet with the parents to determine their perspective on cleanliness. Help them find resources or easy methods for cleaning clothes and children if necessary. Let them know objective reasons for your concern (the child is not making friends or a cut became infected). Explain that in the classroom setting a higher standard of cleanliness is needed for the child to stay healthy because so many children are close together for long periods. Remember that health habits at home are not your main concern, unless the child's health is seriously threatened.

➤ If conditions are extremely bad and the child's health and well-being are truly at stake, refer the family to your local social service agency. Follow your program's policies on referrals—usually a supervisor will make the call. (See "Parents Who May Be Abusive to Their Children" on pages 154 to 157.) Note that the agency may provide the family with a home health worker who is trained to help with these matters.

➤ Offer the child the opportunity to clean himself at school soon after he arrives. Assist with this, if necessary. Provide a clean set of clothes for him to use (donated or secondhand) if he desires. Do this discreetly to avoid embarrassment. (Most children who do this prefer to change back into their clothes from home before they leave school at the end of the day.)

➤ Help the other children maintain respect and consideration for the child. Remind them of the rule about using words that don't hurt. Support the child who gets ridiculed and help him stand up for himself: "Michael is a kind person and a good friend. That is much more important than what his clothes look like."

Resources

Aronson, S. S. "Health Update: Exclusion Criteria for Ill Children." *Exchange* 49 (May 1986): 13-16.

Bosque, Elena, and Watson, Sheila. *Safe & Sound: How to Prevent and Treat Most Common Childhood Emergencies.* New York: St Martin's Press, 1988.

Health in Day Care. Developed by Georgetown University Child Development Center, 3800 Reservoir Road NW, Washington DC 20007, with grants from ACYF and Maternal and Child Health, 1986. Includes, in looseleaf format, *A Manual for Day Care Providers* and *A Training Guide for Day Care Providers.*

Maraty, L.; Puse, J.; and Cross, M. *Health, Safety, and Nutrition for the Young Child.* Albany, NY: Delmar, 1985

Vaughan, Gerard. *Mummy, I Don't Feel Well: A Pictorial Guide to Common Childhood Illnesses.* London: Heinemann, 1977.

Kendrick, A.S.; Kaufmann, R.; Messenger, K.P., eds. *Healthy Young Children: A Manual for Programs.* Washington, DC: NAEYC, 1988.

Footnotes to Part II

[1]Katz, L. and Chard, S. *Engaging Young Children's Minds: The Project Approach*, Norwood, N.J.: Ablex, 1989.

[2]Hohmann, Banet, and Weikart. *Young Children in Action*, Ypsilanti, MI: High/Scope Press, 1979.

[3]Berrueta-Clement, J., et al., *Changed Lives: The Effects of the Perry Preschool Program on Youths through Age 19*, Ypsilanti, MI: High/Scope Press, 1984.

[4]For more information on *Emergent Curriculum* contact Elizabeth Jones or Sydney Clemens, Pacific Oaks College, 5-6 Westmoreland Place, Pasadena, CA 91103. The following books provide examples of *Emergent Curriculum* in action: *Teacher* by Sylvia Ashton-Warner (Touchstone Press, 1985); *The Sun's Not Broken, A Cloud's Just in the Way: On Child-Centered Teaching* by Sydney Clemens (Gryphon House, 1984); *Walley's Stories* by Vivian Paley (Harvard University Press, 1981).

[5]*The Creative Curriculum,* Creative Associates, 4419 39th St., N.W., Washington, D.C. 20016.

[6]*The Crayola Creative Program.* Binney and Smith, Educational Products Division, 1100 Church Lane, PO Box 431, Easton, PA 18044-0431.

[7]*Crossties.* Cole, et al. The Economy Company, PO Box 25308, Oklahoma City, OK 73125, 1977

[8]*PEEK.* Lloyd Dunn, et al. AGS, Publishers Building, Circle Pines, MN 55014-1796.

[9]*The Portage Classroom Curriculum.* Joan Brinckerhoff. Portage Project Materials, 626 E Slifer St., Portage, WI 53901.

[10]*Small Wonder.* Merle B. Karnes. AGS, Publishers Building, Circle Pines, MN 55014-1796.

[11]Williams and De Gaetano. *ALERTA.* Menlo Park, CA: Addison-Wesley, 1985.

Part III
Children Who Are Challenging

1. Suspected Handicaps

2. Children with Handicaps in Your Class

3. Gifted or Talented Children

4. Children Who Are Culturally or Physically "Different" and Biased Behaviors

5. TV/Video Obsessed Children

6. Children with Extreme Fears

7. The Sexually Precocious Child

8. The Child Who Identifies with the Opposite Sex and Sex-Bias Issues

9. Children Who Are Too Responsible

1. Suspected Handicaps

As you are the first teacher for most of your children, you will come in contact with some who have mild handicaps which have not been detected. Sometimes this happens because no one has yet realized that a problem exists, but sometimes parents deny that their child has a problem or the family physician says that the child will grow out of it.

A child in your class who is clumsy and has many accidents on the playground may have gross-motor coordination problems, which should be looked at by a physical therapist. A child (over three and a half) who has difficulty putting together simple puzzles, drawing simple shapes, getting dressed, or eating a meal without making a mess may have fine motor coordination problems, which should be looked at by an occupational therapist. A child who never seems to listen to you or seems lost in her own world may have problems hearing and should be seen by a physician, an audiologist, or an ear, nose, and throat specialist (ENT). A child who bumps into things and has trouble concentrating may not be seeing well and should be seen by an ophthalmologist. A child who says very little or talks in "baby talk" may have speech or language problems (the most common handicap in young children) and should be seen by a speech therapist.

How do you know if the child really has a problem that needs professional help? Observe the child carefully and give a screening test.

If your program has policies and procedures in place regarding screening, observing, diagnosing, and serving children with handicaps, follow these procedures. Use the information in this chapter to determine if the practices are good ones and to strengthen them if needed. If your program has no set policies and procedures, use the information in this chapter to help develop them.

Observing

➤ Write down exactly what you see the child do without interpreting it. Do not include your judgements. For example, you might write the following:

Chris	2/20/90	8:45	Tripped and fell when entered class
		9:00	Slid off chair
		9:05	Knocked over milk glass
		9:20	Bumped into table while running to circle. Bruised leg.

This observation report provides clear evidence of the child's difficulties. Show this list to parents and specialists.

➤ To help you observe a particular concern, use observation checklists. There are checklists for behavior, social/emotional development, language, speech, and more. (For checklists to use, see the resources on page 68.) Some checklists give scores to help you determine the extent of the problem, but most just list behaviors to look for, giving you a general picture of the child's strengths and weaknesses. Checklists often list behaviors you may not think of looking for or may not consider part of the problem. They provide further evidence of real concerns about the child.

Screening

A screening test gives a general profile of a child's strengths and weaknesses. It cannot be used to determine if a child has a certain handicap, but only to determine if a child should receive further testing by a specialist.

➤ Use a screening test that is valid and reliable for the age of your children (See list at the end of this chapter.) Most screening tests take fifteen to twenty minutes, are easy to give, and do not require much special training. If you do not feel able to give the test yourself, find a person who can teach you or who can do it for you. (Most school districts use screening tests and have personnel who are trained to give them.)

➤ Obtain written permission from parents to give a screening test to their child.

A screening test usually consists of questions for you to ask a child or skills, called items, for you to observe a child doing. These items are commonly divided into six areas of a child's development: language, social/emotional, cognitive, self-help, fine motor, and gross motor. The following is a list of items, one in each of the six areas of development, typically found on screening tests for four year olds:

A child who is weak in one or several areas of development should be taken to a specialist by her parents. The specialist will then give her more in-depth tests called diagnostic tests. These will determine if a problem exists and the extent of the problem. The specialist will then develop a plan for helping the child. Make certain that ideas for you to help the child in class are included in this plan.

➤ Use screening tests with caution. They sometimes will identify a child as needing further evaluation who is really not in need (perhaps she is shy) and fail to identify a child who actually does need further evaluation (the test may not be sensitive enough). Use these tests only in conjunction with careful classroom observations of the child (across situations and over time), with information from parents, and with observations made by other adults.

Language	Can use past tense and future tense when talking.
Social/emotional	Engages in dramatic play, e.g., plays house, pretends to be animals.
Cognitive	Counts 4 objects and tells how many.
Self-help	Uses toilet independently.
Fine motor	Copies a square.
Gross motor	Stands on one foot for 8 seconds.

Preventing Problems

➤ Screen all your children. This avoids the problem of singling some children out from others, which may upset some parents or make those children feel different. This procedure will also help you catch any problems that you may have overlooked.

➤ Screen early in the year or soon after any new children enter your class, but give yourself enough time to get to know the children well and for them to feel comfortable with you. (Children must feel supported and relaxed when being tested to get

accurate results.) Don't wait too long however. Act on your concerns about a child as quickly as possible. Note that getting a child seen by a specialist and getting a treatment program started often takes months.

➤ Keep a list of specialists (speech therapists, physical therapists, occupational therapists, pediatricians, ENT's, opthamologists, and audiologists) in your area for referral to parents. Include those specialists who are good with children and with whom other parents have been happy. Write down their addresses and phone numbers.

➤ Keep a file of good observation checklists where they can be easily found. For quick access, categorize and label them by the area of concern they address.

➤ Give all parents a written policy on observing, screening and referring children to specialists. Ask them to sign permission forms for this when they enroll their children. Then they will not be surprised when the time comes to discuss the results of the screening and observation with them. Include the following in your written policy: information about the screening test you use; the reason for screening and observation; a personal

account about how a child was helped by your screening and referral; an assurance of confidentiality; and a guarantee that children will not be labeled (i.e., *mentally handicapped* or *emotionally disturbed*).

➤ Schedule regular conference times with parents at least twice a year. Hold the first one soon after the child is enrolled and screened. Hold the second one towards the end of the program year. This creates a situation where meeting with parents is a given. If there is a concern about the child, a special meeting will not have to be arranged. Asking parents to attend a special meeting may cause them great anxiety and they may refuse to come or just not show up.

Dealing with Existing Problems

Parents Who Deny There Is a Problem

Some parents do not know enough about child development to recognize that their child has a problem. However, once they are shown concrete evidence of the problem, they will usually be very concerned and interested in doing whatever is necessary to help their child.

Some parents may refuse to recognize that their child has a problem, even when they have the knowledge and the evidence. Usually they have good motives for doing this: They do not want their child labeled or considered an outcast. They do not want to feel responsible for the problem or overwhelmed by it. They may not want to admit their own similar weaknesses or problems. They want their child to be liked and treated with respect.

➤ Do not bring up the issue of your concerns with parents until you have won their trust. Be very supportive, friendly, and helpful. Ask questions and consider them the experts on their child. During this time, gather information about the child by observing and screening, as discussed earlier, and by reading more about the particular handicap you suspect. By winning parents' trust and confidence you accept as valid their motives for denying the problem. When they feel you have their child's best interests at heart, they will be ready to listen to your concerns.

➤ If parents avoid talking to you informally, set up a meeting with them. Tell them that the purpose of the meeting is to chat and to find out more about each other. Spend this time just listening, asking questions, and discussing positive things

about their child. (It is important not to "make upe things. Always be honest and up-front.) Note that you may need several meetings like this before you can bring up your concerns.

➤ When you are able to state your concerns, do so by telling the parents only what you have observed. Do not make judgements. Simply say something like the following: "I have seen that Chris falls down and bumps into things quite a bit. Here are some specific examples from notes I took on February 20th." Include information from the screening test. State your own lack of expertise about what this means and request them to let you have someone who knows more observe and test their child. Assure them that nothing will be done without their knowledge and permission. If you will be arranging the evaluation, ask the parents to sign a permission form (this is required by law) to have a trained professional observe and evaluate their child. Also request permission for you to receive the results and to discuss them with the specialist.

➤ Remember that you have a professional responsibility to inform parents of concerns you have about their children no matter how hard this is to face. (See "Telling Parents About the Difficult Behavior of Their Children," on pages 149 to 150, for effective ways to do this.)

Other Professionals Who Believe There Is No Problem

Some physicians, pediatricians, or other health professionals will occasionally downplay a child's

problems. They may even state flatly that there is no problem to be concerned about. "The child will outgrow it" is a typical phrase you might hear.

A health professional will do this because she firmly believes that focusing attention on the problem may make it worse if the problem is not that serious. She believes that the child will be able to compensate for it, especially if the child is strong in other areas of development, and that calling attention to the problem may make the child feel different, damaging her self-esteem.

But if the child's problems are addressed in a positive way by building on her strengths, and the teachers and professionals are sensitive, the child can improve and also feel very good about herself. Children can often overcome a problem much more quickly and easily as preschoolers than they can when older. Many problems will get worse if left untreated. It makes little sense to ignore a problem when you can help the child overcome it, prevent the possibility of it getting worse, and also make the child feel good about herself.

➤ If you are uncertain that a problem exists, get a second opinion from another professional, if possible. If the second professional agrees there is no problem, then leaving the situation alone is probably safe. Throughout this process, write down reports of all meetings and phone conversations and keep these in a safe place. If at a later time the child's problem reappears, gets worse, or another teacher has similar concerns, you will have a record of what you have done.

➤ If you are convinced that the problem is a real one that should not be ignored, you may need a third opinion from another professional. If the second professional you consult agrees with you, follow her recommendations. If, however, she also believes that there is no problem or if it is not possible to get a third opinion and the child's parents also feel there is no problem, keep a record of everything you have done as described previously. You can still do many things in the classroom to help the child in a supportive way, without violating her parents' wishes. Doing those things is just part of individualizing, which all good preschool teachers do. Read as much as you can about the child's particular problem and about ways to help. In the following chapter, you will find more ideas about helping children with handicaps.

Difficulty in Finding or Affording Professional Services

➤ If you work in a program that has no access or funding for the services of a health professional and the parents cannot afford the services, consider other options such as the following:

• Many service and religious organizations, such as Kiwanis, Elks, Lions, Salvation Army, National Council of Jewish Women, Shriners, Easter Seal, and so on, can help out with costs of diagnosing a potentially handicapped child.

• You may tap the services of your local school district, although the response varies greatly among school districts. Many are happy to help while others are overwhelmed with the children they currently serve. However, school districts are required by law (Public Law 94-142 and 99-457) to at least determine, for any child who lives in their district, if she needs to be seen by a specialist. They may use your observation records to make that determination, so make sure your notes are complete. Most school districts go beyond the minimum requirements and will refer a needy child to a specialist for evaluation. Contact the special education coordinator.

• County or state mental health departments or health departments can also be a source for finding specialists. People in these agencies can also inform you of the laws in your state. Many states have laws that mandate services to young children with handicaps. A federal law (Public Law 99-457) mandates that all states provide a free, appropriate, public education to all children with handicaps beginning at age three, through state education agencies (effective 1990-1991).

Observation Checklists

Concerns in Multiple Areas

Banas, N., and Wills, I. *Identifying Early Learning Gaps.* Atlanta, GA: Humanics Press, 1975. (Includes checklists for visual/motor ability, auditory/language ability, behavior, ability to use symbols.)

Bluma, S., et al. *The Portage Guide to Early Education Checklist.* Portage, WI: Portage Project, 1976. (Includes socialization, self-help, language, cognition, motor.)

Cherry, Clare, et al. *Nursery School Management Guide.* Belmont, CA: Fearon, 1973. (Includes gross motor, sensory-motor integration, laterality and dominance, tactile discrimination, perceptual motor, conceptual skills, language.)

Hodgden, L., et al. *School Before Six.* St. Louis, MO: CEMREL, Inc., 1974. (Includes social/emotional, language, small motor, and gross motor.)

Saifer, S., et al. *The Oregon Assessment for 3-5 Year Olds in Developmentally Appropriate Classrooms.* The Early Childhood/Head Start Training Office, P.O. Box 1491, Portland, OR 97207, 1990. (503) 725-4815 (Includes cognitive, problem solving, social, language, motor, play, and dispositions.)

Behavioral or Social/Emotional Concerns

Abelson, W., Naylor, A., and Provence, S. *Teachers' Inventory of Emotional and Behavioral Development in Children Ages 2-6 Years.* Yale Child Study Center, New Haven, CT., 1980.

Bell, D., and Low, R. *Observing and Recording Children's Behavior.* Performance Associates, Richland, WA., 1977.

Screening Tests

Chicago Board of Education. *Chicago EARLY.* Educational Teaching Aids, 159 W. Kinzie St., Chicago, IL 60610. (Ages 3 years to 5 years.)

Lichtenstein, R. *Minneapolis Preschool Screening Instrument.* Prescriptive Instruction Center, Minneapolis Public Schools, 254 Upton Ave. S., Minneapolis, MN 55405. (Ages 3 years, 7 months, to 5 years, 4 months.)

Mardell-Czudnowski, C., and Goldenberg, D. *Dial-R.* AGS, Publisher's Building, Circle Pines, MN 55104. (Ages 2 years to 6 years.)

McCarthy, D. *The McCarthy Screening Test.* Psychological Corporation, 757 Third Ave., New York, NY 10017. (Ages 4 years to 6-1/2 years.)

Meisels, S., and Wiske, M. *Early Screening Inventory.* Teachers College Press, P.O. Box 1540 Hagerstown, MD 21741. (Ages 4 years to 6 years.)

Miller, J. *Miller Assessment for Preschoolers.* KID Technology, Inc., 11715 East 51st Ave., Denver, CO 80239. (Ages 2 years, 9 months to 5 years, 8 months.)

Other Resources

Boehm, A., and Weinberg, R. *The Classroom Observer. A Guide for Developing Observations Skills.* New York: Teachers College Press, 1977.

Cohen, D., et al. *Observing and Recording the Behavior of Young Children,* New York: Teachers College Press, New York, 1983.

Meisels, Samuel. *Developmental Screening in Early Childhood: A Guide.* NAEYC, Washington, DC, 1985.

2. Children with Handicaps in Your Class

Many teachers worry about having a child with handicaps in their class. They worry that they do not have the proper training or expertise to help the child or to deal with the child's problems. They worry that the child will take up so much extra time and energy that the rest of the class will suffer. These are real and valid concerns. However, most teachers find that when they actually have a child with handicaps in their class, the joys far outweigh the problems — real or imagined. When this doesn't happen, the child is either misassigned (perhaps he is too severely handicapped to benefit from a regular classroom) or the teachers have not received the information and support they need.

If you are already using good early childhood practices (an individualized, active, social, playful, child-focused classroom), you will not have difficulty caring for and teaching a child with a mild or moderate disability. You will have to stretch some of the things you already do, but your basic approach and routines will not have to change. For example, many children with developmental delays or mental handicaps have very short attention spans and experience difficulty in focusing in group situations. (Undoubtedly you already have a few children who fit this description, but the child with a disability may have an even shorter attention span and experience more difficulty focusing.) Lower your expectations slightly, but keep challenging the child. Use the same techniques

you already use — small groups, short group times, alternative quiet activities during group times for some children, seating the child next to you, involving all children actively — but employ these techniques sooner, more often, and very consistently for a child with a handicap.

Young children are usually very open and accepting of children with handicaps, even very severe handicaps. Most have not built up many prejudices or misconceptions yet. This makes your job easier, in a way, than the job of teachers of older children.

You will quickly find that children with handicaps are children first and foremost. The similarities between them and children without disabilities are far greater than the differences.

Preventing Problems

➤ Read books and view films with the children about children with a variety of handicaps. (The best ones do not make handicaps the central focus but include children with handicaps as part of a good story.) Use these to talk about individual differences and similarities.

➤ Answer the questions (which are often painfully honest) that children ask about handicaps with direct, simple, and factual responses. If you are unsure or don't know the answer, say so, and seek the answer together from books or professionals. If a child asks, "Why can't he walk?" respond by telling him to ask the child. If the child cannot or will not respond, give a simple answer to the best of your ability: "When he was born his legs didn't work. He gets around very well on his

scooter board, though." Many children are not just curious but are worried that this handicap might happen to them or that they will "catch it." They need some reassurance.

➤ Show children concretely and in a variety of ways how different everyone is from each other, but how ultimately we are more similar than different. To do this, you might want to graph the height of the children. On the graph, draw a human figure to represent each two-inch increment in height. Within each figure add a colored adhesive dot to represent each child whose height is in that range. Invite the children to measure and graph each other; then do the same for a group of children two years older and a group two years younger. (See the chart on the following page.)

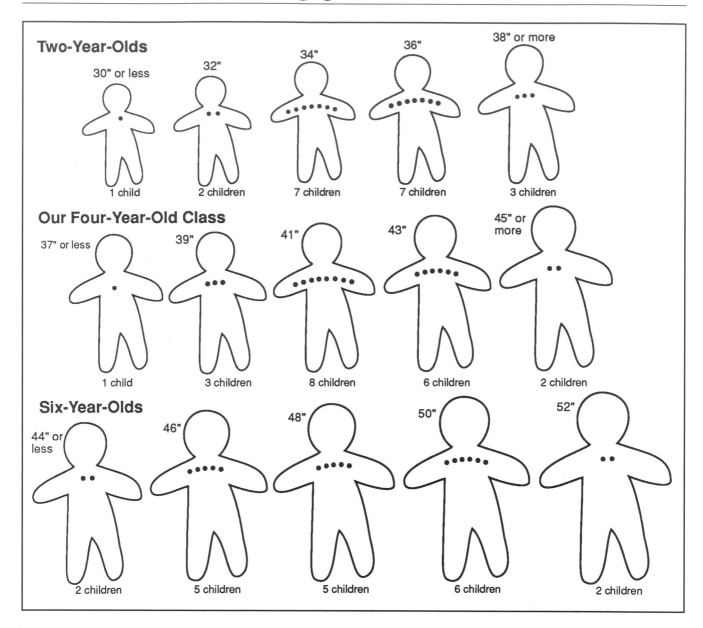

Two-Year-Olds

30" or less — 1 child
32" — 2 children
34" — 7 children
36" — 7 children
38" or more — 3 children

Our Four-Year-Old Class

37" or less — 1 child
39" — 3 children
41" — 8 children
43" — 6 children
45" or more — 2 children

Six-Year-Olds

44" or less — 2 children
46" — 5 children
48" — 5 children
50" — 6 children
52" — 2 children

➤ Point out that in spite of great individual differences between the children in the same class, most of the children are taller than the younger children and shorter than the older children. Note that all children are growing, and that the older ones were once as short as the younger ones and the younger ones will someday be as tall as the older ones.

➤ Take an active approach to replacing children's misconceived stereotypes about handicaps with notions based in reality. Do this through concrete activities such as these:

• Invite people with handicaps who will talk openly about their handicaps to spend time in the class.

• Correct misconceptions as soon as you hear children say them.

• Show specific examples (through films, books, and on field trips) of people with handicaps functioning in a variety of self-sufficient ways and situations.

(See the chapter on "Children Who Are Culturally or Physically 'Different' and Biased Behaviors," on pages 78 to 81, for more ideas.)

➤ Make sure you are part of the team of people who meet to determine the child's goals and services. (This is usually called the interdisciplinary or multidisciplinary team and the goals and services are written in a plan called the IEP [individualized educational plan] or IFSP [individualized family service plan].) If this has already happened, request the parents' permission to become part of future team meetings and to read the plan. Ask questions to make sure you fully understand the plan. Make sure you have a copy of the plan.

➤ If you are part of the planning team, request that educational goals or objectives are written that can be easily met in your active, child-centered classroom. An objective such as "Angie will stack six blocks with 80% accuracy" implies direct teaching, boring repetition, isolating skills, and little choice for Angie. A goal such as "Angie will use blocks daily for creative play and stack them on the storage shelf when done" develops the same skills as the first objective but in a fun, creative way, integrates the skills into routines, and gives choices to Angie.

➤ If possible, meet with all team members (which may include the parents, a physical therapist, occupational therapist, speech pathologist, and other health professionals) individually and before the child is in your class. Discuss their goals for the child, their expectations of you, your concerns, and how the team members can help you. Make sure that the logistics of when and how they will provide therapy to the child are clear and that these logistics will not cause problems for your schedule or routines. Get the phone numbers of the team members so you can contact them quickly if necessary.

➤ Set up a regular system for communicating with therapists to discuss the objectives they are working on and how you can assist the child meet those objectives in the classroom.

➤ Reach a clear understanding that you would like the child in your class on a trial basis to start with. Set up in advance a meeting time (four to six weeks after the child starts) to discuss any problems, concerns, or successes you might have. Be honest and forthright, but reasonable, about what you need for the child to be successful in your class. If you cannot get those needs met, then the child might be better off in a different placement.

➤ Make adjustments to the room, furniture and equipment before the child enters your class, if possible. If the class has already started, enlist the help of the children and explain what you are

doing and why. Show them a photo of the child and tell them all you know about him, not just about his handicapping condition.

➤ Provide a wide variety of equipment and materials that span a broad range of skill levels. For example, have three-piece puzzles as well as twelve-piece puzzles.

➤ Read about the particular handicap of the child and ask knowledgeable people about what to expect to increase your understanding of it.

➤ Maintain daily communication with the parents. Meet regularly to discuss the child's problems and progress.

Dealing with Existing Problems

Conflict with Therapists or Other Specialists

Conflict between teachers and others who serve the special needs of a child with a handicap often arise because each views the child from a slightly different angle. A teacher might see the child's strengths and abilities, whereas a specialist might be more focused on fixing what is wrong with the child. They also have been trained very differently and even use different jargon. Miscommunication can happen easily.

Conflict over Educational Approach. A common area of conflict is over the educational approach. You may, for example, provide many opportunities for children (including a child with a handicap) to learn math skills by manipulating objects, playing dice games, setting the table for the correct number of children, regulating on their own the number of children allowed at the sand table, and graphing. A special educator might approach math development by drilling a child with a handicap on counting beads and reinforcing correct answers with a reward, while keeping careful data by tallying all responses. These two very different approaches may not be easily reconciled.

➤ Find areas of commonality — you both want to help the child learn and grow, your goals for the child are the same, and you agree on the child's strengths and problems. Build on those commonalities and discuss ways on which you can agree to help the child. For example, the specialist can sit with the child during a math game and help her count the dots on the dice, figure out when her turn is, and record her progress. If this fails, at least agree to disagree. The child will not be harmed by being served in two different ways.

➤ Be patient and understand that the special education or therapeutic approach is designed to be precise, clear, and scientific. The therapist was trained in this approach, which comes from good intentions to help the child. This approach often gets good short-term results and children with severe handicaps benefit greatly from it. However, continue to use and advocate your approach even though you may get negative feedback on it from someone who has a more formal education than you do. Children with mild to moderate handicaps benefit greatly from learning to be self-initiating, especially for long term growth. They are young children first and foremost and like all young children they learn best through playful, active, integrated activities.

Fortunately, many special educators and therapists are changing to this approach. More is being written about it, and you can give them some of this written information to support your views. (See the resources on page 74.)

Conflict over Managing Behavior. Conflict also occurs over the use of reinforcement (reward and punishment) systems. Most early childhood professionals manage behavior through setting a stimulating environment, providing an active schedule, encouraging positive behavior, giving children many chances to be successful, using logical consequences, and redirecting children. They do not use punishment. They sometimes reluctantly use rewards as a last resort, but these are curtailed as soon as possible. Even then the results may not be very good and the means do not justify the ends. Some special educators, however, use reinforcement systems through rewards (stickers, stars, food, tokens) or punishment as the first method to deal with a problem. Many self-contained special education classroom teachers use an ongoing reward and punishment system as part of their routine group management. For some very handicapped children, these systems work well and may, indeed, be appropriate.

Some preschools have set policies stating that rewards, especially food and tokens, are not allowed. This frees the teacher to reject the use of a reinforcement system, without having to defend her position.

➤ Work with the special educator to set a specific plan in writing about how you will help the child by using a wide variety of methods — teaching correct behaviors, redirection, child choice, logical consequences, and so on. Agree together to try this out before using a reinforcement system. If this plan fails and a reinforcement system seems to be needed, set a very specific plan to fade out the reward as soon as possible.

The Overly Involved Parent

Parents of children with handicaps care deeply about their children, are very concerned about their growth and development, and tend to be very involved in their lives. If they can afford to stay at home, mothers of children with handicaps are less likely to work than other mothers. Because of this concern, commitment, and available time, a parent might want to spend a great deal of time in your classroom. While this can be extremely helpful, it can also create problems. The child might not get enough time to be independent and the parent may at times be more of a hindrance than a help. She may interact poorly with the other children or with her own child, or she may demand your attention when you need to give it to the other children.

➤ Meet with the parent, preferably before she starts volunteering, to discuss potential problems, to inform her of your approach, and to make expectations clear. Agree to a regular schedule of volunteer hours. Make it clear that you may ask her to curtail her involvement if it does not work out. Meet regularly, at least monthly, to discuss any concerns and to make plans for improvements. Give informal feedback more frequently. Clarify your roles and do quick training sessions about your methods. Ask her to work with other children to give her child time to be independent. Express your appreciation and give specific, positive feedback about what she does well. Provide very specific, factual information about the problems: "This morning you cut Julia's food for her. I then asked you to let her cut it herself. A few minutes later you went back to cutting it for her. Tell me what happened and let's figure out how to solve the problem."

The Child Who Takes Too Much Time and Energy

A child with a handicap requires more time and energy than other children. If the situation becomes too much, however, then you are not getting the support you need. Many children with handicaps need an aide (at least part-time), and often the local school district or early intervention program will provide one. This can be a great help to you and the child, especially if the aide is capable and hard-working. If you have an aide who is not, and you cannot train and motivate her, make sure you provide objective information about her job performance to her supervisors. A year in the life of a young child is too important for her to receive less than excellent services.

➤ Enlist the assistance of other children to help the child with a handicap. Most will be eager to help if the task is reasonable. Children can push a wheelchair, help a child clean up, assist her with puzzles, zipping, buttoning, or tying, and even teach a simple skill. This will also encourage responsibility and altruism, while freeing time for you. However, make sure that other children do not do things for the child with a handicap that she can do for herself. The child needs to develop independence.

➤ Part of the problem may be that you are not getting the information or the equipment you need to be effective. You must have access to a competent professional, who can observe you and the child in the classroom and recommend methods or materials to use that will save time, increase efficiency, and allow the child to be more independent. This person is usually one of the health professionals on the child's team, but she could be a specialist from a hospital, social service agency, or university.

The Child with a Handicap Who Does Not Play with Others

For many children with handicaps, playing with other children does not come naturally. This happens because they have had few opportunities to do so, because their verbal skills are poor, or because they have not developed positive social skills. Most young children with disabilities can learn to play with others, however, if a caring teacher helps. Usually the teacher has to provide direct and specific assistance.

➤ Involve the child as fully as possible in all group games and activities. Physically guide a child with a developmental delay through all the actions in a game of "Duck-Duck-Goose." See that the child has a turn just like everyone else.

➤ Teach the child to pretend. Play pretend games with the child, starting with you pretending to be an animal. Then encourage the child to pretend to be an animal with you. After he feels comfortable, bring in another child and pretend together, eventually pulling yourself out of the game.

➤ Teach the child to imitate. To encourage imitation, involve him in simple games (a noncompetitive game, such as "Simple Simon"). Let other children lead the imitation games so he will get used to imitating children.

➤ Teach the child the right words and actions to use to join children in play. You may need to say them for him and show him how, until the child can do it on his own. Note that the best method of joining play is to start by imitating, in some way, what the children are already doing.

➤ Mediate a play situation. When the child with a handicap is playing alongside another child and they are using the same materials, encourage them to play together by suggesting a slight variation or by introducing a new item: "Sara is building a road and so are you. You can hook your roads together to make a big, long road, and there are more cars on the red shelf."

➤ Set out play materials that are of particular interest to the child with a handicap.

➤ Encourage another child to play with her by providing a special game or unique toy that only two can use.

➤ Adapt toys and equipment to make it easier for

the child with the handicap to use them. For example, add straps to the pedals of a trike to make it possible for a child with a mild physical handicap to use it. She can then be part of the active outdoor play along with the other children.

➤ Encourage the child with handicaps to bring in favorite toys from home, including popular commercial toys, to help her form friendships. (Put some limits on the use of these toys as discussed in "Toys from Home," page 51.)

➤ Help him expand his play skills by imitating what he does and then doing something slightly different. For example, if the child is stacking small blocks, do the same thing until you have his attention, and then stack the blocks by alternating big and little ones.

Resources

Adult Books and Articles

Bredekamp, S., ed. *Developmentally Appropriate Practice in Early Childhood Programs Serving Children from Birth Through Age 8*. Washington, DC: NAEYC, 1987.

Cook, R., Tessier, A., and Armbruster, V. *Adapting Early Childhood Curricula for Children with Special Needs*. Columbus, OH: Merrill, 1987.

Froschl, M., et al. *Including All of Us: An Early Childhood Curriculum About Disability*. New York: Education Equity Concepts, 1984.

Kugelmass, J. W. "The 'Shared Classroom': A Case Study of Interaction between Early Childhood and Special Education Staff and Children." *Journal of Early Intervention* 13(1) (Winter 1989): 36-44.

Musselwhite, Caroline Ramsey. *Adaptive Play for Special Needs Children*. San Diego, CA: College-Hill Press, 1986.

Odem, S.L., et al. *The Integrated Preschool Curriculum: Procedures for Socially Integrating Young Handicapped and Normally Developing Children*. Seattle: University of Washington, 1989.

Safford, Phillip L. *Integrated Teaching in Early Childhood: Starting in the Mainstream*. White Plains, NY: Longman, 1989.

Spodek, B., Saracho, O.N., and Lee, R.C. *Mainstreaming Young Children*. Belmont, CA: Wadsworth, 1984.

Tompkins, Mark. "Special Children: Building on their Strengths." *Extensions: Newsletter of the High / Scope Curriculum* 3 (March/April 1989).

Videos

In the Middle. Fanlight Productions, 47 Halifax St., Boston, MA 02130. (Shows a child, physically handicapped with spina bifida, fully and happily integrated into a Head Start classroom.)

Regular Lives. WETA, Educational Activities, Box 2626, Washington, DC 20013. (Although not focused on preschool children, this video makes a clear case for the value of integrating handicapped and typical children and shows successful examples of integration in action.)

Children's Books

Bellet, J. *A-B-C-ing: An Action Alphabet*. New York: Crown, 1984.

Brown, T. *Someone Special, Just Like You*. New York: Holt Rinehart & Winston, 1984.

dePaola, Tomie. *Now One Foot, Now the Other*. New York: Putnam, 1981.

Hasler, Eveline. *Martin is Our Friend*. Nashville: Abington Press, 1981.

Henriod, Lorraine. *Grandma's Wheelchair*. Chicago: Albert Whitman & Co., 1982.

Greenfield, Eloise. *Darlene*. New York: Methuen, 1980.

Quinsey, M.B. *Why Does That Man Have Such a Big Nose?* Seattle: Parenting Press, 1986.

Rabe, Bernice. *Where's Chimpy?* Chicago: Albert Whitman & Co., 1988.

Stein, S.B. *About Handicaps*. New York: Waler, 1974.

Weissman, Jackie. *Let's Be Friends* and *All About Me*. Overland Park, KS: Miss Jackie Music, 1981.

3. Gifted or Talented Children

About five percent of all children, regardless of family income, age, or race, are gifted or talented. If not nurtured, their abilities will not be fully realized and they may develop behavior problems. In fact, a child in your class with behavior problems may be a gifted child who is unchallenged and bored. By identifying gifted children and providing for their needs, you will help them as well as yourself.

As with other children with special needs, providing a good program for gifted children is not hard if you already have an active, child-centered, individualized classroom. You will just need to provide some additional challenges and opportunities within your current curriculum and routines.

You will find that the suggestions in this chapter can work well with almost all children, not just the gifted. However, for their basic needs to be met, gifted children require these approaches.

Preventing Problems

➤ Provide many opportunities for all children to be creative through open-ended art activities (not crafts that result in a specific, finished product), music, creative dance and movement, story writing, and creative dramatics. A talented child will be excited when participating in her area of interest.

➤ Make available a wide variety of creative materials, which any child can use for any purpose (within reasonable limits) during free choice. Include many different kinds of blank paper, streamers, pieces of foam, different sizes of cups and containers, wood scraps, cotton balls, cloth, buttons, foil, colored chalk, pens, colored pencils, glue, paste, staplers, scissors, tape, and so on. Keep these items in separate boxes.

➤ Know the interests of the children in your class. Give them many opportunities to talk about and pursue their interests. Be aware that talented and gifted children often have areas of specific interest about which they know a great deal, often more than most adults. By giving all children opportunities to pursue interests you will be able to determine which children are gifted and nurture those gifts.

➤ Ask the parents of any new child if their child has any particular talents, skills, interests, or strengths. Parents are usually good judges of their child's abilities, particularly if they have a check-list to use, like the one that follows. (As with any child with special needs, much contact and good communication with parents is necessary to avoid problems and provide the best possible services.)

Identifying Gifted and Talented Children

The following is a list of characteristics of young children who are gifted and/or talented. Most gifted children excel in some areas, but not others.

A gifted child...

- has a very good memory, especially long-term memory.
- has a very good vocabulary.
- can concentrate for long periods.
- retains information easily.
- observes keenly and is very curious.
- has strong and broad interests.
- shows early compassion for others.
- is interested in books.
- exhibits a high energy level.
- is often a perfectionist.
- prefers to play with older children or to be with adults.
- does simple math problems easily and enjoys them.
- is very persistent.
- has a good sense of humor.
- uses common items in uncommon ways.
- shows leadership ability and good social skills.
- shows a strong interest in any or in several of the arts.
- is very sensitive

As most children have at least one area of strength, take a wide view of giftedness or talent. A child may be gifted in the area of social skills and leadership (could she be a future politician?), large motor skills (a future athlete?), empathy towards others (a future psychologist?), small motor skills (a future craftsperson?), or verbal skills such as persuasion and negotiation (a future lawyer?). Remember that there are many different kinds of intelligence and that you need to value all of them equally.

Meeting Their Needs in the Classroom

➤ When planning your activities, devise ways to make them more challenging for gifted children.

If, for example, you will be playing a memory game during small group time, plan to add additional items when your gifted children have a turn. For instance, for most children you would place four items on a tray and take one away (while you cover the items so they can't see which one is removed). Then you would invite a child to guess which one is gone. For gifted children you might place six items and take two away. Plan this ahead of time so the activity will run smoothly. For all the children, including gifted children, increase the difficulty of the activity slightly, once they can do it with little effort. However, start with and end with activities that are not too difficult, so that all the children will feel competent and successful.

➤ Ask gifted children for their suggestions about changing aspects of an activity and follow through on reasonable ideas. (This will stretch their thinking skills and provide valuable feedback about their thoughts and needs.)

➤ Give gifted children many opportunities to make real choices and to be leaders: "You can dismiss the children from circle. How would you like to do it — by first initials, by colors of shirts, or in some other way?"

➤ Allow gifted children to pursue their own interests as far as they can go. Encourage them by providing books and materials related to their interests. (The *Project Work* curriculum described in "Selecting and Using a Curriculum," on pages 44 to 45, is excellent to use with gifted children.)

➤ Give all children, but especially gifted children a five minute warning, at least, before they have to end their activity and move on to the next routine.

➤ Ask gifted children about how they came up with a particular response. (Although some children will not be able to tell you, others will.) For example, if a child says to you, "I think that signs says 'Open,' " ask her how she knows that. Note that her response will give you great insight into how her mind works and help you to plan for her needs. She might say, "I see it every time we go into the store" or "My mother read it to me yesterday" or "I sounded out the letters." The first response indicates that she is a very receptive, quick, and self-directed learner; the second indicates a good visual and auditory memory; and the third reveals an analytical thinker.

➤ Be prepared to modify an activity while you are doing it to make it more challenging. Or, provide an alternative, although you did not plan for it. For example, if you notice that a gifted child is bored during a story that the other children are enjoying, let her choose to look at another book by herself or leave off words at the end of some sentences and have the child verbally fill them in.

➤ Because most gifted children are very active and have broad interests, provide a wide variety of choices including challenging games, puzzles, dramatic play situations, and table toys.

➤ Give gifted children many opportunities to generate ideas through brainstorming rather than through answering questions that have one right answer. (Read the chapter on "Individualizing," on pages 46 to 48, for more ideas.)

Problem Behaviors of Some Gifted Children

Because of their uniqueness, gifted children have a tendency towards certain behaviors that can cause problems for themselves, yourself, their parents, or their classmates. Use the suggestions in the table below to minimize these problems.

Problem	Suggested Solutions
Bored, silly, acts out.	Provide more stimulating and challenging activities. Give the child opportunities and ample time to pursue her own interests at her own pace.
Invents her own methods or systems of doing things, which conflict with yours or the way these things need to be done.	Provide many opportunities for the child to do things her own way when it will not cause a problem. When something must be done your way, be firm about the need for her do it your way, but explain your reasons clearly. Help her generate ways to meet both her needs and those of the group.
Gullible, easily fooled and swayed.	Appreciate the child's sense of wonder, trust, and curiosity which results in her being gullible. Respect her by not teasing her about her gullibility. Point out calmly the truth of the situation. Support and validate her feelings so that she will continue to be open and trusting. Stop others from teasing her.
Perfectionist, discouraged, critical of self and others.	Continue to encourage the child's attempts: "You feel you can do better and you will. You tried hard and worked hard, which is something to be very proud of." Also: "Look how much better you did this time than last time." Tell her specifically what she does well and why it is good. Support and validate her feelings of frustration at the shortcomings of others: "Some children find things more difficult than you do, but everyone has some things they do very well. Let's appreciate how much people try."
Gets impatient or angry at interruptions.	Allow plenty of time for the child to work on things of her own choosing. Give plenty of warning before she has to finish an activity. Have a way and a place for her to save her work to finish at another time. Make sure that she can keep her work safe in this place.
Dislikes repetitious activities or games.	When the child is bored with an activity, offer her an alternative. Help her express her discomfort in a socially appropriate way. When she is restless, encourage her to ask to do something else.
Resists directions.	Give the child many opportunities to have control over her time and routines. Explain thoroughly the reasons for your directions. Give her plenty of advanced warning before changes.

(Continued on next page.)

Problem	Suggested Solutions
Very active and energetic, talks too much, and dominates discussions.	Provide long free choice times with a wide variety of active choices. Redirect the child's energy into activities that are creative and constructive. Limit the amount of time any child can talk in a group setting. When she wants too much of your time, tell her that you will listen to her for one more minute (set a timer), but that you will listen again at a specific time (e.g., "as soon as we go outside").
Overlooks details and skips routines; impatient with things that are not important to her.	Give the child some slack by not putting too much emphasis on formalities and routines. Remind her when she needs to do something for health or safety reasons and explain why: "Tie your shoes so that you don't trip over your laces." You will have to do this often but say it calmly. The child is not forgetful, simply disinterested.

Resources

Bloom, B. *Developing Talent in Young Children*. New York: Ballentine, 1985.

Fewell, Rebecca R., ed. "Gifted Preschoolers." *Topics in Early Childhood Education* 6(1) (Spring 1986).

Karnes, M., ed. *The Underserved: Our Young Gifted Children*. Reston, VA: Council for Exceptional Children, 1983.

Karnes, M., and Johnson, L.J. "Training for Staff, Parents, and Volunteers Working with Gifted Young Children, Especially Those with Disabilities and from Low-Income Homes." *Young Children* 44(3) (March 1989): 49-56.

Kitano, M. "Young Gifted Children: Strategies for Preschool Teachers." *Young Children* 37(4) (1982): 14-24.

Kitano, M. "The K-3 Teacher's Role in Recognizing and Supporting Young Gifted Children." *Young Children* 44(3) (March 1989): 57-63.

Roedell, W.C.; Jackson, N.E.; and Robinson, H.B. *Gifted Young Children*. New York: Teachers College Press, 1980.

Wolfe, Jane. "The Gifted Preschooler: Developmentally Different, But Still 3 or 4 Years Old." *Young Children* 44(3) (March 1989): 41-48.

4. Children Who Are Culturally or Physically Different and Biased Behaviors

Culture is how we live our lives. It is what we eat, how we dress, how we talk, the way we communicate, what we believe in, what we hope for, how we raise our children, the music we listen to, and so on. Everyone is part of a culture or several cultures.

Seeing "culture" broadly is important in order to help children and create a supportive classroom. Our society has many cultures. A culture of poverty, a culture of wealth, a male culture, a female culture, racial cultures, regional cultures based on what part of the country one comes from, cultures based on what language a person speaks (including a deaf culture whose members share American Sign Language), and more. (For ideas on dealing with issues related to males and females see "The Child Who Identifies with the Opposite Sex and Sex-Bias Issues," on pages 90 to 92.)

In many classrooms there are one or two children whose families are from a culture different from the other children. Whether they are the only black children in a predominantly white classroom, the only white children in a predominantly Hispanic classroom, the only girls among boys, the only deaf children among hearing children, or the only poor children among upper-middle-class children, they will need some special attention to feel included and accepted.

Similarly, a group of children who are all different from the predominate culture around them (for example, a class of all Asian children, whose families recently immigrated to Seattle) will need a curriculum and teaching approach that addresses their particular needs.

Children whose cultural backgrounds reflect the predominant culture around them and children in a class with no culturally different children need to learn about other cultures. This broadens their view of the world and teaches them to accept and appreciate the similarities and differences of others.

All children receive great benefit from learning to actively counteract stereotypes. Teachers need to employ a wide variety of methods to help children change misguided beliefs or to prevent the development of those beliefs. This chapter discusses concrete ways to replace stereotypes with truth.

Preventing Problems

➤ Meet with parents to determine their cultural preferences for their children, their goals, and their hopes.

➤ Upon enrolling their children, make sure parents know your policies and procedures about celebrating cultural diversity, your approach to holidays, and your methods of counteracting bias. (This should be in writing in a parent handbook.)

➤ Establish a classroom rule: "Only words that don't hurt people can be used." Include here teasing, name-calling, and excluding others because of what they look like or who they are.

➤ Provide books, puzzles, pictures, and artwork that reflect a variety of cultures and show people of different races, skin colors, and physical attributes (including handicaps).

➤ Invite people with disabilities into your classroom and take field trips to visit people who are handicapped or who have nontraditional jobs. For instance, when doing a health unit, invite to the classroom a male nurse or a black dentist. Invite a female firefighter when doing a unit on community workers. Emphasize the person's abilities more than his differences, without minimizing or ignoring them.

➤ Invite people to your classroom who can share their cultural traditions, dance, dress, and food. Make sure the children know what these people do and how they dress during a typical day. Make clear the differences between costumes or historical dress and daily dress, and between rituals and daily routines.

➤ Involve children in traditions from other cultures. For example, during Halloween, tell children how it is celebrated in other countries. Role play some of these traditions. Invite the children to tell you a joke for an apple or a nickel as the children in Scotland do on Halloween. Because real bonfires on almost every street corner are another Halloween tradition in Scotland, gather the children around a pretend bonfire (piled up branches and wood on top of flashlights, decorated with paper flames in a darkened room) and listen to stories. Share your own traditions with the children.

➤ Use holiday celebrations as a basis for counteracting stereotypes. Tell the story of Thanksgiving from the perspective of native Americans and use cultural activities that represent actual practices rather than stereotypes. Show examples of native American stereotypes (readily found at Thanksgiving time) and explain why they are not accurate.

➤ Use a bicultural and bilingual (if appropriate) curriculum with a class consisting of children who are culturally different from the predominant society. (Many are available. In this approach children learn the values, language, and customs of their own culture as well as those of the predominant one.)

➤ Answer questions about people with differences openly and honestly. For example, if child asks, "Why does that man walk funny?" answer by saying, "He was probably born with legs that work differently from most people, although I don't know for sure. He uses crutches and metal braces on his legs to help support his legs so he can walk for himself. You may ask him yourself politely if he's not busy."

Dealing with Existing Problems

When You See Bias Happening

Children will not change their misguided beliefs about differences (learned from parents and/or assimilated from media and society in general) simply by seeing and hearing positive images of different cultures or by celebrating cultural holidays (Martin Luther King, Jr.'s Birthday, Hanukkah, Kwanza, Chinese New Year, Cinco De Mayo, and so on). To change their beliefs or to minimize the likelihood that they will develop negative beliefs, take direct action (Derman-Sparks 1989).

➤ Give children correct information as soon as they hear stereotypical statements (whether from children or adults) or see biased behavior. Say something like the following: "It hurts deeply inside to be told you can't play because of the color of your skin. This goes against our class rule of using words that do not hurt. People have to get to know each other before they can really tell if they like or don't like each other."

➤ Help the offended stand up for himself. Support his hurt feelings and then help him say such words as "I'm proud of my skin color and I can play where I want to." Continue to encourage nonbiased behaviors in the offending child: "You had a lot of fun today with Maria whose skin is different from yours. Many different children can enjoy each other." Don't try to force friendships or deny a child's feelings of dislike or repulsion. Set up opportunities for friendships to develop through play.

➤ Develop activities that actively counteract the stereotype that was acted upon. Write stories with the children about classroom events in which biases were overcome (e.g., two culturally different children who didn't like each other at first but then became good friends). Use puppets to make up stories about incidents of bias and how people can deal with them effectively.

➤ When you or the children notice examples of prejudice, show them ways to do something about it. For example, on a field trip to a museum, you realize that the museum has many steps and is not wheelchair accessible. Ask the children, "Can all people get up these steps? Which people can't? Can they get into the museum? How would it make you feel if you couldn't go to the museum? What can be done about it?" If they have trouble developing solutions, suggest some, such as talking to the person in charge of the museum or writing a letter to him. Follow through on the idea as a class and share the response. Sometimes you can get dramatic and satisfying results—your actions may result in the building of a ramp! If this happens, take several trips to watch the ramp being built.

➤ Meet with the parents of the child who often expresses bias. Explain how you are dealing with this trait in the classroom and discuss your views on it. Listen carefully to their views and develop a plan together. If they disagree with you and support their child's biases, make clear that in your class you still will not allow the voicing or acting out of biases. (They may choose to use a different program.) Have a parent meeting where all parents can listen and discuss these issues. You may gain good support this way.

Differences in Learning Styles and Priorities Due to Culture

Different cultures emphasize certain values and abilities over others. While some cultures strongly value education, others value hard work and physical labor. Some cultures value promptness, others value a relaxed attitude about time. The visual sense is very important in some cultures (colorful art and clothing) while other cultures place more emphasis on the auditory sense (music, discussion, and literature). Seeing the strength of what each culture values and recognizing how it may be different from those in your classroom is important. A clash between a child's own culture and the culture of the school will result in his feeling less able, less willing to participate, different, and odd.

➤ Once you have recognized the differences between your values and the values of a family, which can be discovered through home visits, meeting with parents, inviting parents to share aspects of the culture in the classroom, and listening to the child, help the child by being flexible about your values and by supporting his. For example, in the culture of the urban poor in

America, many families view time as very flexible and flowing. (There are many exceptions to this and to any generalizations about a culture). The family may have no set meal times, bed times, bath schedules, and so on. When the child enters your class, he confronts a set schedule with specific times for everything. This is very different from what he has always known and therefore internalized as his sense of what time means. Review your schedule with the children and give frequent reminders about what happens and when, give ample warnings before the next routine on your schedule, allow children to finish projects or save them to finish later, allow plenty of time for children to play and choose from a wide selection of activities, and alter your schedule occasionally. This will enable you to help all children develop a sense of time and order (which is highly valued in mainstream society) while supporting the child whose culture views time differently. Apply a similar approach to other cultural issues.

Children from Religious Minorities

Some families are part of a religious group, such as Buddhist, Jehovah's Witnesses, or Jewish, and have many values and practices that may be very different from the common practices in your classroom. Make sure all families know upon enrollment your approach to celebrating holidays and birthdays. Meet with parents from religious minorities to negotiate any altering of your approach that is acceptable to both of you. This may involve inviting a Jewish parent to show the children how Hanukkah is celebrated or supporting parents who are Jehovah's Witnesses who decide to keep their child home during Halloween. If a fair compromise cannot be worked out, the parents may feel more comfortable placing their child in a program affiliated with their particular religion.

➤ Help parents recognize that many religious holidays have secular aspects to them. Dying eggs and egg hunts at Easter and Santa Claus and trees at Christmas have become mainstream American cultural symbols and events, although they have religious origins. Almost all children know about and enjoy these activities and traditions. To deny their existence by never doing these activities nor displaying traditional decorations in a center does children a disservice because they are so important to children. However, limit the amount of time you spend celebrating traditional holidays in typical ways because the children get exposed to them from many other sources. Expand children's cultural understanding and awareness by presenting a wide array of holidays and ways that they are celebrated in different places. Use children's excitement about holidays to foster learning and growth in all areas of development. Invite the children to classify and match Easter eggs of various patterns or make books for Christmas presents. Consider your classroom a place where all children's interests and values are supported and then deepened and expanded.

Resources

Derman-Sparks, Louise and the A.B.C. Task Force. *Anti-Bias Curriculum*. Washington: NAEYC, 1989.

Escobedo, T.H., ed. *Early Childhood Bilingual Education*. New York: Teachers College Press, 1983.

Froschl, M., and Sprung, B. *Resources for Educational Equity: An Annotated Bibliography for Grades Pre-K-12*. New York: Garland Publishing, 1988.

Kendall, F. *Diversity in the Classroom: A Multicultural Approach to the Education of Young Children*. New York: Teachers College Press, 1983.

Quinsey, M.B. *Why Does That Man Have Such a Big Nose?* Seattle: Parenting Press, 1986.

Ramsey, P.G. *Teaching and Learning in a Diverse World: Multicultural Education for Young Children*. New York: Teachers College Press, 1987.

Ramsey, P.G.; Vold, E.B.; and Williams, L.R. *Multicultural Education: A Source Book*. New York: Garland Publishing, 1989.

Saracho, O.N., and Spodek, B. *Understanding the Multicultural Experience in Early Childhood Education*. Washington, DC: NAEYC, 1983.

5. TV/Video Obsessed Children

Some children spend a great deal of time watching television or videos at home. In many cases adults do not limit what is watched, counteract the values promoted, nor help children understand what they see. Children in this situation will often engage in play that is derivative of television shows. This can result in aggressive, repetitive, loud, or dangerous play.

However, when children share a mutual interest based on toys and play from a TV show, it can help them make friends. As this can be very helpful for a child who is new, shy or handicapped, do not eliminate all such play. Instead, put reasonable limits on the play, as discussed in this chapter.

Preventing Problems

➤ Watch the popular shows and videos most often viewed by your children to understand who the characters are and what their appeal is.

➤ Have readily available dramatic play materials that encourage play not related to TV characters. Some examples are: fire hats and pieces of garden hose; stethoscopes, crutches, bandages and other hospital supplies; stamps, envelopes, paper, mail bags, hats, and other post office supplies.

➤ If you have action figures in your class, use generic ones that cannot be identified with currently popular shows. Provide small plastic dinosaurs, lions, bears, and other scary animals with which children can safely play out fears and aggression.

➤ Offer many opportunities for children to be involved in cooperative games and activities such as building projects and group art activities.

➤ Talk to parents about the importance of limiting, monitoring, and discussing what children view. Because of the availability of VCRs and videotapes many more children are watching adult films that confuse and even terrify them.

Dealing with Existing Problems

Noncreative Play

➤ If some children insist that others play according to a particular TV script, talk to them about how the TV show was written by a person who made it up. Explain that children have ideas just as good as these adult writers. Help the children rewrite the script and change it.

Aggressive Play

Play that imitates television is often a problem because of its aggressive nature. Be aware that in this kind of play, children may get hurt or may be dominated by others. However, remember that children need to act out issues related to good and evil or power and weakness.

➤ Set up rules to avoid problems and make sure that roles are rotated. Such rules might include the following: use only gentle contact and any child can call a time out to leave the game or switch roles.

➤ Put a reasonable limit on the amount of time children can spend in play that is based on television shows or videos. After that time, redirect them by suggesting other choices they can make. (See "War, Gun or Violent Play" in "Hitting and Aggression" on page 127, for ideas on dealing with action figures such as G.I. Joe™, He-Man™, and Teenage Mutant Ninja Turtles™, superheroes, and other aggressive play from TV.)

Resolving Conflicts

➤ Conflicts that arise from this type of play provide excellent opportunities for teachers to help children with conflict resolution skills. Encourage the children to talk through problems and help them negotiate compromises. (See "Helping Children with Difficult Behaviors," on pages 110 to 113, and "Hitting and Aggression," on pages 126 to 127, for more conflict resolution ideas.)

Barbie Doll™ Play

Even if these types of dolls are not available in the classroom, many girls (and a few boys) will find opportunities to play out their ideas of "teenage adventures." This is disturbing because it usually reflects stereotypical behavior. It is the female version of boys' war play, as females are taught to gain power for themselves by attracting the "right man" (power by association). We know that this course is dangerous because it discourages self-reliance and intellectual growth. Many more women are hurt by it than win by it. To see young girls practicing behaviors whose goals are to only become popular with boys is cause for concern. However, stopping this type of play is difficult because the messages in the media (particularly advertising) are so strong.

➤ Tell the children of your concerns in simple terms: "Real teenagers like to dress up, but they also spend a lot of time reading and learning and working, so they can take care of themselves when they are grown-ups."

➤ Put a time limit on the play and then redirect the children into an activity that is equally compelling, such as pretending to be teenagers working in a restaurant with many props and clothes.

➤ Provide a wide variety of active, hands-on choices. Stimulate the children's thinking and challenge their imaginations so that they will not need to play with "Barbie" dolls. (See "Toys from Home," on page 51, for additional suggestions.)

Resources

Adult Books and Articles

Abraham, K.G., and Lieberman, E. "Should Barbie Go to Preschool?" *Young Children* 40(2) (January 1985): 12-14.

Honig, A.S. "Television and Young Children." *Young Children* 38(4) (May 1983): 63-76.

Kostelnik, M.J.; Whiren, A.P.; and Stein, L.C. "Living with He-Man: Managing Superhero Fantasy Play." In *Reducing Stress in Young Children's Lives*, edited by J.B. McCracken. Washington, DC: NAEYC, 1986.

Myers-Walls, J.A., and Fry-Miller, K.M. "Nuclear War: Helping Children Overcome Fears." *Young Children* 39(4) (May 1984): 27-32.

Perotta, K. *Taming the TV Habit.* Ann Arbor, MI: Servant Books, 1982.

Tuchsherer, P. *TV Interactive Toys: The New High Tech Threat to Children.* Bend, OR: Pinaroo Publishing, 1988.

Winick, M.P. "Media Damage: Developmental Stress Points." In *Children and Stress: Helping Children Cope*, edited by A.S. McNamee. Washington, DC: Association for Childhood International, 1982.

Winn, M. *The Plug-In Drug.* New York: Penguin, 1985.

Winn, M. *Unplugging the Plug-In Drug.* New York: Viking Penguin, 1987.

Children's Books

Charren, P., and Hulsizer, C. *The TV-Smart Book for Kids.* New York: E.P. Dutton, 1986.

6. Children with Extreme Fears

Most preschool children have common fears, such as a fear of the dark, snakes, or being left alone. These are healthy fears (they protect children) as long as they do not get in the way of children's abilities to play, have friends, and be reasonably independent for their age. These fears are healthy as far as they are connected to reality—if some possibility of danger or harm really exists. Extremely fearful children will be obsessed by their fear. They will talk about it or show anxiety about it often and at times when no cause is apparent.

Possible Causes

Fears develop because preschoolers have active imaginations, are becoming aware of cause-and-effect relationships ("If it is dark then dangers can't be seen, and if they can't be seen then I can't protect myself"), have an increasing awareness of how many ways they can be hurt, have conflicts within themselves over being independent but still needing adult protection, and are egocentric (they see themselves at the center of the world and therefore believe dangers are directed at them).

Some gifted children can develop extreme fears (of things like pollution, fire or diseases) because while they have an advanced intellect, they still have emotions typical of a young child. They understand certain facts and cause-and-effect relationships but lack the ability to put these in proper perspective.

Fears of monsters can represent children's anxieties about not being able to control their own aggression. (See Part V "Children with Difficult Behaviors," on pages 109 to 142, for ideas on teaching self-control.)

For toddlers or developmentally delayed children, some fears develop because the world is still an unsure place. ("Is my brother with a mask on still my brother or is he somebody else?") The ability to know that something is still there even if it cannot be seen is called object permanence. It develops gradually and is why peek-a-boo is fun for children. They also have not developed a good sense of relationships (size, weight, and so on). They think that being washed down the drain along with the bath water is possible.

Extreme fears can develop as a result of the factors discussed above being united with an additional trauma. In most cases, extreme fears are linked directly to a troubling experience, such as fear of fires after seeing a neighbor's house burn or fear of water after a near drowning. In other cases, the connection is less clear. Extreme fears can result from a more general anxiety or insecurity. A child who has witnessed a violent act may become extremely fearful of the dark, for example, although darkness was not connected to the event. A neglected child may have a number of extreme fears, although none are necessarily related to a particular trauma.

Preventing Problems

➤ When the family enters the program, make sure they fill out an intake form that asks about any stressful events in the child's life and about fears the child has.

➤ Maintain regular communication with parents, so that they will inform you of any problems or traumatic events in their children's lives.

➤ Create a sense of security for all children by having a consistent daily schedule, comforting routines, and a child-controlled environment (many choices, child-sized furniture and materials, and equipment accessible on low shelves). Whenever possible, make children aware of all changes before they happen. Remind them of the next event in the schedule. (This provides predictability.)

➤ Support and validate the feelings of all children (even if you can't support the behaviors): "I can hear that you are very angry. You have a right to be angry, and I would be angry, too, if someone teased me. Let me help you talk to him about it."

➤ Provide many opportunities for children to safely express their feelings and fears through a wide variety of methods. Children can talk about fears during a sharing circle, draw on blank paper, make up stories that adults can write down for them (if necessary), use dress-up clothes and props for dramatic play, play with small figures of people and animals, and act out short stories (such as "The Three Little Pigs") that involve fearful events.

➤ Play games that help strengthen the children's sense of knowing something is still there even if it can't be seen (object permanence). Include peek-a-boo, hide-and-seek, what's missing? and similar games.

➤ Read children's literature dealing with fearful events that children overcome. (Original fairy tales do this better than most other forms of children's literature. Stories such as "Little Red Cap" and "Mama Goat and the Seven Little Kids" put children or young animals in extremely dangerous circumstances but through their own abilities, they come out of these adventures alive and even better off. These stories are very healing.)

Dealing with Existing Problems

➤ Children with extreme fears will usually benefit from professional counseling. Recommend this and with the parents' permission, ask the counselor for advice about helping the child in the classroom. Counseling will be of most benefit if the whole family is involved.

➤ Support the child's feelings no matter how irrational. Avoid the temptation to say something like the following: "Come on, there's nothing to be afraid of." Remember that the fears are very real to the child. Do not make the child do something that he is terrified of. Support him by saying: "I know dogs are frightening to you. You can hold my hand, and you don't have to pet her."

➤ Join the child's fantasy about the fear and help him overcome it. For example, if a child is afraid to go into a closet for some art materials because there is a monster in it, go into the closet with him to get rid of the monster. Follow his lead by asking "What can we do to get rid of the monster?" Perhaps you will both need to catch the monster, put it in a garbage bag, and throw it in the dumpster.

➤ Most counselors help people overcome their fears by very gradually introducing the fearful element and letting the person get used to it slowly. You can do the same. For example, you can help a child overcome a fear of water through the following steps, moving on to the next step only when he feels comfortable and in control:

1. Have him play in a gentle sprinkler or hose aimed at the feet and hold his hand.

2. Hold only his little finger.

3. Let go and have him play on his own.

4. Gradually raise the level and intensity of the water.

5. Have him stand in a small wading pool and hold his hand if needed.

6. Have him stand on his own.

7. Have him sit down in the wading pool while you hold his body.

8. Have him sit while you hold his hand.

9. Have him sit while you hold his little finger.

10. Have him sit on his own.

11. Take him to a large pool and have him wade in the shallow end while you hold his body.

12. Hold only his hand.

13. Hold only his little finger.

14. Have him play on his own.

15. Gradually increase the water level.

➤ Be aware that some children can move through these steps more quickly than others or may not need every step to be successful while other children may need even smaller steps. Make sure the child controls the process: "If you need my hand back again, just tell me."

➤ If the child talks about his fears very often, give only minimal attention to his comments and limit them. Say something like the following: "I'll listen carefully to you for one more minute (set a timer), and then you need to do something else." Redirect him into active play with other children.

➤ Give the child many opportunities to be in control: "You can be in charge of turning the lights off and on when we leave and enter the room."

➤ Make up stories or read books directly related to the particular fear the child has. Provide specific, factual information about the object of fear and ways to deal with it. For example, help a child who is very afraid of dogs by explaining that: "Most dogs will not chase you if you don't run. Most dogs will go away if you say 'Go' in a loud, firm voice and stamp your foot. Pet only a dog whose name you know and if the owner tells you it's OK."

➤ Talk with the parents. Find out if they know where the fear comes from. In one case, a child's intense fear of insects was a result of his mother's similar fear. The teacher helped the mother realize that until she was able to overcome her own fear, her child's fear would probably not diminish. Reassure the parents that with support most children grow out of most fears.

Resources

Brett, Doris. *Annie Stories*. New York: Workman, 1988.

Grimm, The Brothers. *Grimm's Fairy Tales*. New York: Pantheon Books, 1944.

Hyson, Marion Carey. "Lobster on the Sidewalk: Understanding and Helping Children with Fears." In *Reducing Stress in Young Children's Lives*, edited by J.B. McCracken. Washington, DC: NAEYC, 1986.

Myers-Walls, J.A., and Fry-Miller, K.M. "Nuclear War: Helping Children Overcome Fears." *Young Children* 39(4) (May 1984): 27-32.

Children's Books

Hill, S. *Go Away Bad Dreams*. New York: Random House, 1985.

Howe, J. *There's a Monster under My Bed*. New York: Macmillan, 1986.

Mayer, M. *There's a Nightmare in My Closet*. New York: Dial, 1976.

Mayer, M. *There's an Alligator Under My Bed*. New York: Dial, 1982.

Ross, T. *I'm Coming to Get You*. New York: Dial, 1984.

Sendak, M. *Where the Wild Things Are*. New York: Scholastic, 1988.

Stein, S.B. *About Phobias*. New York: Walker, 1974.

Viorst, J. *My Mama Says There Aren't Any Zombies, Ghosts, Vampires, Monsters, Fiends, Goblins, or Things*. New York: Macmillan, 1973.

7. The Sexually Precocious Child

This is the child who knows a great deal about sex, acts sexual or provocative, or tries to involve other children in games which simulate sexual activity or include touching each others' genitals. It goes beyond the typical behaviors of young children who are curious about what their bodies look like and want to play doctor. This child is sophisticated, manipulative of others, and wants to do the activities often.

The child who exhibits these behaviors may do so because of the following:

• She has learned that she can get certain children to like her, play with her, and pay attention to her, through the behaviors.

• She is imitating the behaviors she observes from parents, older siblings, baby sitters, or neighbors.

• She has a low self-image and this behavior is a way to get attention, control others, see herself as "grown-up," and feel in control.

• She has been sexually abused and sees herself as worthwhile primarily because of her sexuality.

Preventing Problems

➤ In a natural, relaxed way, provide opportunities for children, who are all naturally curious about bodies, to see what bodies look like. Have boys and girls share bathrooms. At about five years of age children begin to want some privacy, and that should be respected. Give older preschoolers the option of sharing a bathroom or having privacy. Supervise the bathrooms carefully to make sure that no child is being manipulated by a sexually precocious child. A relaxed atmosphere about bodies will help them understand that the human body and its natural functions, such as elimination, is different from sexuality. It will also reduce the desire and need to explore bodies through playing doctor or other games.

➤ Talk to children about protecting themselves from sexual abuse and the importance of getting help if they are being sexually abused. Many good curriculums that deal with the issue in a nonthreatening and very concrete way are available. (See "Parents Who May Be Abusive to Their Children," on pages 154 to 157, for a list of these curriculums.) Children can best protect themselves by telling the adult perpetrator that they will tell their teacher (or mother or other specific authority figure) on them. Saying no is usually not enough. Be available and approachable so that a child who is being sexually abused will tell you about it.

➤ Talk about bodies and use the appropriate names for body parts (penis, scrotum, vulva, vagina, clitoris) in a relaxed, matter-of-fact way.

➤ Provide pictures, puzzles, anatomically correct dolls, and picture books that reflect a relaxed, open attitude about bodies and bodily functions.

➤ As all children are bombarded with many images of subtle and overt sexuality from television and advertising, do not ignore this. Tell the children that these behaviors are OK for adults but that they are *not* OK for children—much like driving a car.

➤ Give all children lots of attention for who they are and for appropriate things they say and do. Build the self-esteem of all your children with this type of attention. Note that the absence of a great deal of positive attention from adults can create an atmosphere where children seek attention from other children or accept attention from abusive/manipulative adults. When children seek attention from other children, the result is a classroom of children with behaviors that are difficult to manage, such as acting out, silliness, and the controlling of some children by others.

➤ Give minimal attention or praise for how they look or what they wear. If a child comes in with a new dress, screeching with delight, "Look what I'm wearing," respond by saying, "It looks lovely on you, but I like you no matter what you are wearing."

➤ Get to know parents, siblings and family routines, so that you can get a sense of where the behaviors might be coming from.

➤ Assure all the children in your class that you will not allow any child to force another child to do what she does not want to do.

Dealing with Existing Problems

Questions about Sex

➤ Most questions about sex reflect a healthy curiosity about how babies are made, about relationships between men and women, and about the human body. Give honest, short, straightforward answers to these questions. However, make sure that you fully understand what the child actually wants to know. For example, if a child asks how a man and woman make a baby, ask her questions to determine if she wants to know what they do physically to make a baby before assuming that this is what she wants to know. She may really want to know about the birth process. Also ask her how she thinks a man and woman make a baby. (This will tell you her level of understanding.) If you determine the question does pertain to the sex act, say something like this: "When a man and woman love each other very much, they lie in bed and hug and kiss. If they want to, the man puts his penis inside the woman's vagina and that feels really good for both of them. Tiny sperm come out of the man's penis, and if one meets a tiny egg

inside the woman's body, a baby will start." (Gordon and Gordon 1974.)

➤ A sexually precocious child may ask questions which reflect an adult knowledge of sex or of unusual sexual practices. This is cause for concern. Try to determine where and how she has gained that knowledge, in case it is through direct experience. See below: "Determining If the Child is Being Sexually Abused."

Mutual Exploration

➤ If you see play where children are exploring each other's genitals and they are both mutually involved and interested (there doesn't appear to be any manipulation), tell them, "It is important to keep your clothes on in the classroom and keep hands or objects away from each other's genitals. This is because our genitals and anus are very delicate and can easily get hurt or sore." Encourage interest in what bodies look like and help the children find some dolls or books to learn more.

The Manipulative Child

➤ Intervene calmly in the situation where a child is getting others to do what she wants them to do. Help the child who is being controlled by the sexually precocious child to stand up for herself. Give her specific words she can use to assert her right not to be taken advantage of: "I don't have to do whatever you tell me to do if I don't want to. Friends do what both want to do." Have both children come up with acceptable ways to play together. Tell the manipulative child that forcing herself on others will not be tolerated. Let her know that the consequences of doing this again will be that she will have to play by herself. Praise her often when she interacts with others cooperatively: "Thank you for playing fairly. It makes our classroom a fun and safe place for everyone."

Grown-up Play in the Dramatic Play Area

➤ If a child spends a great deal of time in the dramatic play area acting out sexually advanced behavior, limit the amount of time any child can stay in that area. Provide materials and a starting structure for the dramatic play area to be a restaurant, office, or a store. (This may be less conducive to the behavior than a house or a kitchen area.) Spend time playing with the children in this area and redirect the play if it goes in a sexual direction by asking for other ideas or bringing in a new, attractive item with which to play.

Appropriate Affection

➤ Provide the sexually precocious child with a great deal of positive attention when she is acting age appropriately. Give her hugs and safe physical affection (stroke her hair, hold her hand) so that she will learn how normal relations between adults and children should and could be. Let her know that she is worthwhile and loved even when she is not being sexual.

Determining If the Child Is Being Sexually Abused

➤ Use a sexual abuse prevention curriculum and read books written for young children about sexual abuse. Provide opportunities for the child to draw pictures and dictate stories about her fears and concerns. Create some secure, private time for the two of you so that she can talk about any abuse that may be happening. If it is happening, tell her that you can help her make it stop. Tell your supervisor about the child's statements so that the appropriate actions can be taken. If a social service agency is involved with the family, ask someone in the agency if she has knowledge that sexual abuse has occurred recently. (See "Parents Who May Be Abusive to Their Children," on pages 154 to 157, for further information.)

Fairy Tales Can Help Heal

➤ Read original Grimm's fairy tales, such as "Little Red Riding Hood" and "Hansel and Gretel," to your children. These can be very therapeutic as they deal with children overcoming the abuse and manipulation of adults.

Resources

Adult Books and Articles

Bettelheim, Bruno. *The Uses of Enchantment: The Meaning and Importance of Fairy Tales.* New York: Vintage, 1976.

Conte, Jon. "Clinical Dimensions of Adult Sexual Abuse of Children." *Behavioral Sciences and the Law* 3(4) (Fall 1985).

Gilbert, Neil, et al. *Child Sexual Abuse Prevention: Evaluation of Educational Materials.* Berkeley, CA: Welfare Research Group, School of Social Welfare, 1988.

Koblinsky, S., and Behana, N. "Child Sexual Abuse: The Educator's Role in Prevention, Detection, and Intervention." *Young Children* 39(60) (September 1984): 3-15.

Money, John, and Tucker, Patricia. *Sexual Signatures: On Being a Man or a Woman.* Boston: Little Brown, 1975.

Morrison, Eleanor, et al. *Growing Up Sexual.* New York: D. Van Nostrand, 1980.

Ratner, M., and Chamlin, S. *Straight Talk: Sexuality Education for Parents and Kids 4-7.* New York: Penguin, 1987.

Wolf, Dennie Palmer. "No Girls Alout: Gender Differences and Early Play." In *Connecting: Friendships in the Lives of Young Children and Their Teachers*, edited by Dennie Palmer Wolf. Redmond, WA: Exchange Press, 1986.

Children's Books

Bassett, Kerri. *My Very Own Special Body Book.* Redding, CA: Hawthorne Press, 1982.

Brenner, Barbara, and Ancona, George. *Bodies.* New York: Dutton, 1973.

Freeman, Lory. *It's My Body.* Seattle, WA: Parenting Press, 1982.

Girard, Linda W. *My Body is Private.* Mt. Flora, FL: Kidsrights, 1984.

Gordon, Sol, and Gordon, Judith. *A Better Safe Than Sorry Book.* Fayetteville, NY: Ed-U Press, 1984.

Gordon, Sol, and Gordon, Judith. *Did the Sun Shine Before You Were Born?* Fayetteville, NY: Ed-U Press, 1974.

Grimm, The Brothers. *Grimm's Fairy Tales.* New York: Pantheon Books, 1944.

Hindman, Jan. *A Very Touching Book.* Durkee, OR: McClure-Hindman Books, 1983.

Junce, Judith. *It's Not Your Fault.* Edmonds, WA. Chas. Franklin Press, 1983.

Stinson, K. *The Bare Naked Book.* Toronto: Annick, 1986.

Sweet, Phyllis E. *Something Happened to Me.* Fayetteville, NY: Ed-U Press, 1981.

Waxman, Stephanie. *What Is A Girl? What is a Boy?* New York: Thomas Y. Crowell, 1976, 1989.

8. The Child Who Identifies with the Opposite Sex and Sex-Bias Issues

In a typical class you will have children with a wide variety of sex-role and gender attitudes about themselves and others. Some feel very comfortable about being a boy or a girl and accept a wide variety of behaviors from others. Others may act very masculine or very feminine with exaggerated and stereotypical behaviors and may also put other children down when they do not act similarly. Occasionally you will have a child in your class who sees himself or herself socially as a member of the opposite sex.

The child who identifies with the opposite sex knows his/her own biological sex by the age of three, but aspires to jobs typical of the other sex (a boy wants to be a nurse; a girl wants to be a truck driver), prefers to dress up in clothes and accessories associated with the other sex, wants to be a character for Halloween who is the opposite sex (a witch for a boy, superman for a girl), and prefers to play with groups of children of the opposite sex. The girl may choose block play almost exclusively; the boy only dresses up.

All healthy children who feel good about themselves will exhibit these behaviors at times. You need to encourage both boys and girls to feel comfortable in a variety of roles and experience a wide variety of activities. The child who identifies with the opposite sex, however, exhibits these behaviors often and consistently. This child may also exaggerate the behaviors by picking up on broad stereotypes, such as a four-year-old boy who spends a great deal of time imitating a cheerleader. This is usually not an acceptable behavior from any child in preschool (except outside in the playground), regardless of sex. The role-playing becomes too loud, and the jumping and kicking can cause injuries.

The child's language will give you important clues to how he/she perceives him/herself. A boy might make a statement like "Teacher, we girls chased the boys all around the playground, and we caught them!" A girl who identifies with the opposite sex might pick many fights and say things like "Me and the other boys are the drivers, you girls be the riders."

The reasons for this development are not totally understood, but they appear to be multiple. A combination of biological factors (prenatal hormone levels, perhaps) and environmental factors (home life) are probably involved. What is known, and what is important for teachers to understand, is that the child *does not choose* to identify with the opposite sex. It is *not* a sign of a problem, disease, or sickness that can be corrected. About five to ten percent of children have these characteristics—this has been documented throughout history and in all cultures. Your goal is to make sure the child feels supported, feels good about him/herself, and is respected by other children. Although these are goals for all children, they are more difficult to achieve with the child who identifies with the opposite sex, because of all the ridicule he/she receives. When the child feels more secure, supported, and accepted, some of the exaggerated, stereotyped behaviors will diminish.

Preventing Problems

The following ideas are designed to help you create a classroom atmosphere where a broad range of sex-role behavior will be accepted and supported. The result will be that the child who identifies with the opposite sex will feel less different and more free to be who she/he is. As there will always be a range of sex-role behaviors within any group of children, it is best to implement these ideas even if you do not currently have a child in your class who identifies with the opposite sex.

➤ In your classroom or your teaching, eliminate anything which points up artificial differences between boys and girls. For example:

➤ Avoid a boy's line and a girl's line.

➤ Avoid counting numbers of girls and numbers of boys during role call. Count children sitting on the left side and those on the right side or just count all children.

➤ Avoid complimenting children when they dress up. Compliment all children for appropriate preschool dress: "Those jeans will be perfect for playing in the sand box."

➤ Teach children the real differences between the sexes. Boys and men have penises. Girls and women have vaginas. Differences between girls and boys are basically physical ones and not related to ability and skill. Tell the children that girls can do anything boys can do and that boys can do anything girls can do. Show and display pictures of girls/women and boys/men in a wide variety of jobs, hobbies, and roles, such as female athletes and men feeding babies.

➤ Actively encourage boys and girls to play with each other, form friendships, and accept a wide range of behaviors from each other.

➤ Include in the dramatic play area a variety of materials and clothing such as plastic tools, ties, sport jackets, and men's and women's shoes.

➤ Place the block area next to the dramatic play area to encourage play between these two areas.

➤ Read stories that include strong female characters and males who nurture. Avoid stories that reinforce stereotypes or leave out female characters.

➤ Include females in songs and finger plays. (Each children's finger during "Where Is Thumbkin?" can be "ma'am" as easily as "sir." It can also be a gender neutral "friend." The monkeys jumping on the bed can be female as easily as male, and the doctor who is called when they are all off the bed can be a woman doctor.)

Dealing with Existing Problems

Building Self-Esteem

➤ Remind the child of his abilities and strengths. Approve of the child's desire to do any activity. If an activity is not appropriate for school, request that it be done at home or on the playground, while respecting the child's desire to do it. Inappropriate behavior at school (such as the cheerleading example already given) is inappropriate for all children, not just the child who identifies with the opposite sex.

➤ Intervene when another child rejects, teases, or pokes fun at the child. Help him to verbally stand up for himself with such statements as, "I have a right to play whatever I want. If you don't like it, play somewhere else." Have him practice saying this. Tell the child who is doing the teasing that you would help him if he were being teased and tell the teaser that you will not tolerate hurtful words. Explain that a consequence of teasing, if it happens again, could be not playing with any children for a while. Explain to him the importance of respecting everyone, especially those who do things differently from most people. When you see him interacting positively with the teased child later, let him know how well he is doing.

Helping Parents

Almost all parents of a child who identifies with the opposite sex know that their child is different. Some parents will try to deny this, and some will want to find out how to help. Parents of girls may be more accepting because "tomboy" behavior is tolerated by society. Parents of boys may have a harder time because society is less willing to tolerate effeminate behavior, which is wrongly associated with homosexuality by many people. The word *sissy* has a much more negative connotation than *tomboy*.

➤ Assure all parents that you accept and care about all children regardless of individual differences in behavior or physical appearance. Assure them that all children are unique—they all have strengths and weaknesses. Let parents know that you will not tolerate teasing and meanness in your class and that children will be taught to be supportive and positive towards others.

➤ Talk with and write notes to the parents often about the positive aspects of their child ("He has a great attention span." "She's a motivated learner." "He's a champ at putting together puzzles.") Let parents know that you are willing and able to help and are available to talk whenever they have any questions or concerns. (See "When You See Bias Happening" on page 80 in "Children Who Are Culturally or Physically 'Different' " for ideas on dealing with sex-biased remarks or behaviors.)

Resources

Adell, Judith, and Klein, Hilary D. *A Guide to Non-Sexist Children's Books*. Chicago: Academy Press, 1976.

Money, John. *Love and Love Sickness: The Science of Sex, Gender Difference, and Pair Bonding*. Baltimore: Johns Hopkins University Press, 1980.

Money, John, and Tucker, Patricia. *Sexual Signatures: On Being a Man or a Woman*. Boston: Little Brown, 1975.

Pitcher, Evelyn G., and Schultz, Lynn H. *Boys and Girls at Play: The Development of Sex Roles*. South Hadley, MA: Bergin and Garvey, 1983.

Sprung, Barbara. *Non-Sexist Education for Young Children*. New York: Citation, 1975.

9. Children Who Are Too Responsible

These children do not show behavior problems in the typical way, and therefore, you can easily overlook them. They are the children who take care of others' needs beyond what is expected or reasonable for young children. They may focus on other children whom they see as weak and vulnerable and "parent" them. They may focus on adults and show unusual concern for their feelings and needs. On the surface, these behaviors are altruistic and positive. However, when these behaviors happen too often and too consistently, when others don't want or need the children's help, and when their own needs are denied, the children have serious problems. These are children who are being robbed of their right to grow up free of adult responsibilities and their right to be taken care of by adults.

Possible Causes and Consequences

Typically, overly responsible children are growing up in homes where roles are reversed. The children are taking care of their parents, psychologically, if not actually. Whether the parents are not functioning well because of alcoholism (most common), drug dependency, poor health, emotional problems, mental illness, or other reasons, the effect on children is similar. They learn to take on the parent role in the household for their own survival. These children often are the oldest child in the family or have no siblings.

Children who feel they are worthless because of years of negative feedback can also exhibit these behaviors. They have found that they can get positive feedback and satisfaction from doing something that comes easy to them—putting themselves last.

Most often, these children are girls, because these behaviors are more socially acceptable in females and modeled more by females. In fact, women who spend their lives sacrificing for their families and years volunteering in service organizations are considered to be exemplary people. Some are, because they truly enjoy the work and can afford to do it, but many others bury their own dreams, desires, and needs.

If this pattern of behavior continues, it will have a profound effect on the children's lives. They will continue to deny their own needs and may develop destructive behaviors, such as never questioning authority, dropping out of school, marrying abusive spouses, having more children than they can handle, living with poor health, or abusing drugs or alcohol.

Preventing Problems

➤ Make the development of self-esteem a vital part of your curriculum and integrate it throughout all parts of the day. During lunch, discuss the children's accomplishments that day. Help them evaluate themselves in positive ways by asking what they have done that makes them proud of themselves. One of the best self-concept building strategies is to challenge children without pushing them. This sends the following message: "I believe you are smart and capable."

➤ Help children switch roles in dramatic play situations. This will reduce the amount of time some children dominate others or some children spend in inferior roles, such as the "Baby" or the "Dog."

➤ Inform the children through books, puppets, and role-plays about the appropriate roles of adults and children. Show situations where children are told to do unacceptable things, such as a five-year-old being told to care for younger siblings for several hours. Make sure the children know that this behavior is not acceptable. Tell them how they can get help by talking to a caring adult, such as yourself, or by using the telephone for help if they are frightened or if they are facing an emergency.

➤ Serve as a role model of an appropriately responsible adult. Explain how some responsibilities in their classroom belong to the children (using toys correctly), some to the teacher (providing safe toys) and some to both the children and the teacher (developing a new dramatic play area).

➤ Show children how to be helpful without completely doing things for others. For example, explain that they can help another child with a puzzle by doing one or two pieces and letting her finish or by showing her how to match the color of a puzzle piece to the color on the puzzle frame.

➤ Meet with parents regularly and do home visits if at all possible. (This will give you great insight into family situations, values, and problems.)

Dealing with Existing Problems

➤ Intervene when you see overly responsible behaviors. Tell the child that you appreciate her helpfulness (these are children with fragile self-concepts) but that she needs to play. Redirect her into a more appropriate situation and spend a few minutes making sure she is on the right track.

➤ Help the child who is the focus of the caretaking behaviors by giving her the words she needs to assert her independence: "I can do it myself, thank you." Another need the child may have is to learn to negotiate dramatic play roles to be more equal: "Let's both be doctors, and the doll can be the patient."

➤ Set up games that involve children taking turns and being in equal relationships. (Board games and lotto games, store bought or teacher made, are good for this.) Make sure the games are easy enough for children to do on their own but challenging enough to make them inviting. Guide the overly responsible child to these games and try to have her play with a child who will stand up to her but not dominate her.

➤ Work on the root of the problem. If you discover, for example, that the child lives with an alcoholic parent, seek help from local agencies that deal with helping alcoholics. Note that these agencies will suggest ways to assist the family and the child without violating trust or scaring them off. Read the children's books about alcoholic families and use puppets to role-play, for the whole class, situations specific to alcoholic families. Remember that all children can relate to and benefit from learning about how to help and heal children in difficult situations.

➤ Find quiet time to spend with the child—not too near other children. Read a book or make up a story related to her problem. Establish rapport and be open, empathetic, and ready to listen so she will talk about her situation. Remember that this will take much time and patience as most young children have difficulty knowing that they have a problem (they assume everybody lives the same way). Articulating this problem is very difficult for them.

Resources

Adult Books and Articles

Ackerman, R.J. *Children of Alcoholics: A Guidebook for Educators Therapists, and Parents 2nd Ed.* Holmes Beach, FL: Learning Publications, 1983.

Brett, Doris. *Annie Stories.* New York: Workman Press, 1988.

Deutsch, Charles. *Broken Bottles, Broken Dreams: Understanding and Helping the Children of Alcoholics.* New York: Teachers College Press, 1982.

Children's Books

DiGiovanni, K. *My House is Different.* Center City, MN: Hazelden, Center City, 1986.

Hammond, M., and Chesnut, L. *My Mom Doesn't Look Like an Alcoholic.* Pompano Beach, FL: Heath Communications, 1984

Hasting, J.M., and Typpo, M.H. *An Elephant in the Living Room.* Minneapolis: CompCare, 1984.

Stanford, D. *I Know the World's Worst Secret: A Child's Book About Living with an Alcoholic Parent.* Portland, OR: Multnomah Press, 1987.

Vigna, J. *I Wish Daddy Didn't Drink So Much.* Niles, IL: Whitman, 1988.

Part IV
Children Who Must Cope with Major Changes

1. New to the Class

Almost all new children will have a hard time at first, especially with separating from parents at the start of the day. Usually this gets better within a few weeks when the child knows she will be picked up regularly and when she is familiar with the new surroundings or the new teacher.

Preventing Problems

➤ If at all possible, visit the child in her home before she starts in your class, if she has not met you before. Leave a picture of yourself or snap a picture of her and yourself to leave or to send when developed.

➤ Invite the child and her parents to visit the class for about an hour before her first full day. Put no pressure on her to participate in any way. Respect her need to observe. If possible, have her visit several more times, gradually increasing the visiting times until her first full day.

➤ Request that a parent (or relative or friend) stay in the classroom the first few times the child attends, if at all possible. Ask the parent to sit quietly on the sidelines and not push the child into participating.

➤ Encourage the new child to bring in favorite toys from home, including some popular commercial toys, to help her form friendships. (Put some limits on the use of these toys as discussed in "Toys from Home" on page 51.)

Dealing with Existing Problems

➤ Recommend to parents that they drop off and pick up their child at the same time each day. This will establish a clear routine and routines create security.

➤ Encourage the parents to arrange for their child to spend time outside of school hours with another child who is in the class. This will help the child establish a special bond with a classmate and help her look forward to coming to the new program.

➤ Read children's books dealing with the issue of starting and/or moving. (See resources on page 97.)

➤ The child who still has separation problems a month after being in the program with the same teacher(s) has a problem most likely due to causes other than the newness. Ask yourself if the child is gaining anything by the behavior—such as extra attention. Can you change things so that the child will gain extra attention by separating easily and joining the activities quickly? (The attention can be in the form of encouraging remarks, smiles, and hugs.) Meet with the parents to discuss possible

causes and brainstorm solutions together. Determine if the child has excessive fears. Ask about the child's situation before entering the class and about major changes at home (a new sibling, divorce, or remarriage) that you can help the child work through. Face the possibility that the child might be better off in a different child care arrangement, such as family day care or fewer days of preschool, for now. (See "Starting the Day Off Right," on pages 17 to 19, for additional ideas on helping a child who is having trouble separating from her parents.)

The Child Who Has Recently Moved

➤ If the child has recently relocated, read books about moving and provide many opportunities for her to talk about her move. Ask her to show pictures, if she has them, of her old house and her friends from her former neighborhood. Help her write letters to these old friends.

➤ Help the child's parents learn about activities and resources for families in the area. These can include fun parks and playgrounds, places to swim, short hikes, zoos, museums, libraries, campgrounds, amusement parks, skating rinks, restaurants that welcome children, community centers, health clinics or pediatricians, social service agencies that help families, and family oriented organizations—from Parents without Partners to the YMCA.

Resources

Adult Books and Articles

Balaban, N. *Starting School: From Separation to Independence*. New York: Teachers College Press, 1985.

Jalongo, M.R. "When Young Children Move." *Young Children* 40(6) (September 1985): 51-57.

Kleckner, K.A., and Engel, R.E. "A Child Begins School: Relieving Anxiety with Books." *Young Children* 43(5) (July 1988): 14-18.

Children's Books about Attending a New School

Brand, J., and Gladstone, N. *My Day Care Book*. Mt. Rainier, MD: Gryphon House, 1985.

Cohen, M. *Will I Have A Friend?* New York: Macmillan, 1967.

Rockwell, H. *My Nursery School*. New York: Puffin, 1976.

Rogers, Fred. *Going to Day Care*. New York: G.P. Putnam's Sons, 1985.

Soderstrom, M. *Maybe Tomorrow I'll Have A Good Time*. New York: Human Sciences Press, 1981.

Tompert, Ann. *Will You Come Back for Me?* Niles, IL: Whitman, 1988.

Children's Books about Moving

Gretz, S. *Teddy Bear's Moving Day*. New York: Macmillan, 1981.

Malone, N.L. *A Home*. New York: Bradbury, 1988.

McKend, Heather. *Moving Gives Me a Stomach Ache*. Windsor, Ontario: Black Moss Press, 1988.

O'Donnell, E.L. *Maggie Doesn't Want to Move*. New York: Four Winds, 1987.

Rogers, Fred. *Moving*. New York: G.P. Putnam's Sons, 1987.

Watson, J.W., et al. *Sometimes a Family Has to Move*. New York: Crown, 1988.

2. Divorce and Remarriage

Although divorce has become an almost commonplace experience for children today, the emotional effect of divorce on a child is no less devastating. When a child experiences a divorce, you will most likely see behavior changes, such as silliness, negativeness, a short temper, increased aggression, nervous habits, more toileting "accidents," shorter attention span, temper tantrums, whining, and crying. Recent studies on divorce indicate that the effects on children can be long lasting and profound, extending into their adult lives.

Children who fare best under this difficult situation are those whose parents remain civil and mature towards each other, do not play "tug of war" with their children or with their children's loyalties, speak well of the other parent to their children, keep in close contact with the children, and help them realize that they are not responsible for the divorce.

As the child's teacher, you may not have a big role in influencing these factors, but you can give parents this information. You can also be a great support, a source of stability, and someone who clarifies information for the child. You can certainly help him realize that the fault for the divorce is not his.

Preventing Problems

As the chances are good that at least one child in your class will experience divorce in his family during the year, discussing the topic at any time will be helpful. Use chidren's books, stories, puppets, and films. As several children in your class are probably dealing with this problem, they can be helped by this and can contribute to the discussion.

➤ Provide information through books and pictures about many different kinds of families. Let the children know that children are loved and cared for in families with a wide variety of configurations: single moms, single dads, gay parents, joint custody, grandparents, foster parents, adoption, and so on. Discuss the different family arrangements of the children in your class.

➤ Give children helpful information about changing and about separating, through concrete experiences. (See the section on themes in "Selecting and Using a Curriculum" on pages 42 to 46.)

➤ Provide many outlets for the children to express their feelings and emotions. Include drawing, painting, sand play, water play, play with clay and playdough, creative movement, and making up stories.

➤ Provide places in your classroom where children can have privacy and quiet.

Dealing with Existing Problems

After their parents separate, many children go through a grieving process over the loss of their family and/or a parent who has left. Note that children in foster care go through this repeatedly. The stages in this process are the following:

Denial	They deny the divorce is really happening.
Anger	They show their anger through misbehaviors.
Hope	They try to bring their parents back together.
Sadness	They begin to accept the reality of the situation and express their feelings.
Acceptance	They find ways to be at peace with themselves and their new situation and return to their usual behaviors.

➤ Be aware of these stages so that you can help children move through them at their own pace. Accept their feelings but help the children express these feelings appropriately. In the anger stage do not deny their need to express their anger but help them direct the emotion in a way that does not hurt others or themselves. You might say the following: "I can't let you hit another person, but you can work with clay or hammer nails." Some of these feelings will emerge again for the child whose parent is remarrying.

➤ Make clear to the child that the divorce was not his fault and nothing he could have done or not done would have prevented it. Use books and stories to reinforce this message. Be aware that a child coping with a remarriage needs assurances that his parent does not love him any less because of the new spouse and perhaps new stepchildren. Assure the child that adults, like children, can love many people and love them all in different ways.

➤ Give the child many ways to express his feelings through open, creative activities. Ask him if he would like to write a story with you about a bunny who loses his parents. (Using animal characters helps give the child some distance from the issue, allowing him to risk expressing his inner feelings.) Ask him if he would like to draw a picture of his family.

➤ Help the child see the positive side of the divorce: "Your parents will be happier if they are not fighting so much. If they are happier, then it will be more fun to be with them and easier for them to make you happy." Do not deny the pain and the negative feelings the child is experiencing, but present another perspective. Point out that remarriage holds the possibility of more loving grown-ups to care for the child and maybe new brothers and sisters with whom to play.

➤ Avoid overprotecting or overindulging the child because of his pain. Remember that he will be better off with clearly defined, consistent limits. Give him support for appropriate behavior and redirect him towards this behavior. The last thing he needs now is to feel "different" because of being treated differently from the other children.

➤ Be loving and empathetic but do not allow a dependent relationship to develop between you and the child. Make sure he spends most of his time engaged with other children and not clinging to your leg. If this happens, say something like the following: "I'll give you one great big hug, and then you need to go play."

➤ All children and families undergoing this major change could benefit from professional counseling. Recommend this to parents as a way to ease the stress for everyone and to prevent future problems. Increasing lines of communication with parents by meeting and talking more often is crucial at this time.

Resources

Adult Books and Articles

Atkinson, Christine. *Step-Parenting: Understanding the Emotional Problems and Stresses*. New York: Thorsons, 1986.

Bettelheim, Bruno. *The Uses of Enchantment: The Meaning and Importance of Fairy Tales*. New York: Vintage, 1976.

Block, Joel D. *To Marry Again*. New York: Grosset & Dunlop, 1979.

Brett, Doris. *Annie Stories*. New York: Workman, 1988.

Diamond, Susan A. *Helping Children of Divorce: A Handbook for Parents and Teachers*. New York: Schocken, 1985.

Eckler, James D. *Step-by-Stepparenting: A Guide to Successfully Living with a Blended Family*. Crozet, VA: Betterway, 1988.

McNamee, Abigail S. "Helping Children Cope with Divorce." In *Children & Stress: Helping Children Cope*, edited by A.S. McNamee. Washington, DC: Association for Childhood Education International, 1982.

National Institute of Mental Health. *Caring About Kids When Parents Divorce*. NIMH, Public Inquires, 5600 Fishers Lane, Room 15-C-05, Rockville, MD 20857. (301-443-4536). (free publication)

Salk, Lee. *What Every Child Would Like Parents to Know about Divorce*. New York: Harper & Row, 1978.

Simon, Anne W. *Stepchild in the Family: A View of Children in Remarriage*. New York: Odyssey, 1964.

Skeen, P.; Robinson, B.E.; and Flake-Hobson, C. "Blended Families: Overcoming the Cinderella Myth." *Young Children* 39(2) (January, 1984): 64-74.

Skeen, P., and McKenry, P.C. "The Teacher's Role in Facilitating a Child's Adjustment to Divorce." In *Reducing Stress in Young Children's Lives*, edited by J.B. McCracken. Washington, DC: NAEYC, 1986.

Troyer, Warner. *Divorced Kids*. New York: Harcourt Brace Jovanovich, 1979.

Wallerstein, J.S., and Blakeslee, S. *Second Chances: Men, Women, and Children a Decade after Divorce*. New York: Ticknor & Fields, 1989.

Wallerstein, J.S., and Kelley, J.B. *Surviving the Breakup: How Children and Parents Cope With Divorce*. New York: Basic Books, 1980.

Visher, E.B., and Visher, J.S. *Step-Families: Myths and Realities*. Secaucus, NJ: Citadel, 1979.

Children's Books about Divorce and Step-Families

Adams, Florence. *Mushy Eggs*. New York: Putnam, 1973.

Christansen, C.B. *My Mother's House, My Father's House*. New York: Atheneum, 1989.

Dragonwagon, C. *Always, Always*. New York: Macmillan, 1984.

Drescher, Joan. *My Mother's Getting Married*. New York: Dial, 1983.

Grimm, The Brothers. *Grimm's Fairy Tales*. New York: Pantheon Books, 1944.

Kirkland, D.C. *I Have a Stepfamily . . . But It's Not the End of the World*. Southfield, MI: Aid-U, (no date).

Lexau, Joan. *Emily and the Klunky Baby and the Next Door Dog*. New York: Dial Press, 1972.

Paris, Susan. *Mommy and Daddy Are Fighting*. Seattle: Seal Press, 1986.

Sanford, D. *Please Come Home: A Children's Book about Divorce*. Portland, OR: Multnomah Press, 1985.

Sinberg, Janet. *Divorce Is a Grown-up Problem*. New York: Avon, 1978.

Stenson, Janet Sinberg. *Now I Have a Stepparent and It's Kind of Confusing*. New York: Avon, 1979.

Stinson, K.. *Mom and Dad Don't Live Together Any More*. Willowdale, Ontario, CA: Annick Press, 1985.

Children's Books about Families

Bosche, S.. *Jenny Lives with Eric and Martin*. London: Gay Men's Press, 1983.

Boyd, Lizi. *The Not-So-Wicked Stepmother*. New York: Viking Penguin, 1987.

Bunin, C., and Bunin, S. *Is That Your Sister?* New York: Pantheon, 1973.

Caines, J. *Abby*. New York: Harper & Row, 1973.

Caines, J. *Daddy*. New York: Harper & Row, 1977.

Caines, J. *Just Us Women*. New York: Harper & Row, 1982.

Clifton, L. *Everett Anderson's Friend*. New York: Holt, 1976.

Drescher, J. *Your Family, My Family*. New York: Walker, 1980.

Eichler, Margaret. *Martin's Father*. Carrboro, NC: Lollipop Power, 1971.

Greenberg, P. *Rosie and Roo*. Washington, DC: The Growth Program Press, 1988.

Quinlan, P. *My Dad Takes Care of Me*. Willowdale, Ontario, CA: Annick Press, 1987.

Schaffer, P. *How Babies and Families Are Made*. Berkeley, CA: Taber Sarah Books, 1988.

Simon, N. *All Kinds of Families*. Niles, IL: Whitman, 1975.

Surowrecki, S. *Joshua's Day*. Carrboro, NC: Lollipop Power, 1977.

Tax, M. *Families*. Boston: Little Brown, 1981.

Watson, Jane, et al. *Sometimes a Family Has to Split Up*. New York: Crown, 1988.

Williams, V. *A Chair for My Mother*. New York: Greenwillow, 1982.

Williams, V. *Something Special for Me*. New York: Greenwillow, 1983.

3. New Sibling

Whether by birth, remarriage, or adoption, a new sibling in the family will mean major changes. Children who have good preparation for this will weather the changes more easily, minimizing the feelings of uncertainty, jealousy, and insecurity that can develop. Teachers can be a great source of information and comfort.

Preventing Problems

Keep your children informed about how babies are made and are born. Many good books are available to help you do this in a simple way appropriate for young children. Some teachers like to do this in the spring when farm animals are giving birth, but doing it occasionally throughout the year is important because new siblings can come at any time.

➤ Discuss the wide variety of family configurations, including adoption. Tell the children why people adopt children and how this process works.

➤ Use terms such as *uterus* or *womb* to explain where the baby grows as many children believe the child grows in the stomach, which confuses and disturbs them.

➤ Make sure that the children understand that a long time passes before a baby grows old enough to be much fun to play with. Explain to the children that babies require a great deal of care so adults tend to fuss over babies and ignore older siblings.

Dealing with Existing Problems

➤ Inform the parents of the child that the more they involve their child in all aspects of the preparation, birth, and caregiving, the more the child will feel needed and important. This reduces feelings of being displaced. (Some families print out birth announcements that read: "Amy Rubin would like to announce the birth of her new baby brother, Angelo James, on July 26, 1989.")

➤ Parents also need to know the importance of giving special time just to the older sibling. Although giving this time on a regular, scheduled basis is hard because new babies are so unpredictable, striving for this is wise. Perhaps parents could have a story time with the older child each time the baby naps.

➤ Give the child many opportunities to proudly share the progress of the baby's prenatal growth, birth, and care. Follow the progress of the fetus by showing the children photos or pictures in a book depicting the growth inside the womb, such as Nilson's *How Was I Born?* (see resources for complete listing). Invite the mother and father to come to class, as often as they can, so that the children can see the mother's expanding middle and ask questions about the pregnancy and birth. Have the parents bring the baby into the class and teach the children about diapering and baby care. Let the older sibling take the lead, as much as she can, in showing how to care for the baby. Invite the child to make books about the new baby and her concerns as well as her good feelings. Have her illustrate the book with pictures.

➤ Accept any feelings of jealousy or hatred that the child has toward the new baby. Be aware that soon after the new baby arrives, many children want to "give the baby back." Offer the child many outlets to express her feelings in a way that will not hurt herself or others. Include drawing, throwing a beanbag at a large target, talking about her feelings or writing about them, pounding playdough, dramatic play with dolls, and sand and water play. Give her specific ways to get attention without angering her parents. Help her practice such questions as "Can you pay attention to me when the baby is napping?" "Can you take me to the park while Daddy watches the baby?"

Resources

Adult Books and Articles

Calderone, M., and Ramey, J.W. *Talking with Your Child about Sex: Questions and Answers for Children from Birth to Puberty*. New York: Ballentine, 1982.

Koblinsky, S.; Atkinson, J.; and Davis, S. "Sex Education with Young Children," In *Reducing Stress in Young Children's Lives*, edited by J.B. McCracken. Washington, DC: NAEYC, 1986.

Woods, S.B., and Woods, R.F. "Who Am I Now That Someone Else Is Here Also?" In *Children and Stress: Helping Children Cope*, edited by A.S. McNamee. Washington, DC: Association for Childhood Education International, 1982.

Children's Books

Alexander, M. *Nobody Asked Me If I Wanted a Baby Sister*. New York: Dial, 1971.

Baker, S. *Before I Was Born*. Swindon, England: Child's Play, 1987.

Banish, R. *Let Me Tell You about My Baby*. New York: Harper & Row, 1982.

Clifton, L. *Everett Anderson's Nine Month Long*. New York: Holt, 1978.

Collins, M.J. *The Knee Baby*. Toronto: Sunburst, 1988.

Edelman, E. *I Love My Baby Sister (Most of the Time)*. New York: Puffin, 1985.

Foreman, M. *Ben's Baby*. New York: Harper & Row, 1987.

Gordon, S., and Gordon, J. *Did the Sun Shine Before You Were Born?* Fayetteville, NY: Ed-U Press, 1974.

Hoban, R. *A Baby Sister for Frances*. New York: Harper & Row, 1964.

Holland, V. *We Are Having a Baby*. New York: Charles Scribner's Sons, 1972.

Kitzinger, S. *Being Born*. New York: Gosset & Dunlop, 1986.

Lasky, K. *A Baby for Max*. New York: Macmillan, 1984.

Manushkin, F. *Baby, Come Out!* New York: Harper & Row, 1972.

Nilson, L. *How Was I Born?* New York: Delacorte, 1975.

Rogers, F. *The New Baby*. New York: G.P. Putnam's Sons, 1987.

Stein, S.B. *That New Baby*. New York: Walker, 1974.

Sheffield, M. *Where Do Babies Come From?* New York: Knopf, 1972.

Walsh, E.S. *Brunus and the New Bear*. New York: Doubleday, 1979.

Watson, J.W., et al. *Sometimes I'm Jealous*. New York: Crown, 1986.

4. Hospitalization

Because young children typically have experiences in the hospital due to emergencies, it is important to present this topic even if you do not have a child in your class who is scheduled to enter a hospital.

A hospital experience can be very traumatic to a young child because he may be in much pain, the environment is so different from anywhere else (strange equipment, unusual smells, workers in masks and uniforms), the atmosphere is formal and rule-bound, and many hospitals are not very child oriented.

Preventing Problems

➤ Read books about hospitals and answer questions children have that the books raise.

➤ Make sure the children understand that for most illnesses that are treated in hospitals (appendectomy, having ear tubes put in), children are not at fault and did not cause the problem.

➤ Visit a hospital. Prepare for the field trip well in advance and make sure that the children receive a tour from someone who relates well with young children. Have a paramedic visit the classroom with an ambulance the children can tour. Visit a doctor's office to give the children additional information about health care. (See "Field Trips Are Supposed to Be Fun" on pages 49 to 50 for more information.)

➤ Set up a hospital dramatic play area. Include cots, blankets, bandages, stethoscopes, pads of blank paper and pens, old X-rays, pictures of hospitals and doctors' offices, several toy doctor's kits, and crutches. Extend the play by having the children build an ambulance and role play paramedics.

➤ Have small toy ambulances as part of your set of cars and trucks. Provide props that can be used with small figures of people to play out hospital scenes. Do this inexpensively by making small stretchers, beds, operating tables, surgical masks, and so on, out of cardboard and cloth.

Dealing with Existing Problems

If you find out that a child in your class will be hospitalized, do the activities described above unless you have done them very recently. If more than six weeks has gone by, repeat the activities.

➤ Create opportunities for the child who will be hospitalized to talk about his concerns, make books about his concerns, draw pictures, and listen to picture books about hospitals. Meet with the child's parents to gain a full understanding of why, when, and for how long he will be hospitalized. Ask them what you can do to help their child.

➤ Make up a package for the child in the hospital. Include pictures of the class on field trips and at school, an audio tape made by the children and a tape of favorite songs from records, drawings made by the other children, and blank books to write and draw in. Present this package to him in the hospital or just before he leaves for the hospital.

➤ Provide information to other parents so that they can take their children to visit the child in the hospital.

➤ Visit or call the child while he is in the hospital. If possible, call from the classroom so that the other children can talk to him.

➤ When a child returns to the classroom after a hospital stay or emergency room visit, provide many chances for him to share his experiences with the other children. Set up a hospital dramatic play area if this was not done before the stay. In one classroom a child's real experiences with a broken arm in the emergency room led to rich and exciting dramatic play, which led to investigating bones and skeletons, which then led to exploring organs and the inside of the body.

Resources

Adult Books and Articles
Association for the Care of Children's Health. *A Guide for Teachers: Children and Hospitals* (brochure), *A Child Goes to the Hospital* (brochures), ACCH, 3615 Wisconsin Avenue NW, Washington, DC 20016.

Fassler, D. "The Young Child in the Hospital." In *Reducing Stress in Young Children's Lives*, edited by J.B. McCracken. Washington, DC: NAEYC, 1986.

Rouck, L.A. "Children's Response to Hospitalization." In *Children & Stress: Helping Children Cope*, edited by A.S. McNamee. Washington, DC: Association for Childhood Education International, 1982.

Trawick-Smith, J., and Thompson, R.H. "Preparing Young Children for Hospitalization." *Young Children* 39(5) (July 1984): 57-62.

Children's Books
Burton, N., and Burton, T. *First Time at the Hospital*. London: MacDonald, 1980.

Hautzig, D. *A Visit to the Sesame Street Hospital*. New York: Random House, 1985.

Howe, J. *The Hospital Book*. New York: Crown, 1981.

Reit, S. *Jenny's in the Hospital*. Racine, WI: Western, 1984.

Rockwell, A., and Rockwell, H. *The Emergency Room*. New York: Macmillan, 1985.

Rogers, F. *Going to the Doctor*. New York: G.P. Putnam's Sons, 1987.

Rogers, F. *Going to the Hospital*. New York: G.P. Putnam's Sons, 1988.

5. Death of a Loved One

When a loved one dies, most children will go through a grieving process that can last a year or more, depending on the importance to the child of the person who died. Be aware of where the child is in the process so you can help in a meaningful way.

The following details the steps of the grieving process:

Denial The child believes the dead person will come back.

Anger The child expresses strong feelings of being abandoned and rejected by the person who has died. The child may express these feelings through misbehaviors and acting out.

Grief The child mourns over the loss. She cries often and feels despondent.

Acceptance Gradually the child returns to more typical behaviors and attitudes. She comes to a new understanding of herself and her place in the world.

Preventing Problems

➤ Read books about death to the children occasionally. Allow time for children to process the ideas and to ask questions. Many original versions of fairy tales, such as "Cinderella," deal with the death of a parent and the healing that comes from grieving.

➤ Read simple versions of tales and myths that deal with death, from a variety of cultures and lands. Point out how different people believe different things about what happens to people when they die. Discuss how people cope with loss. A beautiful American Indian legend/dance is about a shrouded widow—the cocoon of a caterpillar who mourns for a year. She then realizes all she is missing in life and removes her shroud to reveal the colorful butterfly underneath.

➤ Talk about famous people when they die. The children will usually be aware of the death from the news and adult conversation. Explain in simple terms what made them important or famous and how their deeds will live on after them.

➤ Note that many children's songs are about death ("Blue," "Who Killed Cock Robin?" "Go Tell Aunt Rhodie," "The Ruben James," and others). Sing these songs with the children so that death does not become a taboo subject.

➤ When a child finds a dead insect or small animal, use it as an opportunity for the children to learn what death means in concrete terms. Even very young toddlers can understand that death means no movement, stiffness, silence, and no response.

➤ Take a field trip to a cemetery. Get parent approval and prepare the children well for what to expect and what you will do there. Before going, talk with a friend so you can work through your own discomfort or anxiety about visiting a cemetery. If legal, make stone rubbings at the cemetery and take photographs. Bring flowers to lay on gravestones. This will bring out many questions about death and give the children a fuller understanding of how society deals with death. (For more ideas on a field trip to a cemetery see S.S. Riley's article, "Pilgrimage to Elmwood Cemetery," in the January 1989 issue of *Young Children* (Riley 1989).)

Dealing with Existing Problems

➤ If you find out that a child in your class has experienced a recent death in her family, do the activities described above. Explain to the child's parents or guardians your approach to helping the child in the classroom and request their approval. Negotiate any activities that they feel uncomfortable with or would like to see included. Assure them that young children are aware of death and greatly benefit from information and outlets for expressing themselves, provided they are not pushed or given more information than they can handle.

➤ Ask the child's permission before talking about the death with the whole class. Take your cues from her about how much detail to go into. Have children direct questions to the child, unless she would prefer that you do the talking. Check each response you give with the child for accuracy and approval.

➤ Be aware that all children and families who have recently experienced the loss of a loved one, especially if the death was sudden and unexpected, could benefit from the help of a professional counselor. Recommend this to the family.

➤ Because young children cannot put their feelings into words and because they usually act on their feelings, you will encounter difficult behaviors. Help the children express their feelings without hurting themselves or others. Provide them with outlets for expression such as pounding clay and playdough, hammering nails, climbing, running, and riding.

➤ Help children to soothe and calm themselves. Remember that they can generate their own ideas and/or you can suggest that they listen to music, sing, look at a book, talk, draw, or play with sand or water.

➤ Write books about the person who died and the wonderful things he or she did while alive. Be aware, however, that some children cannot or prefer not to talk about a recent death. Respect the child's feelings and instead write stories about young animals who have lost a loved one. (This will be less threatening and will be very healing.)

➤ Use the words *death* and *dead* instead of euphemisms such as *loss, gone to sleep, passed away,* and so on.

➤ If the death was due to an illness, be sure to help the children understand that ordinary illnesses do not result in death.

➤ Help parents see the importance of including the child in the funeral and in all aspects of the death and mourning. This is the only way they can know and benefit from the rituals and ceremonies our society has for death.

Questions about Death

➤ Answer questions simply and honestly. If a child asks, "What happens to people when they die?" answer by saying, "No one knows for sure. Different people believe different things, and when you are older, you can learn about it and decide for yourself. We do know that their bodies become stiff and cold, and the person can never talk, play, laugh, or move again. This makes us very sad because we will miss them."

➤ Be aware that children who ask questions about death often and regularly are working through the issue and may have had a recent experience with death. In some cases, the questions reflect a general insecurity or fear related to other issues. As your best approach, provide loving reassurance to the child. If she asks, "When will I die?" respond with, "I hope you live a very long time because you bring joy to everyone and many people love you a lot." If the questions and concern continue for more than a few weeks, talk to the parents about getting help from a professional counselor.

➤ The causes of death are of great interest to most children. (This is natural, as they are trying hard to understand all aspects of the world around them.) If they ask a blunt question to a grieving child or parent about the cause of the death when the person is not ready to talk about it yet, help by saying (if you don't know the cause yourself), "Julia isn't ready to tell you now because it makes her very sad. Maybe in a few days, if she's ready, she will tell us." If you do know the cause, give a brief explanation, "Julia's father was in a car accident. Let's talk more about it after circle time, because it makes Julia uncomfortable to talk about it now."

Death of a Classroom Pet

➤ Be aware that the death of a classroom pet provides an excellent opportunity to explore the subject of death with your children, so don't minimize the event. Let each child hold the dead pet so she can learn concretely what death is. Encourage her to feel the stiffness, coldness, and lack of response of the animal. Compare that to how the animal used to be. Take plenty of time to read books about death, sing songs, and talk about feelings and beliefs. Have a ceremonious funeral and bury the pet outside under a marker. Invite each child who desires to do so to say something about the pet. Put together a book of remembrances. Plant something in memory of the pet.

Resources

Adult Books and Articles

Brett, D. *Annie Stories*. New York: Workman, 1988.

Elkind, D. "Life and Death: Concepts and Feelings in Children." *Day Care and Early Education* 5(1) (January/February 1977).

Furman, Erna "Helping Children Cope with Death." *Reducing Stress in Young Children's Lives*, edited by J.B. McCracken. Washington, DC: NAEYC, 1986.

Hoch, D. "What Do You Do with Death?" *Early Childhood Education* 22(1) (Winter 1988-1989): 9-11.

Leming, M.R., and Dickinson, G.E. *Understanding Dying, Death, and Bereavement*. New York: Holt, 1985.

LeShan, E. *Learning to Say Goodbye: When a Parent Dies*. New York: Avon, 1976.

MacIsaac, P., and King, S. "What Did You Do with Sophie, Teacher?" *Young Children* 44(2) (January 1989): 37-38.

Parness, E. "Effects of Experiences with Loss and Death among Preschool Children." *Children Today* 4(6) (November/December 1975): 2-7.

Riley, S.S. "Pilgrimage to Elmwood Cemetery." *Young Children*. 44(2) (January 1989): 33-36.

Schaefer, D., and Lyons, C. *How Do We Tell the Children?: A Parents' Guide to Helping Children Understand and Cope When Someone Dies*. New York: Newmarket Press, 1986.

Watts, D.W. "Fantasy and Violence in Children's Folklore." *Early Childhood Education* 22(1) (Winter 1988-1989): 12-16.

Whitley, E., and Duncan, R. "Coping with Death: Early Childhood Experiences." In *Children & Stress: Helping Children Cope*, edited by A.S. McNamee. Washington, DC: Association for Childhood Education International, 1982.

Children's Books

Buscaglia, L. *Fall of Freddie the Leaf*. Thorofare, NJ: Charles B. Slack, 1982.

Clifton, L. *Everett Anderson's Goodbye*. New York: Holt, 1983.

Dodge, N.C. *Thumpy's Story: A Story of Love and Grief Shared by Thumpy the Bunny*. Springfield, IL: Prarie Lark Press, 1984.

Evans, C., and Millard A. *Greek Myths and Legends*. London: Usborne, 1985.

Evans, C., and Millard A. *Norse Myths and Legends*. London: Usborne, 1986.

Greenberg, J.E., and Carey, H.H. *Sunny: The Death of a Pet*. New York: Franklyn Watts, 1986.

Grimm, The Brothers. *Grimm's Fairy Tales*. New York: Pantheon Books, 1944.

Martin, B., and Archambault, J. *Knots on a Counting Rope*. New York: Holt, 1987.

Mellonie, B. *Lifetimes: The Beautiful Way to Explain Death to Children*. New York: Bantam, 1983.

Miller, M. *My Grandmother's Cookie Jar*. Los Angeles: Price Stern Sloan, 1987.

Munsch, R. *Love You Forever*. Willowdale, Ontario: Firefly, 1986.

Rogers, F. *When a Pet Dies*. New York: G.P. Putnam's Sons, 1988.

Stein, S. *About Death*. New York: Walker, 1974.

Viorst, J. *The Tenth Good Thing About Barney*. New York: Macmillan, 1987.

Wilhelm, H. *I'll Always Love You*. New York: Crown, 1985.

6. Moving on to the Next Class

Helping children make a successful transition to the next grade or age level will be a great benefit to the children and to their next teacher. It will also help you by reducing the anxiety the children may have, especially as the end of the year approaches. Whether children are excited and feel big, or are worried and scared, moving to the next class is a major change and will affect everyone.

You also need to help the teachers and the children who are in the classes or age groups below yours to ease the transition into your class. You can implement the ideas in this chapter both for your children who are going into the next class and for the children who will be entering your class. Show care and interest in those children. They will feel positive toward you and feel happy to be in your class. When children start out with a positive attitude, you prevent many behavior problems.

Many early childhood teachers are concerned that by following good practices such as giving children choices with active, hands-on materials in classrooms with self-directed learning centers, they are doing them a disservice. In the next grade, children may be required to sit at desks for long periods, take directions from the teacher, do paper and pencil tasks, and line up. While this may be true in many cases (although this is changing rapidly as primary programs adapt more appropriate methods), subjecting children to a curriculum that does not meet their needs and will cause stress and misbehaviors because of what they may face next year makes no sense. Children who feel good about themselves, are self-motivated learners, and have learned self-control will do better when faced with a stressful curriculum than will children who do not possess these qualities. However, teachers do need to help children prepare for what they will encounter and help smooth the transition.

Preventing Problems

➤ Set up field trips to visit some of the classrooms your children will be attending. Invite teachers from the next level to visit your classroom and talk with your children. Prepare the children to ask questions of the teachers. Invite several children who were in your class last year to talk to your current group about what being in the next room is like.

➤ With the permission of parents, send information to the next teacher about the children in your class. Stress their strengths and abilities. Express any concerns objectively and cautiously. You do not want the new teacher to prejudge the child, as he might act very differently in the new class or mature a great deal by then.

➤ Talk to several teachers in the next age grouping to understand their expectations for children.

(This does not mean you will change your curriculum to meet what may be inappropriate expectations. You may find, however, that the expectations are lower than you anticipated.) You may learn some helpful information, such as the style of writing used in that grade. To ease the transition for your children, use this style when printing names and writing stories.

➤ Organize a few meetings during the year when all the teachers in your grade/age level meet with all the teachers in the next level. Exchange information, coordinate, and clarify philosophies and goals.

➤ Read books and create stories about children who go to a new class.

➤ Develop a dramatic play area, which includes the materials and equipment used in the next grade. Observe the spontaneous play that develops for misconceptions about what the children believe will happen in the next grade. Allow them to freely work through their concerns or their excitement.

➤ Near the end of the school year, role play situations the children are likely to encounter in the next class. Help them learn the actions and words to use to get their needs met. For example, if a child is given a math worksheet to complete, he can raise his hand and ask if he can use his crayons to figure out the problem. Most teachers will not object, if children ask politely. Children can also ask for materials to use to make projects more creative and for blank sheets of paper for writing stories during transition times.

➤ With parental permission, give all the children and their families class lists with addresses and phone numbers so that friendships can be maintained. Give all the children a class photo.

➤ Meet with parents to discuss the importance of helping their children move to the next grade. Invite a teacher or the principal to meet with the parents and to answer questions they have about the new class. Request that the guest bring a copy of the report card used in the next grade. Help parents with ways to cope with different expectations and levels of involvement in the new school or class by providing specific information: "At Jefferson School, taking your concerns to the school's parent advisory committee is best. Make positive suggestions rather than complaints." Brainstorm together strategies to help their children get the most out of their new program.

Dealing with Existing Problems

➤ For children who are expressing fears and concerns about going into the next class, try the following ideas:

• Determine, if possible, who the teacher will be and talk with her about the child. Set a time for the child to visit the teacher and the classroom. (Fear of the unknown is often the worst fear.)

• Set up a time when a child from the next class can talk to the child in your class about what he can expect.

• Determine, if possible, the specific concerns the child has. You may be able to clear up some misconceptions easily.

• Role play with the child situations he might encounter in the next grade. Having a chance to practice some new skills, before facing the real situation, always helps.

• Help the child stay in touch with a good friend from the class. Talk with his parents to arrange a photo exchange and to share addresses and phone numbers. Encourage the parents to set up visits with the other child.

Conflicting Styles and Expectations among Teachers in the Next Grade or Age Group

If your children are going to a number of different classrooms with teachers who all are very different, the transition from your

class to the next can be very confusing. In some cases, the teachers' educational approaches may differ radically from one another. The best approach is to role play and discuss two or three (at the most) of these approaches, particularly those most different from your own. Note that all children benefit from learning that different adults have different expectations and styles.

➤ If, for example, a variety of writing styles is used, pick the one to use in your class that you believe is the most appropriate for young children. Base your decision on the ease children will have in writing and reading it. If you have no preference, choose the one that is most common.

Celebrations Not Graduations

In many programs a great deal of time, energy, and money is spent on graduations. Most of these events are designed to meet the needs of the parents and put the children under stress. The children often have to spend a great deal of time sitting and they have to perform as a group. Young children do neither very well. However, parents consider graduation from preschool to be a major milestone in their children's lives and like to mark it in some way. Meet both the needs of the parents and of the children by having an informal celebration. Invite the children to prepare special snacks and to serve them to their parents at a short, early evening gathering. Present a short (fifteen minute) video tape or slide show of some of the highlights of the year. Invite the children to sing a favorite song that they have been singing all year and ask the parents to join in. Send a "diploma" to each child in the mail. Remember that most children love receiving mail and rarely get any, so your sending the "diploma" will make it very special.

➤ Plan your celebration with parents so they will understand your goal of involving the children in a meaningful, enjoyable occasion. Work out compromises and accept the good ideas of the parents. Be aware that they will take more responsibility for organizing the event if the ideas come from them.

Resources

Adult Books and Articles

Bredekamp, S. , ed. *Developmentally Appropriate Practice in Early Childhood Programs Serving Children from Birth Through Age 8*. Washington, DC: NAEYC, 1987.

"Easing the Transition from Preschool to Kindergarten: A Guide for Early Childhood Teachers and Administrators." Head Start Bureau, Washington, DC: ACYF, 1986.

Greene, E. "Continuity: Building Bridges between Settings." *Extensions: Newsletter of the High/Scope Curriculum* 3(6) (May/June 1989).

"Ideas That Work with Young Children: Children's Performances," *Young Children* 40(3) (March 1985): 17.

Ziegler, P. "Saying Goodbye to Preschool." In *Reducing Stress in Young Children's Lives*, edited by J.B. McCracken. Washington, DC: NAEYC, 1986.

Media

Transition: From Preschool to Public School (slide/tape), Chapel Hill-Carrboro Head Start Outreach Project, Lincoln Center, Merritt Mill Road, Chapel Hill, NC 27514 (919-967-8295).

Children's Books

Cohen, M. *The New Teacher*. New York: Macmillan, 1972.

Howe, J. *When You Go to Kindergarten*. New York: Knopf, 1986.

Osborne, J. *My Teacher Said Good-Bye Today: Planning for the End of the School Year*. Cambridge, MA: Spaulding, 1978.

Part V
Children with Difficult Behaviors

1. Helping Children with Difficult Behaviors

You may have noticed that a child who is difficult to deal with seems to act much better in one teacher's class than in another. You may also have observed that some teachers seem to have many children with behavior problems and some teachers seem to have few. The difference is not luck. Teachers do specific things that can make problem behaviors worse, keep them the same, or make them decrease. The chapters in this section reveal some of the strategies good teachers use to decrease behavior problems.

Your Goal: Teaching Self-Control

Always keep in mind that your ultimate goal in helping young children with behavior problems is to get them to control their own actions and reactions.

➤ Before a problem occurs, discuss choices children can make about how to act. If several children usually argue over one particular trike, help them to figure out various ways to solve the problem just before they go out to use the equipment.

➤ Remind the children of the reason behind any rule or consequence to a behavior, at the time the rule is being enforced. Have them repeat the reason back to you: "Punching can seriously hurt a person. It only makes people angry and does not get the problem solved." Ask them to list some other ways to deal with the problem. Help them with ideas if necessary.

➤ If a child is given a consequence — such as having to choose a solitary activity because of hitting another child — tell her that she can join the other children when she feels able to use her voice to express her feelings. Respect her own internal time clock even if it lasts only a few seconds. Repeat the consequence if she repeats the negative behavior.

➤ Actively teach children how to make friends, keep friends, and be liked by others. (This is called teaching prosocial skills.) For example, when a group of children are playing together, a child may be able to enter the group by listening to the play and figuring out a role to take that will fit in. She should then ask to join by taking that role — "I'll be the sister, O.K.?" Barging in, changing the direction of the play, demanding a leadership role, or being too unassertive will result in rejection.

➤ Help children to negotiate solutions to conflicts. Sit with them and write down the ideas they generate: "You both want the same toy so what can happen that will make you both happy?" Ask them to think through the consequence of each idea: "What might happen if you grab it? If you ask for it? If you ask me for help? If you wait for it?" Summarize and then ask the children to agree on a solution they both like. (Elizabeth Crary's *Children's Problem Solving Books* are great for helping you do this. See resources on page 106.)

Use Alternatives to Reinforcement Systems

Remember that rewards (stickers, stars, and so on) for good behavior or negative reinforcement for bad behavior (taking privileges away) do not teach children self-control. They are tempting to use because they can be very effective at changing behaviors quickly, but they give all the control to the teacher. Redirection, logical consequences, prevention strategies, and other techniques (described in this and subsequent chapters) will teach self-control better than reinforcement techniques and will also effectively reduce problematic behaviors.

A danger of reinforcement systems is that they are so effective that teachers never fade them out to allow children to act appropriately on their own. Another problem with them is that the children who are not getting rewards feel cheated. This sometimes leads teachers to have a reinforcement system for the whole class, even though it is not really needed.

On its own, praise such as, "Good work," is a teacher-controlled form of reinforcement. It is a verbal reward system rather than a tangible reward system, but it is really no different from stickers and so on. In classrooms where teachers use a great deal of praise, children are less cooperative with others and are more unsure of themselves (Brophy 1981).

However, social or verbal encouragement is something everyone needs. This entails letting children know what they are doing well by giving them specific information that is helpful: "You picked up the blocks quickly and neatly. They will be easy to find and play with tomorrow and everyone enjoys being in a neat room."

Modifying behavior through reinforcement systems can be beneficial to children with moderate to severe handicaps or with behaviors that are inappropriate the majority of the time. However, use this reinforcement as a starting strategy (with the intention of eliminating it as soon as possible) and with the advice and support of a professional psychologist or special educator. Most children who have these conditions will not be served best in a regular early childhood program. However, they may be mainstreamed part of the time with the intention of integrating them fully (with continued support services) as their behaviors or skills improve.

Reinforcement systems are powerful manipulators of children; however, the teacher's role is to empower children, not to manipulate them.

Use Child Choice Not Time Out

Time out (placing a child off by herself for a period of time) rarely works because the consequence is not related to the misbehavior. After a minute the child has forgotten why she is there. She is also angry because she is being punished and humiliated. She may be using "time out" to think of ways to get back at you.

If a child needs to be removed from an area because of being continuously disruptive, let her choose a quiet activity away from others. (This is called "child choice.") Before doing this, give her at least one chance to improve her behavior by telling her that she will have to choose a different activity if she continues to be disruptive. If she does have to do this, tell her that she can return when she feels calm and ready to attend. Help her learn and develop the skills she needs to do the appropriate behavior. Ask her to watch the other children to see how they play in school. Give her verbal encouragement when she does well. (This eliminates the punishment aspect of time out and gives control to the child.)

Determine the Root of the Problem

A cause exists for all behaviors. However, if the cause is not apparent (known abuse, a recent move, excitement about a birthday, and so on), determining what it is can be difficult. Meeting with parents to support their efforts in dealing with their child's behavior problems can open the door to discovering the cause. If possible, request a home visit. A great deal is often revealed during a home visit. Family values, priorities, approaches to discipline, and attitudes about food and toileting can all become evident. Parents are more likely to open up when they feel comfortable on their own turf.

Check the child's files for any medical information that might tell you something (perhaps there is a history of severe allergies). Request a medical checkup, as it may reveal the cause of the behavior problems. This is often a good place to start the process of helping the child because it takes the blame off the parents, the child, or yourself for the behaviors.

In one case, a three and half year old child had a problem of occasionally but regularly biting other children very hard. He was a wonderful child in every other respect. The teachers tried everything they could think of to eliminate the behavior. They blamed themselves for not being consistent enough. They felt frustrated and like failures. Eventually the child was referred to a special agency that dealt with emotionally disturbed children. During the interview process, it was discovered that the child was on medication for a physical problem. The medication was changed, and the biting stopped.

Continue to work on determining possible physical causes for problem behaviors, while you work on changing the behaviors in the classroom and helping parents change the behaviors at home. Although you may not be able to solve the behavior problems by determining the cause, you will gain useful insights that will make you more empathetic to the child's problems. If you cannot find the cause, you can still do many things to help the child and to reduce the behaviors, as discussed in subsequent chapters.

Resources

Brophy, J.E. "Teacher Praise: A Functional Analysis." *Review of Educational Research* 51(1) (1981): 5-32.

Clewett, A.S. "Guidance and Discipline: Teaching Young Children Appropriate Behavior." *Young Children* 43(4) (May 1988): 26-31.

Crary, E. *Children's Problem Solving Series.* Includes: *Mommy Don't Go, I'm Lost, I Want It, I Can't Wait, I Want to Play, My Name Is Not Dummy.* Seattle: Parenting Press, 1982.

Faber, A., and Mazlish, E. *How To Talk So Kids Will Listen and Listen So Kids Will Talk.* New York: Avon, 1980.

Gartrell, D. "Viewpoint. Assertive Discipline: Unhealthy for Children and Other Living Things." *Young Children* 42(2) (January 1987): 10-11

Gartrell, D. "Punishment or Guidance?" *Young Children* 42(3) (March 1987): 55-61.

Gottfried, A.E. "Research in Review: Intrinsic Motivation in Young Children." *Young Children* 39(1) (November 1983): 64-73.

Hitz, R., and Driscoll, A. "Praise or Encouragement? New Insights Into Praise: Implications for Early Childhood Teachers." *Young Children* 43(5) (July 1988): 6-13.

Katz, L.G. "From Our Readers: Katz Responds to Daniels." *Young Children* 40(2) (January 1985): 2-4.

Katz, L.G. "The Professional Early Childhood Teacher." *Young Children* 39(5) (July 1984): 3-10.

Kamii, C. "Viewpoint: Obedience is Not Enough." *Young Children* 39(4) (May 1984): 11-14.

Miller, C.S. "Building Self-Control: Discipline for Young Children." *Young Children* 40(1) (November 1984): 15-19.

Osborn, D.K. Osborn, J.D. *Discipline and Classroom Management.* Athens, GA: Education Associates, 1977.

Rogers, D.L. and Ross, D.D. "Encouraging Positive Social Interaction Among Young Children." *Young Children* 41(3) (March 1986): 12-17.

Trawick-Smith, J. "'Let's Say You're the Baby, OK?': Play Leadership and Following Behavior of Young Children." *Young Children* 43(5) (July 1988): 51-59.

Turecki, S., and Tonner, L. *The Difficult Child.* Toronto: Bantam, 1985.

2. Preventing Behavior Problems

Some of the children will enter your classroom with anger, little ability to get along with others, depression, a self-image of being "bad," the need for constant attention, a very high energy level, or all of these problems. Although you have no control over how they got this way, you can do many things to reduce the negative behaviors that often result from these feelings or needs. You can help such children most effectively by preventing behavior problems from happening in the first place, or at least from happening very often.

In order to prevent behavior problems in your classroom, work on three major areas: the physical environment of the classroom; your schedule and curriculum; and your own attitudes, actions, and reactions. Because the environment, scheduling, and curriculum are dealt with in previous chapters of the book, this chapter focuses on the third area.

Your Own Attitudes, Actions, and Reactions

Attitude: Focus on the Positive

Feel positively towards the child with behavior problems. View him as a valuable gift, as he will provide you with an opportunity to learn a great deal. You may learn about the causes of behavior problems, new approaches to helping, the nature of your own biases, parenting skills, and the availability of community agencies and resources. He will provide you with a chance to help turn a life around for the better.

A child with difficult behaviors also can help you improve your program. A highly active child may be the first (or the only one) to let you know that your activity is boring. A child who cries often can tell you that you may not have enough inviting things to do (he probably has too much time to think about his unhappiness.) Although you may feel that this difficult child has come into your life just to make you miserable, he has not. He is acting the best and only way he knows how. Understanding the difficult child will help you feel positive and loving towards him and may be the single most important thing you can do to reduce the behaviors.

Attitude: The Child Can Do Better

Although in some extreme cases years of help, treatment by a professional counselor, a special education program, or intervention by a social service agency may be necessary, you *must* believe that you can help the child. Even if you are the person who only starts the process, you will have done something important. Don't be tempted to pass a problem off as a phase. Although it might actually be a phase, such as biting, you can still help improve the behavior. Don't shrug off the problem as being due to the child's terrible parents, over whom you have no control. Many children learn to behave positively at school while acting differently at home. They come to see themselves as worthwhile because of a loving teacher. Don't ignore the problem hoping that it will go away, that the child will move, or that nine months will pass quickly. Too many children get passed on this way and never get the help they need. Often they grow up to be troubled teens who cause serious problems for society. Changing problem behaviors when the child is young is much easier than waiting until later. Believe in the child and your own ability to help him.

Action: Have a Positive Classroom

➤ Make many more positive statements, and make them more energetically, than admonishments or corrections. Catch children doing well and let them know that they are doing well. At the same time, give them useful information about their behavior, without judging their characters. "Good boy" is a judgment. Saying, "You cleaned up the blocks so quickly and thoroughly; it makes our class look neat and it will be easy to find all the blocks tomorrow" is helpful. Tell them often how much you enjoy being with them, but only if you can be honest about this sentiment: "I love seeing all your beautiful faces every morning."

Action: Make Expectations Clear and Reasonable

➤ Establish few rules and enforce them consistently. One important rule to have is the following: Use your body and words without hurting other people. To make this rule work you must deal with behaviors that violate it almost every time they happen. (If a child breaks the rule ten times and experiences a consequence only one of the times, the child will be confused and angry.) After a rule has been established well enough that the behavior is rarely seen, add an additional rule, if needed.

➤ Remind children of rules ahead of time: "Please walk when we get inside the room." Let your expectations be known immediately before the event. Remember that young children have short memories and are primarily interested in the here and now: "After you hang your coat up, please sit on the circle."

➤ State all rules and expectations positively because young children behave better when they know what to do. Instead of saying "Don't yell," say, "Please use a quiet voice."

Action: Make Sure the Children Feel Important and Respected

➤ Give all the children many chances to do jobs vital to the running of the classroom. Create a job chart where children's names are displayed next to the names and pictures of their jobs. Rotate the names daily. Examples of jobs are listed in the box below.

Create as many jobs as possible. If possible, have one job for each child every day.

➤ Give children many chances to make real decisions such as what song to sing, what book to listen to, or what movement game to play. If necessary, give a choice between two or three songs, books, or games, as some choices may not be acceptable to you. Ask an individual child to make the choice, as opposed to the whole group, if you do not want to take the time to vote or decide by consensus. Make this the task of the "Teacher" on the job chart (you may want to have several "Teachers") so your choice of which child will be the "Teacher" will not seem arbitrary or unfair.

➤ Make sure that the children have easy access to sponges and soapy water to clean up messes after themselves, easy ways to put away toys where they belong when they are finished playing, and simple methods to dress and take care of themselves. (Even a two year old can put her own coat on by laying it flat on the ground — front of the coat facing up — standing behind the top of the coat, putting her arms in the sleeves and flipping it over her head.) Encourage the children to help each other with buttoning, zipping jackets, putting on mittens, and so on. Remember that anything you can do to give children responsibility over themselves or each other, with little or no adult assistance, will make children feel powerful and will reduce behavior problems that stem from feelings of insecurity and powerlessness.

Action: Provide for Success

➤ Give each and every child many opportunities to be and feel successful and challenged. Individualize games and activities. For example, ask a

Zookeeper 1	(Feed the fish.)
Zookeeper 2	(Feed the guinea pig.)
Waiter	(Set the table.)
Weather Reporter	(Draw or place a symbol of the weather on the calendar.)
Dentist	(Lead the toothbrushing and collect the toothbrushes.)
Environmentalist	(Turn the lights off each time the class leaves the room; collect the litter off the playground.)
Teacher	(Decide what song we will sing; lead the song; dismiss the children from the circle.)
Custodian	(Wipe the tables and sweep the floor.)
Librarian	(Decide what book will be read, distribute books that children request for book browsing; collect and account for all books.)

child who does not yet name colors to match colors during a color/shape lotto game; ask a child who can name colors to find the color on his card; ask a child who can name colors and shapes to find the square that has both attributes. When all play together, the less able or the younger children learn from the more able or the older ones. To make this work, look at the card you are holding, and if the child who can name colors and shapes has a picture that matches it, ask "Who has a red triangle?" without showing him the card. If the child who can name colors but not the shapes has the picture, ask, "Who has a red shape with three sides?" (Draw a triangle if she can't get the shape.) If the child who can match colors has the picture, hold up the card for him to see and ask, "Who has this card?" (He can then match it.) Once children can be successful with little effort, challenge them with a slightly harder task.

➤ Another way to ensure feelings of success is to provide sand and water play daily. Have fun equipment in each, such as plastic bottles, funnels, tubing, spoons, and measuring cups. Give children plenty of time to play. Note that these activities are satisfying because children cannot fail at them. (There is no right way or wrong way to do it.) Be aware that the smoothness, softness, and texture of sand and water are very soothing to young children. (They help comfort and relax them.) Keep a small broom and large dustpan (for sand) and large sponges and a bucket (for water) nearby so children can clean up after themselves.

Action: Meet Individual Needs

➤ A child who needs extra attention and asks for it in a positive way should get extra attention from you. If a child is having a rough day because his mother went out of town, permit him to spend more time on your lap than other children do. Let him know that you are doing this today because you know he feels sad, but that tomorrow you will do it less. Let the other children know you would do this for them if they were sad. Be aware that you do not have to provide the same kind of attention for the other children. Being fair with young children means meeting their individual needs, not treating every child exactly the same.

➤ Do not neglect any child's needs. However, be aware that a child who demands an unreasonable amount of attention cannot be accom-

modated because you will be depriving other children of their needs. (This is a hard balancing act. You might need help from another teacher or your director to determine what is an unreasonable need for attention.) In classrooms where children know they will get their share of attention, especially when they need it most, competition for attention by acting out is greatly reduced.

Action: Actively Teach and Promote Cooperation

➤ In the absence of a strong set of cooperation skills, aggression and competitiveness in children flourish. Set the following classroom rule: "Ask three before you ask me." This requires children to learn to seek help from and give assistance to their classmates. Some children will need your help initially to learn how to ask for help in a way that will get a positive response and to give help without doing everything for the other child.

➤ Use cooperative games often. "Islands" is an example of one. Lay down about ten rug squares or pieces of cardboard. Explain to the children that

the object of the game is for everyone to help each other get on the islands (rug squares) and be safe. When the music plays, invite the children to "swim" (walk) all around the islands, but when it stops tell them that they must get out of the water and onto an island quickly. Before you start the music again, remove two or three rug squares. Keep repeating the game until only one square is left. This game has no winners and losers, but it offers a challenge and a great deal of fun (Torbert 1980).

➤ Modify existing games and equipment to make them more cooperative. For example, play "Farmer in the Dell" with two farmers and two of each character. Add more characters if needed so that everyone can be in the circle by the end. Here the "Cheeses" stand in the middle at the end and invite everyone else to make a circle around them. Sing "The cheese has lots of friends," instead of "The cheese stands alone," and have the "Cheeses" move around the circle shaking everyone's hands.

➤ Promote cooperation when situations arise in the classroom. Ask a child to help another child who has broken a class rule: "Everett, please tell Amelia the rule about running in class and give her ideas about how to remember it."

➤ Set up a dramatic play situation involving exciting adventures where all children work together against a shared problem. (Firefighting, rescue squad activities, catching a big fish, and working in a hospital are some examples.) To avoid chaotic or silly play, provide many safe materials and guide the action at first, if necessary.

Action: Use Your Voice Effectively

All teachers with good control of their classrooms have mastered the art of voice control. If you speak in a moderate voice most of the time, the very few times that you do raise your voice slightly or lower it, you will immediately have a big impact on the children.

➤ Bring the noise level down in a room by starting out with a loud voice and by gradually bringing your voice down in volume as you speak.

➤ Vary your voice greatly. Get louder and faster when children start losing attention; use a deep, slow voice when making an important point; and talk softly to set a quiet, peaceful tone. Remember that voice variety keeps children from being bored and tuning you out, leading to misbehaviors.

➤ Use a tone and words that convey respect for children. You can check this by asking yourself if this is how you would talk to an adult friend.

Expressions like "Use an indoor voice" or "You need to clean up now" are contrived and patronizing, while "Please speak quietly" and "Please pick up the toy" are more respectful. Another common trait of early childhood teachers is the use of an exaggerated, sweet tone of voice which condescends to children. If you show respect for children, they will respect you. (This will eliminate many potential discipline problems.)

Reaction: Mistakes Are OK

➤ Treat mistakes and errors children make as a natural part of their learning. If a child drops a container of milk, calmly say, "It's all right. You can get the sponge and wipe it up. I'll help you if you need help." Later, ask him, "What can you do the next time to avoid a spill?" Offer a few suggestions if he has no ideas.

➤ Tell children about mistakes you make (e.g., scheduling a field trip to the zoo on the day it is closed), so they will know that adults still learn from their mistakes.

➤ Strive for the ideal of a supportive classroom in which all the children will thrive. Remove barriers that prevent children from being successful. A child who has a difficult time sitting still during an art project can stand and work on it or lay on a soft pillow and work on it, as long as safety precautions are taken. Perhaps he can work on a different activity. Encourage children to think of these solutions themselves. Be flexible, avoid arbitrary rules, and focus on helping, not fixing, children.

➤ Remember that when you create a classroom atmosphere where failing is difficult, even very discouraged children can feel good about themselves. Once children feel competent, challenge and encourage them to take risks. Be assured that being both challenged and feeling that failing or making a mistake will be accepted results in motivated and engaged children with few behavior problems.

Reaction: Teach the Correct Behavior

➤ If a child grabs a toy, hits another child, crashes his trike into another's, or does some similar problematic behavior, assume that the child does not know the correct behavior. Keep telling and showing the child the appropriate behavior even if you have told him several times. Young children need repetition to learn, and they do not carry over information from one situation to another very easily. They may know not to crash their trikes into the fence, but do not realize that crashing their trikes into another trike is not OK. At the same time remind him of the rules and give consequences to the behavior. Continue to teach correct behavior.

An example of teaching correct behavior would be to help a child understand that using words to negotiate the use of a toy is better than grabbing it. Help him to generate ideas for getting what he wants if he has trouble thinking of any on his own. Make yourself available if additional help is needed. Give only as much assistance as is necessary so that the children work out solutions on their own.

Reaction: Redirect Behaviors

➤ Redirecting behaviors means helping a child follow her impulse or need, but in an acceptable way. For example, if a child is angry with another child she may not hit her, but she can express her anger in words or work with clay to release her feelings. A child who starts throwing blocks must be stopped, but she can be given a foam ball to throw instead. The key to successful redirection is to stay calm and find an activity that is very similar to the one the child is doing, but safe or socially acceptable. If you express anger or use redirection as punishment, your attempts to change behavior will not work. When done well, redirection lets children know that their feelings are valid and that they can act on their feelings. It teaches them that they can make choices as to how to act on their feelings in acceptable ways.

Reaction: Logical Consequences

Logical consequences are responses to problematic behaviors in which the natural result of doing the behavior is allowed to occur. If a child misuses a piece of equipment, the logical consequence is that she will help fix it, if possible, and then not get to use that piece of equipment for a period of time. The logical consequence of tripping another child is to help the hurt child get up, and to get a bandage for her.

➤ The key to making logical consequences successful is to have the consequence be immediate (not going outside *tomorrow*, because of misbehaving on the playground *today*, will not work for young children) and to make the consequence relate directly to the misbehavior. Always tell the child that she is free to return to any activity when she feels ready to act correctly.

➤ Remember that logical consequences must never be punishment or retribution. Logical consequences should be used only as a last resort when repeated attempts at teaching correct behaviors or redirection are not working well. Before using any logical consequences, tell the child what the consequences will be the next time she misbehaves in the same way. She must know these ahead of time so that she has an opportunity to work on avoiding them. Continue to teach correct behavior and use redirection while also using logical consequences.

Reaction: Stay Calm

➤ Whatever approach you take, react calmly to negative behaviors. Many young children with difficult behaviors are used to getting a big response from adults as a result of their behaviors. They thrive on the attention, excitement, anger, and chaos they can create. If they see that you will react the same way, you will experience difficulty getting them to reduce the behaviors. If they see you are not reacting strongly, they might step up the behaviors at first, but eventually they will give them up.

Resources

Adcock, D., and Segal, M. *Play Together Grow Together: A Cooperative Curriculum for Teachers of Young Children.* White Plains, NY: Mailman Family Press, 1983.

Cherry, C. *Please Don't Sit on the Kids: Alternatives to Punitive Discipline.* Belmont, CA: David S. Lake, 1983.

Crary, E. *Kids Can Cooperate: A Practical Guide to Teaching Problem Solving.* Seattle: Parenting Press, 1984.

Dreikurs, R., Stolz, V. *Children: The Challenge.* New York: Dutton, 1964.

Ginott, H. *Teacher and Child.* New York: Macmillan, 1971.

Goffin, S. "Cooperative Behaviors: They Need Our Support." *Young Children* 42(2) (January 1987): 75-81.

"Ideas That Work With Young Children. Avoiding 'Me Against You' Discipline." *Young Children* 44(1) (November 1988): 24-29.

Judson, S. ed. *A Manual on Nonviolence and Children* Philadelphia: New Society, 1977.

Leatzow, N., et al. *Creating Discipline in the Early Childhood Classroom.* Provo, UT: Brigham Young University Press, 1983.

Torbert, M. *Follow Me: A Handbook of Movement Activities for Children* New York: Prentice Hall, 1981.

Tudge, J, and Caruso, D. "Cooperative Problem Solving in the Classroom: Enhancing Young Children's Cognitive Development." *Young Children* 44(1) (November 1988): 46-52.

Wolf, D.P., ed. *Connecting: Friendship in the Lives of Young Children and Their Teachers* Redmond, WA: Exchange Press, 1986.

3. Children with Severe Behavior Problems

Some children have behavior problems so severe that they endanger the safety of the other children, themselves, or you. Severe behavior problems usually reflect emotional problems. Some signs of emotional problems are the following:

The child with emotional problems...

- destroys property.
- acts completely withdrawn.
- has extreme fears and phobias.
- obsesses about a particular detail or item.
- plays with feces.
- eats items that are clearly not food.
- kills or tortures pets or animals.
- displays unusual emotions such as laughing when hurt.

- has strange and intense habits such as hair pulling, rocking, or head banging.
- runs away.
- makes suicidal statements.
- places herself in physical danger.
- hurts herself.
- acts violently or very cruelly towards others.

Children who exhibit these behaviors often and over time, usually have been traumatized by abuse, neglect, or a violent event. Or, there may be an organic reason, such as birth trauma or autism.

Logic, reason, redirection, consequences, and all your tried-and-true guidance techniques that work with most children, are not effective with these children. Sometimes the behaviors seem very deliberate, clearly planned to get others to dislike them and to get themselves in trouble.

Unless you or an assistant are specially trained to help a child with severe behavior problems and have professional support services, you may be doing a great disservice to the child by keeping her in your class. You also will be spending so much time helping this one child, that the needs of the other children in your class will not be met. If the child is in a treatment program and the behaviors are improving, integrating her into your class may be appropriate, but probably not on a full time basis. Usually the most appropriate placement for a child with severe emotional problems is either in a therapeutic preschool, in a treatment center, or in individual therapy. Rarely is a regular group setting appropriate.

Do everything you can to convince the parents that their child needs to be referred for evaluation and placement. Keep detailed and objective notes of the behaviors you observe in the classroom to help other professionals determine the best placement for the child. (See "Observing" in "Suspected Handicaps" on page 64.) In most places, your local school district serves as the place to make a referral. Check with your local department of special education, mental health center, or the state agency that deals with services to families and children for other sources of help.

If the parents refuse or deny there is a problem, keep written, dated records of your conversations. There have been cases where parents have successfully sued preschool programs for failing to make them aware of their child's problem while she was attending. For the benefit of the child, you are obligated to tell parents what you have observed about the child and to seek a referral. If you can get no evaluation, support, and assistance from a professional psychologist, have your supervisor ask the family to find a better placement for their child.

Resources

"Ideas That Work with Young Children: The Difficult Child." *Young Children* 43(5) (July 1988): 60-68.

Magid, K., and McKelvey, C. *High Risk: Children without a Conscience.* Toronto: Bantam, 1987.

Miller, S.M. *Child-Stress!* Garden City, NY: Doubleday, 1982.

4. Active and Distracted

Almost every classroom has at least one child who has difficulty concentrating or sitting still for a short time, compared to other children his age. The causes for this are many and varied.

Most children like this have little control over their problem, although they want very much to control it. This chapter offers numerous ideas for helping active and distracted children feel successful and gain some self-control and self-respect.

Preventing Problems

➤ To avoid a classroom that is overly stimulating for the children, reduce the busyness in your room. Use warm, soft colors; cover or store teacher supplies and materials; arrange things neatly; and reduce the number of pictures, mobiles, and signs on ceilings and walls.

➤ Label all shelves and containers. See that everything has its proper place in the classroom. (This will help the active or distracted child as he often has trouble organizing himself and his surroundings.)

➤ Inform all children of what to expect ahead of time. Tell them, "We will be going outside for forty-five minutes. When the bell rings, we will come inside for snack. Now put your coat on and walk to the door." Note that this is of particular help to the active child.

➤ Set up and follow daily routines and rituals. Make your daily schedule essentially the same every day, with active times and sitting times alternating. (A "good morning song" to start each day is an example of a ritual.) This provides a sense of security to a child whose world feels unsteady.

➤ Appreciate the positive aspects of having an active or easily distracted child in your class. Look at the child as being very *attracted* to the wonderful things you have provided. Use the active child as your barometer for determining if your activity has gone on too long or is not very interesting to the children.

➤ Provide a curriculum and activities that do not require a great deal of sitting or paper and pencil tasks. Have at least forty-five minutes of free choice and thirty minutes of outside or gym play for every three and half hours of class time.

➤ Keep group times short and meet in small groups. (Many active children have a hard time concentrating in groups, but do much better when receiving individual instruction.)

➤ Give instructions clearly and specifically for any task you are requiring children to do. Do not give more than two or three directions at a time. Reinforce the directions visually by demonstrating them and by drawing a picture to which the children can refer frequently while carrying out the activity.

Dealing with Existing Problems

➤ Use a small, freestanding cardboard divider to keep visual distractions from interfering with an active child's attention while he works at a table activity. Use a large divider during nap or rest times.

➤ Physical contact helps some active children feel more in control of themselves. To help a child attend better during circle time have him sit on an adult's lap, rub his back gently, or hold his hand.

➤ Some children benefit from individual, specific instructions. Tell the child specifically how to attend and remind him often: "Look at the line on the paper, put your scissors on top of the line, and then cut."

➤ For the overly energetic child, you will want to provide many outlets that will not cause problems.

Give him beanbags to throw and a gym mat to roll around on. Stroking a stuffed animal or squeezing a foam ball while sitting in group can help him release some extra energy, without disrupting the activity.

➤ Change your expectations. Allow the child to spend less time at activities and to move around during some activities. Whenever possible, substitute items that are easier to use or less likely to get the child in trouble. If he can't keep his chair still while seated at the table, let him sit on a beanbag chair that is not easily moved around.

➤ Use redirection to give the child a nondestructive or even positive outlet for his energy. A child who can't sit still during a flannel board story can place the flannel figures on the board and move them around.

➤ Suggest to the child's parents that they take the child for a physical examination by a pediatrician because a physical cause for the problem may be found. (In extreme cases, where the child has been overly active since birth and is active in all situations—called Attention Deficit Disorder or ADD—medication may be prescribed. Many parents are reluctant to put a young child on continual medication, so the decision must be theirs.)

Such medication (Ritalin™ is most common) is controversial because many people feel it is overused for the convenience of teachers and school systems. (It is very effective at reducing active behaviors, however, which is why it may have become overused.) If prescribed, use this medicine in conjunction with making changes in the classroom and the home to improve the child's ability to thrive there. The goal should be to help the child come off the medication as soon as possible.

➤ As often as you can, catch the child when he is calm and let him know when his overactive behavior is improving: "You've been concentrating for a long time. You must feel very proud of yourself."

➤ Although many in the medical community claim there is no proof of a link between food and behavior, many teachers and parents have seen clear evidence that certain foods, food additives, chemical substances, or even some synthetic fabrics affect behavior. An allergist or pediatrician can test for these reactions. Working on changes in the diet often makes for a positive first step for teachers and parents to help a child. There is no blame on anyone and positive, direct action is being taken. Some diets can be very difficult to maintain, however, and will require great effort and vigilance. A dietary approach to dealing with active behavior should be used along with the other approaches discussed. If a child is on a modified diet and his behavior does not change, help the parents seek family counseling and work on other solutions.

Resources

Barkley, R. *Hyperactive Children: Handbook for Diagnosis & Treatment*. New York: Guilford Press, 1986.

Bloomingdale, L. *Attention Deficit Disorder, Identification Course & Rationale*. New York: S.P. Medical & Scientific Books, 1986.

Fagan, J. "Helping Hyperactive and Inattentive Children by Changing Their Diets: Truth or Myth?" *Early Childhood Education* 21(1) (Winter 1987-1988): 12-15.

Feingold, B.F. *Why Your Child Is Hyperactive*. New York: Random House, 1974.

Franklin, J. *Food Allergy in Children: A Guide to Its Diagnosis & Management*. Park Ridge, NJ: Parthenon, 1988.

Friedrick, B.A. "ADD: A Common Cause of Problems at School." *Early Childhood Education* 22(1) (Winter 1988-1989): 17-18.

Haslam, R., and Valettutti, P. *Medical Problems in the Classroom — The Teacher's Role in Diagnosis and Management*. Austin, TX: Pro-Ed, 1985.

Jellinek, M.S. "Current Perspectives on Hyperactivity." *Drug Therapy* 11(10) (October 1981).

Leverton, S.M. "Toward Positive Social Behavior in ADD-H Children." *Early Childhood Education* 22(1) (Winter 1988-1989) 19-21.

Nichamin, S.J., and Windell, J. *A New Look at Attention Deficit Disorder*. Waterford, NJ: Minerva Press, 1984.

Nichamin, S.J., and Windell, J. *Coping with Your Inattentive Child*. Waterford, NJ: Minerva Press, 1985.

Smith, L. *Improving Your Child's Behavior Chemistry*. New York: Dell, 1982.

Stevens, L.J. Stoner, R.B. *How to Improve Your Child's Behavior Through Diet*. New York: Doubleday, 1979.

Taylor, E.A., ed. *The Overactive Child*. Philadelphia: J.P. Lippincott, 1986.

Taylor, J.F. *Special Diets & Kids: How to Keep Your Child on Any Prescribed Diet*. New York: Dodd, 1987.

Turecki, S., and Tonner, L. *The Difficult Child*. New York: Bantam, 1985.

5. Biting

Children who bite usually do so because they are frustrated or angry. Typically, they want a toy or a privilege that another child has and bite less out of aggression towards the other child than as a way to get what they want. They often act quickly and impulsively, too young or immature to think through other choices. The age when biting is most frequent is between thirteen and twenty-four months. Some children bite because their language skills are not good enough to say what they want. Teething can also be a cause of biting, but it is much less common. Frustrations due to overcrowding and too many children and/or adults in one classroom can lead to biting as well.

Preventing Problems

➤ Have at least two of each toy for toddlers. (This prevents disputes over particular toys, which causes frustration.) Make sure you have an ample supply of toys that are interesting to toddlers.

➤ Create a setting with few frustrations by doing the following: Give children easy access to many materials, set clear limits but few absolute requirements, offer a great deal of time for free choice, set regular routines, and provide a flexible schedule and activities.

➤ Attend to the teething needs of toddlers through use of teething rings and other safe, soothing things to bite on.

➤ Provide many ways for children to express their feelings and frustrations by providing toys to pound, nails to hammer, clay or playdough to mold, sand and water play to experiment with, and beanbags to throw at a target. Provide ample time and space for gross motor play outdoors.

➤ Help children calm themselves down when they are upset. Remember that children often know what activities will calm them down. If not, you can suggest that they listen to music, look at a book, sing, talk, draw, or ask to be held.

➤ Help children express their feelings with words, (vocalizations for very young children.) Interpret their words to other children for them, if necessary: "Rosa, Sara is saying 'Me, Me'; she is telling you she would like a turn."

➤ Provide a great deal of individual attention and affection. Some children bite out of the frustration of feeling "invisible."

Dealing with Existing Problems

➤ Toddlers are often too young to connect the negative consequences (separation from other children, anger from an adult, and so on) with the biting that preceded it. That is why any type of punishment rarely works. Instead, comfort the child who has been bitten and say in a sharp voice to the biter, "That hurts." Use a stern face so she will know that you disapprove. Be brief so as not to give the child who has bitten too much attention and take no further action towards this child.

➤ Watch the child who bites carefully to determine what, if anything, causes this behavior. Check for times of day, interactions with certain other children, or particular situations. If at all possible, catch the child just before she is going to bite. Stop her and say in a sharp voice, "That would hurt." If the biting was not provoked or connected to a frustrating situation, give her a teething ring to bite on. Move her quickly away from other children and give her an engaging toy.

➤ If the biting was about to occur because of a frustrating situation, such as a toy being grabbed from her, help the child to vocalize her needs: "Use your voice" or "Tell him want you want." Help her to practice vocalizing her need. Then help resolve the dispute by doing one of the following things: give the child who grabbed the toy away another toy, set a timer for turns, present a toy they can use together, or give the two children two different toys. Remember that even screaming when frustrated is far preferable to biting. Encourage the child whenever she vocalizes and doesn't bite: "Using words is a great way to get what you want." Work on the screaming to gradually reduce the volume and ultimately to have her use actual words.

➤ If the child seems to bite only one particular child, keep them separated. Consider moving the child to another class. (When a child who bites is with children who are slightly older, the biting often stops because they won't let her do it.)

➤ Make changes in your routines or schedule. If biting happens most often close to lunch time, make sure the child has a midmorning snack to ward off hunger or have lunch a little earlier.

➤ In extreme cases, you may have to ask the child's parents to take her out of the program for a period of time and to put her in another type of setting. Note that some children do not thrive in a large group setting and may stop biting when attending a program with fewer children.

➤ The solution to biting, unfortunately, usually involves very careful, persistent, and tireless observation of the child who bites, something that is difficult for teachers to do with other children and activities to attend to. A teacher must be able to step in as soon as she sees any signs of frustration. The more staff people in a classroom, the easier the task will be. Volunteers can be a big help in such cases.

Resources

Garrard, J.; Leland, N.; and Smith, D.K. "Epidemiology of Human Bites to Children in a Day Care Center." *American Journal of Diseases of Children* 142 (1988): 643-650.

Solomons, H.C., and Elardo, R. "Bite Injuries at a Day Care Center," *Early Childhood Research Quarterly* 4(1) (March 1989): 89-96.

6. Clingy and Dependent

Clingy and dependent behaviors are normal for children who are new to a program or who are going through a difficult change. However, some children are clingy and dependent because they have learned that it gets them what they want. In either case indulging the behaviors is not helpful to the child. The ideas in this section will help you to be supportive without being indulgent, and to balance the needs of the clingy and dependent child with the needs of the rest of your group.

Preventing Problems

➤ Provide a wide variety of fun, active, hands-on activities. Give the child plenty of time to make choices from those activities.

➤ Move around the classroom during free choice time. Spend some time with each of the children, but spend more time with those who have greater needs.

➤ Reduce the children's insecurities by letting them make choices and have control, by setting a predictable schedule and by helping them keep track of this schedule.

➤ Meet children's individual needs as much as

possible because this will reduce insecurities. (See "Individualizing," on pages 46 to 48, for further information.

➤ Promote responsible, age appropriate behavior by teaching the children self-help skills and by giving them many jobs, access to sponges and materials to clean up after themselves, and easy ways to put away materials when done using them.

➤ Try to find out why the child is clingy or dependent. Are there family changes, such as a new baby, a recent move, a parent's illness, or a recent death?

Dealing with Existing Problems

➤ If the child is facing temporary difficult changes in his life, give him extra attention and affection for a while. Ask him to request this attention in acceptable ways, such as by using words or signaling you. Let the child know that you are giving him extra support temporarily.

➤ Put a strict limit on the amount of time the child can spend by your side. Set a timer and say, "In two minutes I will give you a hug and help you find a place to play."

➤ Create a simple system for taking turns for children who would like to sit next to you at a meal or during a circle time. Post a list of the children's names (have them write their own if they are able) and have them cross off their names when they have had a turn. (This is a concrete way for those children to know that they will get to be near you, to visibly see when that will be, and to know that the system is equitable.)

➤ Don't reinforce the child's dependency by hugging or holding him too much. Give him very little attention when he is clinging and physically guide

him to an area in which he can play. Don't push or drag him, as this will only increase his insecurity. Give him positive feedback when he is playing away from you.

➤ Engage him in a game or a more social, positive interaction with you. Tell the clingy child, "Sit (or stand) across from me. That way I can see your handsome face and hear you better." Guide him across from you. Play with table toys or do a board game together. Move away when other children join or when the child is happily playing on his own.

➤ Guide him and another child to an activity that is specifically designed for two, such as a board game.

➤ Meet with the child's parents to discuss together possible causes of the problem and ways to deal with it. Suggest that they arrange to have their child spend time outside of class with a child from the class. (This usually establishes friendships and will give the child an incentive to move away from you and play with another child.)

7. Cursing, Name-Calling, and Hurtful Language

This is a difficult problem for many teachers because they do not want to ignore foul language, yet they know paying attention to it may make it worse. Children use swear words because it gets a big response and this makes them feel powerful. The key to eliminating the behavior is to take away the power of the words, to make children feel powerful in acceptable ways, and to teach better responses to anger or frustration.

Some parents are concerned that their children will learn foul language from other children. The reality is that most of your children heard these words before they came to your class but they may now be of an age when they are interested in trying them out. You can reassure parents that you are taking a multi-faceted approach to preventing and reducing the problem, as described in this chapter.

Preventing Problems

➤ Establish a classroom rule that only words that do not hurt other people can be used. Periodically remind children of this rule.

➤ Talk about the words that go with negative feelings—*frustrated, embarrassed, hurt, put down, angry*, and so on. (These are socially acceptable expressions and alternatives to cursing.) Encourage children to talk about what makes them feel this way. Give them practice in saying the words.

Let them know that negative feelings are OK and that everyone has them.

➤ When children express their feelings by using appropriate phrases such as "I'm angry because she pushed me" or "You really make me mad," praise them energetically. Say, "It's great that you used words that let us know how you feel. Now we can help you solve the problem."

Dealing with Existing Problems

Usually a child uses swear words for one of the following reasons:

• To get attention by causing adults to focus energy and time on correcting or admonishing them. Or to get attention from other children by making them laugh, look at her, or talk to her.

• To empower herself by causing adults or other children to get upset, agitated, concerned, or excited.

• Because these words are an automatic response when she gets angry or frustrated. She hears her parents use these words at home, has learned to do this too, and has no reason to do otherwise.

• To act and sound like an adult.

You can usually tell which of these reasons causes cursing by examining how she does it. Is she looking or waiting for a response from you?

Does she increase the volume of her voice? Or does she just say the words in a matter-of-fact way? Base your approach to dealing with the problem on the reason.

➤ If the reason for using swear words is to get attention or empower herself, ignore the language completely. If other children respond by "telling you" about what was said, say to them calmly, "I heard the words. I am ignoring them, and you can ignore them too." Show no agitation or anger as this is just what the child wants. A few minutes later, talk to the child who used the bad language about the "respectful language" rule. Tell her how much you appreciate her using good words because they tell you how she is feeling and they don't make other people angry. Help her find other words she can say instead. For example, if she is saying these words to get other children to laugh and get excited, she may make up silly rhymes instead. If saying these words involves hurting others, help the child practice expressing her feelings in words instead of using her swear words. Talk with the other child involved in the altercation about his options. This child can practice saying, "You have no right to call me names" and then walk away.

If using these words is an automatic response or an imitation of adults, intervene quickly but calmly. Tell the child to use different words because those words can hurt and upset others. Ask her, "What other words can you use?" Recommend some if she can't think of any. Have her practice saying the more appropriate words out loud. (As you will be helping her break an established habit, you will need to intervene many times before she will use better language.)

Complaints of Parents about Swear Words

If a parent complains that her child learned bad language from other children in your classroom, you can involve the parent in solving the problem.

➤ Don't contradict the parent or act defensively because, after all, the allegation may be true.

➤ Tell the parent that you are concerned about cursing and hurtful language in the classroom and explain your rules and strategies for dealing with this behavior.

➤ Ask for the parent's help and suggestions for dealing with the problem.

➤ Ask the parent what you can do to help her child.

➤ Brainstorm together ways that you can help each other and ways to use similar methods for dealing with the problem so there is consistency between home and school. (See "Complaining Parents," on pages 144 to 146, for more ideas.)

Resources

Crary, E. *My Name is Not Dummy.* Seattle: Parenting Press, 1982.

8. Excessive Crying or Whining

This behavior is more common in children who are new to the center. (See "New to the Class," on page 96, and "Starting the Day Off Right," on pages 17 to 19, for ideas on helping a new child. See "Preventing Problems" in "Clingy and Dependent," on page 123, for ideas on preventing excessive crying or whining.)

Dealing with Existing Problems

➤ Ignore the crying or whining in children three years old and older. Tell the child kindly: "Use words I can understand and I'll be glad to help you." Support the child's feelings while redirecting his behavior.

➤ Give positive attention to the child when he is not crying or whining. Say something like the following: "I appreciate it when you use a regular voice. I can understand you better, and you're fun to be with."

➤ Cut off a whiny voice as soon as it begins by saying, "Please use your regular voice so I can understand you better."

➤ Tell the child who is crying excessively that he can cry as much as he needs to where his crying won't disturb everyone else. Help him move to an area that is safe, visible to adults, but away from the other children. Tell him, "When you are ready to talk about what is making you cry, come back because I'm very interested in helping you." This will let him know that crying and feelings are OK but that you won't let this behavior disrupt the classroom, worry other children, or become an attention getting behavior.

➤ Talk with parents to determine possible reasons for the behavior. Brainstorm solutions together. Suggest a physical examination from a doctor to rule out any physical problems.

➤ Ask your supervisor or a respected coworker to observe you with your children to make sure you are not inadvertently reinforcing the behavior. (Ignoring this behavior can be hard and any attention you are paying to it may be giving the child just what he wants from the behavior.)

➤ Observe carefully to determine if the behavior happens mostly at particular times during the day, when the child plays with certain other children, or when he is with specific staff members. For example, the child may cry more near lunch time because of hunger or in the middle of the afternoon because of tiredness. Be flexible and make any necessary changes needed to meet his needs.

9. Hitting and Aggression

This is probably the greatest single behavior concern of teachers. Realizing that a certain amount of this behavior is normal and to be expected with young children is important. Many children are not fully able to control their strong feelings, and they act impulsively. They are also not able to understand the consequences of their actions. At home, some children are actually encouraged to hit and act aggressively. They see this behavior modeled by adults in their neighborhoods and homes and in the media. However, young children can learn to act differently in different places. In fact, this is a very helpful skill to give them. They can learn to accept that hitting may be allowed at home but words must be used at school.

These behaviors are seen more often in boys than girls. The reason for this is probably a combination of male hormones, expectations, child-rearing practices (boys are handled and talked to differently from girls, almost from the moment of birth), modeling, and reinforcing environments. Many girls have aggressive tendencies, too, but girls tend to express their aggression verbally. (For aggression more typically found with girls see "Mean and Cruel," on pages 123 to 124.)

Read the first two chapters in this section, on pages 110 to 117, carefully for important ways to prevent these behaviors. Make sure that the behaviors you are seeing are truly aggressive and not meant to be playful. Many children will try to engage other children in rough play as a way of being friendly or simply because this is the only way they know how to interact with others. (See "Roughhousing," on pages 130 to 131, for ways to deal with this behavior.)

A child who continues to be very aggressive, endangering the safety of other children, even after you have tried the ideas in this chapter, will most likely be better served in another program. Somehow the child's needs are not being met and perhaps a program that is smaller or specializes in children with difficulties would be the best situation for this child.

Dealing with Existing Problems

For a child who continues to hit while being taught appropriate behavior, use words that give the child a choice: "You must tell other children what you want. If they won't listen to you, then ask me for help. Now you can choose an activity to do on your own like a puzzle, a book, or a table game. When you think you can play with other children and talk with them about what you want, you can join the other children."

Grabbing Toys

➤ Use this situation as an opportunity to teach good social skills. Help the child use words to negotiate a turn-taking system or some fair method of sharing the toy. Give as much help as necessary, but no more. Make sure that all the children have easy access to a timer or a clock so that they can negotiate a solution on their own.

➤ If, after many attempts to teach her better methods, a child continues to grab toys, provide a consequence while continuing to work with her on the correct behavior. One possible consequence would be for her to have the second, not the first, turn to use the toy. When she uses words, give her the first turn with the toy. This encourages the appropriate behaviors. Remember that this child is most likely a little less mature than other children but that she will certainly develop better behavior with patience and kind guidance.

War, Gun or Violent Play

Although play in which children act out violent scenes (including superhero play) may not involve direct acts of aggression against other children, many teachers find this kind of play disturbing. Some teachers limit the play by allowing it only outside. Others are opposed to the play totally and see it as limiting and harmful to children's development.

Young children have a strong need to work on issues related to good and evil (right and wrong) and power and powerlessness. They develop for themselves clear lines of who are "good guys" and who are "bad guys," usually aligning themselves on the side of good. The bad guys must come to a bad end so that everything is right with the world and the children are safe. This type of play is important because it helps young children develop a sense of who they are in the world, how to control their own desires to be "bad," gives them a chance to grapple with what is acceptable behavior and what is not, and gain enough control to be safe. Because of this, children spend a surprising amount of time involved in this type of play.

The challenge for teachers then becomes how to give children opportunities to play out these themes and concepts while supporting play that is not aggressive or violent.

➤ Use aggressive play as an opportunity to expand the children's understanding of issues of violence. For example ask, "What makes that person bad? Is there a way you can help the bad guy become good?"

➤ Set clear rules, such as the following:
"Use your body and words without hurting others or yourself."

"Remember that anyone can call a time out, leave the game, or rotate roles at any time."

➤ Help the children rotate roles so that all children get to be the "bad guy" as well as the "good guy."

➤ Provide alternative scenarios that do not involve weapons yet give children power. For example, set up firefighting play or tracking down a wild animal to give it medicine to get well or to be moved to a safer place. Move the evil or danger away from residing in another person and place it in something else — like fire or a dangerous animal.

➤ Redirect children into cooperative games that involve working together to complete a task, overcoming an obstacle, or winning against time. (See "Action: Actively Teach and Promote Cooperation," on page 115, in the chapter "Preventing Behavior Problems" for ways to do this.) Read original fairy tales and other books, and make up stories that deal with issues of power and control.

➤ Remember that in classrooms where children have many opportunities to be truly powerful by making choices, being leaders, taking responsibility, being treated with respect, and having their feelings supported and their frustrations attended to, the amount of violent play is minimal.

Resources

Carlsson-Paige, N., and Levin, D.E. *The War Play Dilemma: Balancing Needs and Values in the Early Childhood Classroom*. New York: Teachers College Press, 1987.

Carlsson-Paige, N., and Levin, D.E. *Who's Calling the Shots? How to Respond Effectively to Children's Fascination with War Play and War Toys*. Philadelphia: New Society, 1990.

Feeney, S.; Caldwell, B.M.; and Kipnis, K. "Ethics Case Studies: The Aggressive Child." *Young Children* 43(2) (January 1988): 48-51.

Kostelnik, M.J.; Whiren, A.P.; and Stein, L.C. "Living With He-Man: Managing Superhero Fantasy Play." *Reducing Stress in Young Children's Lives*, edited by J.B. McCracken. Washington, DC: NAEYC, 1986.

Torbert, M. *Follow Me: A Handbook of Movement Activities for Children*. New York: Prentice Hall, 1980.

Watts, D.W. "Fantasy and Violence in Children's Folklore." *Early Childhood Education* 22(1) (Winter 1988-1989): 12-16.

10. Lying

All young children lie occasionally. In most cases they do not see this as doing something wrong or immoral. They believe it is acceptable to lie if the lie prevents them or a friend from being punished. Because young children think very differently than adults, moral lectures will not change the behavior. Instead, adults can avoid putting children in situations that force them to lie in order to save face. We can also forgive the occasional lie as a typical behavior of young children.

Preventing Problems

➤ Help children see the difference between reality and fantasy whenever the opportunity arises: "It's fun to play Batman, but is he real?" If necessary, explain that he is a character someone made up and wrote about in books and movies, although it would be exciting if he were real.

➤ Avoid putting children in the position where they feel like they have to lie to protect themselves from consequences. Say, "Tell me what happened in your argument over the toy" instead of "Did you grab the toy away?" If you help children solve their differences fairly and dole out consequences only as a last resort for behavior that is hard to change, children will not feel the need to protect themselves by lying.

➤ Build self-esteem by making sure children are accepted and appreciated unconditionally for who they are and not only for what they can do or say. Do this by saying many positive things to all children: "Your beautiful smile brightens my day" or "I really enjoy being with you every day." Be physically warm and affectionate. Give children many opportunities to be responsible and expect that they can handle their responsibilities, even if this means offering a little assistance.

➤ As lying can often be an attention-getting behavior, give all children a great deal of individual attention. Know their strengths and weaknesses well and be responsive to their needs.

Dealing with Existing Problems

Young children will often make up improbable stories and insist that they are true. This is not so much lying as it is fantasizing. Support the child's ability to imagine and the fulfillment he gets through the story: "You tell wonderful stories that are fun to listen to." This gives the child a completely positive message and at the same time lets him know that you know the story is a fantasy. Avoid asking if the story is true as that only puts the child in a position of having to lie.

Compulsive lying, or lying that happens frequently and consistently, is a sign that the child feels a great deal of shame about himself. He has the need to build himself up and to be seen as always good and right, in order to protect his weak sense of self from further damage. Build this child's self-esteem through a wide variety of methods: Help him to see all that is positive in himself: "You really know how to be a good friend to Amanda. That must make you feel very proud."

➤ When the child lies directly to you, do not confront him with the lie. If the lie has to do with telling about an untrue incident ("Jamie pushed me") then ignore the statement as much as possible. Try to determine if there is a purpose for the lie, such as to get sympathy, attention, or affection. Tell the child how he can achieve his purpose in a better way: "If you need a hug, ask me for one, and I will be very glad to give you one. If I can't because I'm busy, I will give you a hug as soon as I can." Follow through by helping the child figure out what he can do if someone does push him: "You can tell someone who pushes you that you are angry and you don't like it and you are going to play with someone else. What else can you do?"

➤ If the lie has to do with denying wrongdoing ("I didn't take Celia's doll"), say: "I know you're a very good person. Everyone does things he shouldn't sometimes and it's OK. Let's talk with Celia and figure out how to solve the problem." Again do not confront him with the lie.

➤ Work with parents to determine the root cause of the problem and discuss approaches for helping the child. Help the parents to see the importance of being positive with the child as opposed to punishing the problematic behavior. Recommend counseling, as a young child who lies compulsively has a quite serious problem with his sense of self.

11. Mean and Cruel

Mean and cruel behaviors are very disturbing to see. We worry about children who seem to be without a conscience and we wonder if they will grow up to be adults who commit criminal acts without regard to the pain and suffering of others. Children who exhibit mean and cruel behaviors, often and in the extreme, may do so because they have not been securely bonded with a loving adult or because they have seen these behaviors in their homes or neighborhoods.

Teachers can help these children by being empathetic, rather than seeing them as "problems." Let them know that you think they are good people worthy of love, although you don't approve of some of their behaviors. Accept their anger and rage as legitimate feelings to have and then show them better ways of expressing it. "I know you are angry and it is O.K. to be angry. If you don't like what Sara is doing you can use words or choose someone else to play with." Give them a great deal of positive encouragement and attention when they are acting in acceptable ways. Children develop consciences as a result of knowing that an adult cares deeply about them. You can provide this for children and make a difference in their lives, even if no other adult can.

Preventing Problems

➤ Establish a classroom rule: "Use your body and words without hurting others or yourself."

➤ Assure all children that you will not let anyone be mean to them and that you will not let them be mean to anyone else.

➤ Teach the children the correct words to use and the correct actions to take in difficult situations. Let them know that being angry is OK and help them express their anger without hurting others.

➤ Provide many outlets for children to express their strong feelings safely. Be available to talk to and write stories with them and give them plenty of time for large motor play. Provide the children with blank paper and pens with which to draw, sand and water to sift and pour, playdough and clay to mold, hammers and nails to bang, and beanbags to throw at a target. Validate their feelings often: "You really are very angry and that's OK." Help them express their feelings safely and verbally, and then help them deal with the cause of the anger.

➤ Give children ways to express positive feelings and words about other children. Have them say something good about another child during a small circle or group time. Rotate until all the children have had a turn at both expressing and receiving positive comments about themselves and what they do. Make books throughout the year about each child. Invite every child to draw a picture and write or dictate positive information about the child whose book is being composed. Then put all the papers together to form a book. When a child does something positive for another, such as helping to zip up a coat, make sure the child who received the help expresses appreciation.

Dealing with Existing Problems

Actions

Cruel actions, such as picking on a vulnerable child, hurting small animals, or causing excessive pain to others, are signs of a child who is in a great deal of emotional pain herself. She may have been or is being hurt emotionally and/or physically and is acting out her rage. (See "Children with Severe Behavior Problems," on page 118, and "Parents Who May Be Abusive to Their Children," on pages 154 to 157, for ways to deal with this.)

Words

Verbal cruelty is more common with pre-schoolers, particularly girls. Girls tend to express aggression with words and with indirect actions such as excluding others. This may be because they tend to have more advanced language skills than boys; they see the behaviors modeled by women at home, in their neighborhoods, and in the media; and their behavior is reinforced by their success at hurting others. Seeing sophisticated verbal cruelty in very young children is startling, but it is not uncommon.

The children who do this use a variety of methods, including rule-making, forming cliques, placing certain children in subservient roles, and making cruel comments directly to others just within hearing range or "behind their backs."

➤ Intervene when this happens and make children aware of the impact of their behavior. Help them use different words to express their feelings in ways that are not hurtful: "When you told Anita, 'We don't want to play with you, go away,' she felt hurt. Speak only for yourself and use words that don't hurt. Try 'I don't feel like playing with you right now, thank you.' " (See "When You See Bias Happening," on page 80, in "Children Who Are Culturally and Physically 'Different' and Bias Behaviors.")

➤ Realize that the child who is being cruel is building herself up by putting others down. Help her see the good in herself that is independent of comparisons to others: "Everyone is special and important. You really enjoy art and are fun to play with." Use many other methods to build her self-esteem. Be physically affectionate and tell her when she is being kind: "You helped Jason tie his shoes. You are a good friend, and you help make this a fun classroom."

➤ Help the child who is the object of the cruel behavior to stand up for herself by coaching her to say such words as: "I can play where and when I want to." Remember that you can never make children play with each other, but you can make sure that all children have equal access to all equipment and materials. Make sure that the child who is sometimes cruel knows ways that will help her successfully join in play (See "Helping Children with Difficult Behaviors," on pages 110 to 112, for more information.)

12. Roughhousing

Roughhousing is part of childhood. Teachers will never be able to eliminate the need some children have for it. For many children, it is a way of expressing affection for another child. The following suggestions will give you ways to allow rough-and-tumble play in the classroom or outdoors, while keeping it to a safe and reasonable level.

Preventing Problems

➤ Teach children other ways to interact: "Use words. Say to your friend, 'Let's play with the blocks.' " Assist the children in this process until they are able to do it on their own, relying less on roughhousing as the major form of interaction.

➤ Provide many opportunities for children to make physical contact with each other in a safe way. For example, play movement games and teach simple dances, yoga, or exercises in which children interact physically with partners. Make the rules and directions very clear to avoid anyone getting hurt.

➤ Before the start of an organized activity, physically separate children who have a hard time keeping their hands off each other. (This will reduce the strong temptation to interact.) Teach children other ways of expressing physical affection for each other, such as hugging, holding hands, and putting arms around each other's shoulders. Suggest to children that they ask before they touch others: "Kim, would you like to hold hands with me?" Follow this suggestion yourself. Remember that some children dislike being touched and all children need to be sensitive to and respect the feelings and the bodies of others. (However, most children enjoy spontaneously receiving and giving physical affection.)

➤ Provide a gym mat where children can roughhouse safely. Establish some ground rules such as the following:

"No punching."

"When one child says stop the other must do so."

"No shoes or hard objects on the mat."

If children have trouble stopping or if others are waiting to use the mat, limit the time on it. Offer roughhousing on the mat as a free choice activity.

Dealing with Existing Problems

➤ If children are roughhousing at an inappropriate time, such as during circle time, tell them "Now is a time for listening (or singing, sharing, and so on). During free choice time, you may choose the gym mat." Separate the children from each other. Tell them that if roughhousing happens again, they will have to choose a quiet activity away from other children. Follow through if necessary, giving the children the opportunity to return to the group when they are ready to listen without roughhousing.

➤ Give children who roughhouse during sedentary times something active to do with their hands (hold a book or a stuffed animal), an adult lap to sit on, the option of holding a friend's hand, or an alternative activity to do. Involve them more actively in the work.

13. Running Inside

Young children need to be active, and running is a natural way for them to move. Changing this behavior to assure their safety requires doing many things. You have to eliminate the temptation to run, establish clear expectations, give many reminders, and give children plenty of time during the day to run outdoors or in a gym.

It is often best to redirect children who are running inside into another, safer activity, rather than trying to get them to walk. For example, a chasing game can only be played by running. It makes no sense to walk and chase someone. By redirecting both children into a different game (such as lotto, puzzles, dramatic play, block play, etc.), the running will stop. Remind them that they can chase each other outside or in the gym during large motor time.

Preventing Problems

➤ Establish a class rule: "Only walk inside." Be very consistent about enforcing this rule. Explain that the reason for the rule is to make sure no one falls or runs into another person and gets hurt.

➤ Remind children before they enter the classroom from outside and before transitions to other activities, to walk in the room.

➤ Arrange your equipment and furnishings so that there are no long open corridors that invite running.

Dealing with Existing Problems

➤ Stop the child who is running and have her tell herself to please walk. Recognize that the reason for the behavior is usually because the child is excited and wants to get to an activity as soon as possible. Tell her: "It's great that you want to get to the activity quickly, but walking will keep you from getting hurt." Start walking with her to get her going successfully. Show her how to walk quickly without running.

➤ If logical consequences are needed, have the child walk with a teacher holding her hand. Next time the situation arises, ask the child ahead of time if she would like to walk on her own or have help. The common consequence of making a child go back to where she started and walk rarely works because it is punitive and frustrates the child by forcing her to do the opposite of her intentions (getting there quickly). Teach correct behavior in a helpful, instructive way that helps children get what they want *more* effectively.

➤ Pair the child up with another child who is good about walking. Have them be partners when walking somewhere is necessary.

➤ Remind the child of the reason that walking is important. Through a role play, demonstrate in slow motion how a person coming around a corner can have a serious accident with a child who is running.

➤ Reassure the child that when she is outside, she will get to run all she wants.

➤ Let children know, when they are walking, that you recognize the appropriate behavior: "Thank you for walking in the room. You know how to keep yourself and others safe."

14. Shy and Withdrawn

This personality characteristic can stay with people throughout their lives, even though shy people express a lot of pain and unhappiness about the condition. The causes can be numerous, but shy children tend to have shy parents, and many shy children have low self-esteem. They feel that they will be laughed at or not accepted by others if they assert themselves or that they are not as worthy as other children.

Preventing Problems

➤ Make all children feel loved, desirable, and respected.

➤ Rotate assignments and classroom jobs and provide opportunities for the children to make choices and be leaders in a way that is optimal for each child. A shy child may blossom when given formal opportunities to be a leader (e.g., the opportunity to choose children to leave the circle time area by the colors of their clothes). Give the child many opportunities to do this.

➤ Provide a wide variety of challenging activities that involve different amounts of children. See that some activities are only for one (a puzzle), some for two (a board game), some for three (a lotto game), and so on.

➤ Accept and appreciate every child's feelings, ideas, and statements, even if these are just attempts at vocalizing.

➤ Do most of your group activities in very small groups because shy children tend to be less shy around fewer children.

Dealing with Existing Problems

➤ Accept a reasonable level of shyness as a normal individual difference. Intervene only if shyness causes the child to have problems making friends, playing, and being involved in activities that he really wants to be involved in.

➤ Don't push the shy child. Respect his need to stay back and move slowly. Continue to offer opportunities and suggestions for participation, however. Be patient, be positive, and be persistent. Expect changes to come gradually.

➤ Start a game or activity together with the child. In a while invite one or two other children to join. When he is actively engaged with the other children, quietly move away to another part of the room.

➤ Set up a game that involves only two children. Encourage another, less shy, child to ask the shy child to join him in that game.

➤ Actively teach the child specific social skills and ways to enter play with other children. (See "Helping Children with Difficult Behaviors," on pages 110 to 112.) The fear of involving himself in play with others may come from failed attempts to do so. Help him say the words and do the actions needed to join others. Gradually do less for the child as he develops the skills.

➤ Incorporate the child into play activities without making him change his behavior. For example, if you have involved a group of children in acting out "The Three Little Pigs," acknowledge the shy child's important role as a watcher and listener: "Thank you for being an attentive audience member. Plays aren't much fun without an audience." As the child feels more comfortable, incorporate him even more in the activity by having him take the role of a house or a guard. (This requires little movement or talking.) Again show appreciation for his important role. Continue to encourage him to take more and more of an active part. (Chenfeld 1989).

➤ Give positive feedback to the shy child whenever he involves himself with others: "It's nice to hear you talk and laugh. I feel good that you are having fun and like being here."

➤ Give the shy child several options for participating. For example, if he refuses to join a movement game ask him if he would like to lead the game or keep track of who had a turn. Provide other options such as being the "Audience" or having the last turn (there is security in first seeing how everyone else participates).

➤ Limit the amount of time the child spends in a private, quiet area in the room. Tell him that other children want opportunities for quiet also.

➤ For a child who uses a very quiet voice, stop him quickly and encourage him by saying, "I love hearing your big five-year-old voice (or four-year-old voice). It's so beautiful to listen to!" Avoid saying, "Don't use that quiet voice" or "Speak up, we can't hear you" as this further embarrasses the child.

➤ Suggest to the child's parents that they arrange to have him spend time with another child outside of school. (This can often cement friendships that provide more play opportunities back at school.)

➤ Encourage the shy child to bring in favorite toys from home, including popular commercial toys, as a way to help him form friendships. (Put some limits on the use of these toys as discussed in "Toys from Home," page 51.)

Resources

Chenfeld, M.B. "From Catatonic to Hyperactive: Randy Snapped Today." *Young Children* 44(4) (May 1989): 25-27.

Honig, A.S. "The Shy Child." *Young Children* 42 (1987): 54-64.

Trawick-Smith, J. " 'Let's Say You're the Baby, OK?': Play Leadership and Following Behavior of Young Children" *Young Children* 43(5) (July 1988): 51-59.

Zimbardo, P.G., and Radle, S.L. *The Shy Child.* Garden City, NJ: Doubleday, 1982.

15. Silliness

This common behavior in preschool children, especially four-year-olds, can become a problem if it happens too often or at inappropriate times.

Preventing Problems

➤ Give many opportunities for children to be silly and even encourage silliness at times that are appropriate, such as free choice and outside. When the children are silly, let them know that this is a good time to be silly because it doesn't disturb others or make talking about important things hard.

➤ Set rules for activities that require earnest behavior:

"Listen while someone else is talking."
"Be serious during important talks."

➤ Don't require that everyone participate, as some children will find serious discussions too difficult, but do require that everyone show respect.

➤ Give children many opportunities to express their innermost feelings safely and confidentially.

➤ Give a great deal of individual attention and affection to all children.

Dealing with Existing Problems

A child who is silly a great deal of the time is probably using the behavior to avoid dealing with some important issues in her life. When you try to have a serious discussion, the pain she may have to face during that discussion is too great. Acting silly is her way of escaping this pain. (This is also known as the "class clown syndrome.")

Silly behavior can also develop because a child learns that it gets the attention and the admiration of other children and adults. A child who feels unloved can successfully make herself feel better this way.

➤ Meet with parents to determine the root cause

of the problem — the pain that the child is avoiding (perhaps an alcohol problem exists at home). Help in any way possible to ease the child's problems.

➤ Try to spend one on one time with the child away from other children. Note that if she is not near her peers, she might be willing to talk seriously. Use books, puppets, and made-up stories to help bring out her inner feelings. Give her opportunities to draw pictures that do not have to be shown to anyone else.

➤ Stop the child as soon as she starts silly, inappropriate behavior by saying: "Now it is important to be serious. In ten minutes when we're outside, you can be as silly as you want. I'm very interested in what you have to say if you would like to talk seriously." Tell the child that if this silly behavior happens again, she will have to choose an activity away from the group (child choice). Follow through if the behavior does happen again, and tell her she can join the group when she feels able to be serious.

16. Stealing

Unless a child is being encouraged to steal by an adult, which is very unusual, most children who steal do so because they feel deprived. They feel they are missing something that other children have. Because they cannot get affection and attention, they obtain material objects for themselves as a substitute. This is, of course, not satisfying, so they do it again and again. Adults often do this, too, by buying themselves presents when they feel unhappy or unloved.

A younger child may pocket small toys and not realize or understand that this action is stealing. Explain that school toys must stay at school so that all children can play with them. Remind the child that the toys will be there to play with when he returns to school.

Preventing Problems

➤ Build your children's self-esteem. Make this an important part of your curriculum.

➤ Maintain good parent communications in order to know what problems a child might be facing. You can then be helpful, empathetic, and supportive to that child.

Dealing with Existing Problems

➤ If you're not sure that a child actually is stealing, ask him to empty his pockets at the end of the day. Do this when no other children are around. If nothing was taken, explain your reasons for suspecting him and apologize.

➤ If you catch a child stealing, calmly ask him to put the object back so it will be there to play with tomorrow. Do not shame him.

➤ Give a child who is stealing positive verbal feedback hourly or daily (depending on how often he steals) when he does not steal. Tell him: "Thank you for leaving things here at school, then you can play with them tomorrow. I know how much fun it would be to have these toys at home, so you have great self-control when you leave them." Give the

child a hug or a pat on the back so he will know that acting appropriately will get him positive attention and affection.

➤ Meet with the child's parents to coordinate strategies to deal with the problem. Make them aware of the importance of being empathetic and positive. Ask them if they are aware of any possible causes for the behavior. Help them develop ways to build their child's self-esteem.

➤ Give the child many opportunities to be a leader and helper in the classroom. This will make him feel important.

➤ If the other children are aware of the stealing, talk to them about being friendly and about helping that child. Act positive yourself to provide a model for the children.

➤ Ask another teacher or supervisor to observe your classroom to determine if any pattern to the behavior is apparent or if you may be unintentionally contributing to the behavior.

➤ If the problem persists, team with the child's parents to get help from a mental health specialist.

17. Tattling

This is usually an attention-getting behavior and also serves to boost the ego of the child who tattles by casting others in a bad light.

Preventing Problems

➤ Give a great deal of positive, individual attention to all children as often as possible. Give extra attention to children who are more emotionally fragile.

➤ Give children practice saying positive things about other children. Have them say something good about another child during a small circle or group time. Rotate until everyone has had a turn at both expressing and receiving a positive statement.

➤ Make books throughout the year about each child. Invite every child to draw a picture and write or dictate positive information about the child whose book is being compiled. Then put all the papers together to form a book.

➤ When a child does something positive for another, such as helping to zip up a coat, make sure the child who received the help expresses appreciation.

➤ During a small group or circle time, talk with the children about tattling. Help them understand what is wrong with the behavior and what they can do instead. (See below for some ideas.) Do role plays of alternatives to tattling so they can practice the skills.

Dealing with Existing Problems

➤ Give minimal attention to the tattling but do not stop it or cut it off. (There is no way to know if the child might be giving you some important information about other children.) When she is finished talking and you know that she truly is tattling and not saying something you need to act on, then you can work to minimize the tattling.

➤ Tell the child to talk about the behavior to the child on whom she is tattling, not to you.

➤ Put the problem back on the child by asking her what she can do about her concern.

➤ Ask the child who tattles to tell you about the positive behaviors of other children: "I'd love to hear about the good things your classmate is doing."

➤ Say nothing but simply redirect the child into an activity. The lack of response on your part will reduce the behavior eventually.

➤ Encourage the child when she is talking to you without tattling: "I enjoy talking with you when it is not about other children."

Resources

Katz, L.G. "The Professional Early Childhood Teacher." *Young Children* 39(5) (July 1984): 3-10.

18. Temper Tantrums

This behavior is fairly common in toddlers, but if seen in children older than three and a half, it is a cause for concern. Toddlers throw tantrums because they do not have the language to express their needs. All their frustrations in understanding and coping with the world of "giants" build up to the point where they explode. Preschool children, however, usually can express their needs with words, can think abstractly enough to get their needs met with other people, and have more self-control and emotional maturity.

The preschool child who does have temper tantrums and who is not developmentally or language delayed may be under great stress and could possibly benefit from professional counseling or other assistance. The causes of emotional stress can be numerous—expectations from parents that are too high or too low, abuse or neglect, or fighting and tension in the family.

Other possible causes of tantrums are: having a medical problem that causes pain, having been overly indulged, lacking social skills, or having been reinforced for such behaviors.

Preventing Problems

➤ Provide many outlets for children to express their emotions and feelings.

➤ Reduce frustrations by offering children many choices of a wide variety of hands-on, self-directed activities for most of their time at school. Make sure your activities are not too difficult for children. Have reasonable expectations of the abilities of your children. Do not make them sit and listen for more than a few minutes at a time. (See "The Daily Schedule: An Active and Purposeful Program" on pages 16 to 17, for more information on the appropriate length of time for various activities.)

➤ Observe situations carefully as soon as you see children get frustrated. If necessary, step in to help them solve their problems. Do only as much as necessary so that they can gain the skills to be self-sufficient.

Dealing with Existing Problems

➤ Ignore the temper tantrum, except to insure the safety of the child. Remember that the goal of the behavior is for the child to get what he wants or to let off steam. In either case, giving any attention (negative or positive) to the behavior will result in an increase in the number of tantrums because you will be reinforcing the child's goal.

➤ If the tantrum is causing a disruption, move the child quickly to a safe area away from other children. Tell him calmly, "It's OK to be frustrated and angry, but it's not OK to disturb others. When you're ready to be calm, you may join us."

➤ Watch the child carefully to observe when the tantrums occur most frequently or what tends to set them off. Make adjustments in your schedule or environment to help the child. If an interaction with one particular child triggers the tantrum, separate the children after a few minutes of play to ease the tension. Help both children interact with each other differently and more amiably.

➤ Invite a respected peer or your supervisor to observe in your classroom. (She can help you see if you may be inadvertently contributing to the behavior.)

➤ Meet with the child's parents to discuss possible causes of the problem. Brainstorm possible solutions together. Recommend counseling or the help of a social service agency if the above strategies do not significantly decrease the tantrums.

Fits of Anger

A child who is out of control may hurt himself or another child. If you cannot reason with the child, lead him to a safe place, within your sight, such as to a gym mat, to vent his feelings. Tell him that when he feels calm, he can join the group or choose a quiet activity to do on his own. If he may hurt himself, stay close by him (or have an assistant stay by her). If he is not too resistant to your touch, hold him and assure him that you will not let him hurt himself.

➤ Help the child find ways to calm himself down. (He can generate his own ideas and/or you can suggest that he listen to music, look at a book, sing, talk, draw, or play with sand, water, or clay.)

➤ When the child is calm, help him determine how he could deal with the problem that made him so angry. Help him practice the words and actions he can take to get his needs met. For example, he can tell the child who has just knocked over his block structure to help him build it back up again. He can also ask an adult to assist him in dealing with the other child.

Resources

"Ideas That Work with Young Children. Discipline: Are Tantrums Normal?" *Young Children* 43(6) (September, 1988): 35-40.

19. Thumb-Sucking

For children under four years old, thumb-sucking is not a problem and should be ignored. Some doctors and dentists consider it a concern at four years of age and older because the risk of dental problems increases (Friman 1987).

If a child who sucks her thumb has many other emotional problems, ignore the thumb-sucking and concentrate on getting her help. Thumb-sucking may be an important comfort for that child.

Take no action on thumb-sucking without consulting the parents. (They may want you to ignore the behavior, or they may have some good ideas about how to deal with it.)

Preventing Problems

➤ If the thumb-sucking is a new behavior or has recently returned, meet with the parents to determine if there are any new changes at home that might be causing stress. If the stressful situation will be temporary, ignore the problem for now.

➤ Often children will stop sucking their thumbs at around four years of age because other children will poke fun at the habit. This can be an effective way of ending the habit, but the child will need your support to help keep up her self-esteem and to find alternative ways to deal with her stress.

Dealing with Existing Problems

➤ Redirect the child when she sucks her thumb into something equally comforting. Suggest holding and stroking a stuffed animal or lying on a soft pillow and looking at a book.

➤ Remember that comforting habits are difficult to break. When she has not sucked her thumb for a time, tell her often, but privately: "You really must be proud of yourself for keeping your thumb away from your mouth."

➤ Be aware that even a child who is ready and wanting to stop thumb-sucking will most likely need some help. Because habits become unconscious behaviors, the child will sometimes not realize that she is sucking her thumb. Use a mutually agreed upon visual cue to remind the child that she is sucking her thumb. For example, scratch your head or pull your ear. Be discrete so as not to cause embarrassment.

Resources

Adult Books and Articles

Friman, Patrick C. "Thumb-Sucking in Childhood." *WIC Currents* 13(4) (1987).

Heitler, S.M. *David Decides about Thumbsucking: A Motivating Story for Children, An Informative Guide for Parents*. Denver, CO: Reading Matters, 1985.

Children's Books

Tobias, T. *The Quitting Deal* New York: Puffin, 1975.

Heitler, S.M. *David Decides about Thumbsucking: A Motivating Story for Children, An Informative Guide for Parents*. Denver, CO: Reading Matters, 1985.

20. Too Loud

A healthy, happy classroom full of active learning is one that has a fairly constant, medium noise level. Expect your class to sound that way. Don't be jealous of the ultra-quiet class next door. Important learning about social skills, language development, self-concept, or a variety of other skills are probably not developing there. Young children cannot get their learning needs met without actively talking and doing. In your classroom, focus on dealing only with talking that is overly loud or strident.

Preventing Problems

➤ Establish a classroom rule: "Use quiet voices inside." Enforce it consistently. Explain the reason for the rule: "A quiet room will keep us all from getting a headache and we will be able to hear each other. Using a quiet voice will also keep you from getting a sore throat."

➤ Remind the children of the rule before entering the classroom from outside or before they begin a free choice activity.

➤ Use a calm, quiet voice yourself. Remember that children will raise their voices to match your noise level. Give children plenty of opportunities to talk and to be loud when such behavior is appropriate — outside, in the gym, or when singing an energetic song.

Dealing with Existing Problems

➤ Tell all the children to remind other children of the classroom rule about quiet voices when they hear someone being loud.

➤ Ask the child who is being too loud to tell you the rule about quiet voices. Remind him that he will get a chance to be as loud as he wants to be when you go outside: "You have a big strong voice, use it when you get outside."

➤ For the child who continues to be loud after numerous reminders use child choice. Invite him to pick a quiet, solitary activity and return to the group when he feels ready to use a quieter voice.

➤ If possible, allow the child to go outside and shout for a few minutes. Make sure he is supervised by an adult.

➤ Remind the child of the quiet rule just before coming in from outside or before free choice. Tell the child individually.

➤ Thank the child when he uses his voice correctly: "Thank you for speaking quietly. I can easily hear what other children are saying."

21. Won't Listen

Follow the suggestions in this chapter to help children who seem to ignore other people, pay little attention to what others say to them, do not follow through on rules or directions, or seem to experience difficulty in focusing on the speaker.

Preventing Problems

➤ Remind yourself that young children have short memories, focus almost entirely on the here and now, and do not transfer information from one situation to another situation easily. Note that they need much repetition and practice before gaining a new skill or new information. If you can remember this, you will be more understanding.

➤ Don't expect your children to listen to very much for very long.

➤ Make listening times as active as possible by asking questions and giving the children useful things to do with their hands.

➤ Most young children listen better when told something individually rather than as part of a group. Your undivided attention directed at a child tells her clearly that the information is meant for her; it makes the child feel important and helps her to attend. When individual attention is not possible, meet in very small groups with some individual follow-up.

➤ When talking with children, remove distractions, such as extraneous noises and enticing toys.

➤ If possible, back up your verbal information with something visual and with physical action. Most people (children especially) are visual learners but everybody learns best by actually doing or practicing the skill. For example, if you want your children to wash their hands properly, tell them how to do it while showing them. Then have them practice. As a reminder, post pictures above the sink showing proper hand washing.

➤ Ask the children to repeat back to you, individually, the information they received. (Expressing it verbally helps to set it in their minds.)

➤ Use a great deal of variety in your voice. Change the pitch (high and low), speed, and volume often. When you need to make an important point use a slightly louder and faster voice or a lower and slower voice than you normally use.

Dealing with Existing Problems

➤ If a child doesn't listen, have her hearing tested because a physical problem may be the cause.

➤ Some children can't listen because they are overwhelmed by their feelings and emotions. They have too much anxiety. Be patient, nurturing, and supportive. (Follow the suggestions in the first two chapters of this section, on pages 110 to 117.) In time, her anxiety will ease and it will be easier for her to pay attention.

➤ Experiment with a variety of methods to get the child to attend. Different children have different learning styles. Some children may be able to listen at any time, while others may only be able to focus their attention in certain circumstances.

➤ Ask the child to look at you before you talk.

➤ Give the child a specific visual cue along with your words. For example, if you want the child to remember not to touch other children, fold your arms across your chest when you tell her each time. Have her do this, too. Eventually you can just give the visual cue, and she will recognize it.

➤ Because some children listen better when touching something or using their hands, teach the child some words in American Sign Language. Or, give the child a stuffed animal or other item to hold when she has to listen.

➤ Remember that some children listen better with some minor distractions, such as soft music or pictures to look at. (These, undoubtedly, are the ones who will grow up to study with their stereos playing!)

➤ Allow the child to lie down or change her position to be more comfortable. This can greatly improve listening skills for some children.

➤ Try using a slightly louder voice, a quieter voice, or a slower voice to get the child's attention.

➤ Make physical contact with the child (a hand lightly on the shoulder) when talking to her.

Part VI
Working with Parents

1. Complaining Parents

Most parents are very reasonable and simply want the best for their children. Provide an easy, comfortable way for them to give you feedback. Don't ignore legitimate complaints. Take their input seriously and act on requests whenever feasible. When parents see that you are responsive you will win their favor and support.

Some parents, however, make unreasonable requests or complain very often. If you teach long enough you will eventually have to deal with such a person. The suggestions in this chapter will help you minimize complaining behaviors from parents and give you constructive ways to deal with unreasonable complainers.

Preventing Problems

➤ Meet with parents before or soon after the child enters your class. At this meeting, make your goals, philosophy, and expectations clear to avoid misconceptions.

➤ Give parents a parent handbook about your center, school, or classroom. If your program does not have a handbook, volunteer to be on a committee to develop one. Write one for your classroom because they are a must for good parent relations.

➤ Ask for input from the parents about what they would like their child to gain.

➤ Ask parents to help in the classroom if possible or to help in another way (go on a field trip, make a pillow for the book area, and so on).

➤ Welcome parents to be involved with your class in any way or on any level with which they feel comfortable.

➤ Provide information about your goals, philosophy, and expectations to all new parents. Provide this through written materials (in the parents' native language) and verbally (to reinforce the written information and to help parents who are uncomfortable with reading).

➤ Before presenting information to your children that may cause some parents concern, (sex education, sex-abuse prevention strategies, anti-racism education, and so on), send written information home about what you will be doing and arrange a meeting with all interested parents to discuss the issue.

➤ Tell parents often about the great things their children said and did. Write these comments down for them. Send notes home often to let parents know the wonderful things you and the children are doing.

➤ Schedule regular parent meetings (perhaps one every other month) with the parents of the children in your class to allow parents to speak their minds, express concerns, and ask questions. Whenever you meet with a group of parents, arrange the chairs in a circle. When you meet with individual parents, sit near them rather than across a desk. This sets the stage for working together as partners, not adversaries.

➤ Communicate with parents and encourage parents to communicate with you as much as possible. Use bulletin boards, letters home, forms for parents to return, a notebook that children can carry between school and home daily (this makes children feel grown-up too), informal chats, meetings, conferences, and so on.

➤ Request to visit the children in your class and their parents at their homes. At least once during the year invite all the families to your home (perhaps for a backyard barbecue) or on a field trip. Or, if you prefer, invite the families to your home one at a time.

Dealing with Existing Problems

Chronic Complainers

➤ Set up a meeting with the complaining parent, yourself, and the director to get at the root cause of her unhappiness. (It may have to do with the rates, a recent loss of income, marriage problems, guilt about not being home with her child, or some other cause over which you have little control.) Remember that a sympathetic ear may be a big help. Ask for the parent's advice about how you can assist her in solving the problem.

Behind Your Back

A parent, or a few parents, may be unhappy about the program, a policy, the food, or another concern but not let you or the director know. Instead, they will network with other parents to get support for their cause. In time everyone's anger will build up and suddenly, one day, you will feel as if you are being confronted by an angry mob. Worst of all, you will not even realize that there is a problem. Parents do this because they want their perceptions verified and because there is safety in numbers.

➤ Don't try to deal with the problem without preparation and help from the director, supportive parents and other staff. Arrange for a meeting where all the people involved can get together. Invite to the meeting a neutral third party, such as a supportive parent or a sympathetic board member.

The Angry Parent

➤ When confronted with an irate parent, regardless of the cause, just listen at first. Don't defend yourself, even if the parent is clearly misguided or misinformed. Remember that challenging the person only fuels the fire of her anger. Listen intently and sympathetically and use active listening techniques such as reflection ("What happened is really upsetting," "That really is terrible") and clarification ("What I hear you saying is that…," "Tell me more about exactly what happened next"). Note that this will diffuse much of the anger.

➤ Apologize. Even if the problem was clearly not your fault, you can apologize for the anguish that the misunderstanding caused the parent. In many cases, this is all the parent is looking for.

➤ Tell the parent that you will do what you can to ease her concern. If you need more information or

advice about the problem, tell her what you will do and when you will get back to her. Waiting a day or two will often put the problem in its correct perspective, even if the parent felt that the end of the world had come at the time. Remember that some form of compensation can help a great deal: "I wish I could replace the lost jacket. I can't, but I *can* offer you one of the jackets from our extra clothes box. I'm sorry I can't do better."

➤ When the immediate anger has cooled, you may be able to offer an explanation or rationale— your side of the story. Be aware, however, that some people are not interested in reasoning or are not able to reason. If this is the case, empathize with their concern and say what you've done to make sure the problem will not happen again. Leave the situation at that.

Complaints about Your Curriculum or Style

This problem typically happens over clashes in values. You believe, for example, that children have the right to know the facts (appropriate to their age level) about sex or death. However, some parents believe that young children should not hear this information or that it should come only from parents. These parents may get very emotional and let you know clearly of their concerns.

➤ Meet with the parents to give them a forum for their concerns. Let them know that arguing with you in your classroom during class time is not acceptable. Invite all interested parents. Make sure that some are there who support your approach. Discuss your perspective calmly using documented principles of early childhood development or recommendations from experts. Invite a local child development expert to the meeting. Acknowledge the validity of the parents' concerns and feelings. In *Anti-Bias Curriculum*, Louise Derman-Sparks recommends the following options:

• Request that the parents allow their child to participate in the activities and meet again to discuss the results.

• Continue discussions and meetings while the activities are carried out.

• If the vast majority of parents agree with you, let the majority rule.

• If possible and if acceptable to you, come to some

compromises, such as dropping one or two activities or modifying your approach slightly, but don't abandon your curriculum or style.

A Last Resort

The director or the parent may ultimately decide that the parent might be happier using another program. This is a difficult decision, but it may be a necessary one if the parent's expectations or wishes cannot be realistically met. Remember that your program cannot meet every family's needs.

Resources

Bernstein, A.J. and Rozen, S.C. *Dinosaur Brains: Dealing with All Those Impossible People at Work.* New York: John Wiley & Sons, 1989.

Bramson, R.M. *Coping with Difficult People in Business and in Life.* New York: Ballentine, 1981.

Carter, M. "Face-to-Face Communication: Understanding and Strengthening the Partnership," *Exchange* 60 (March 1988): 21-25.

Derman-Sparks, L. *Anti-Bias Curriculum: Tools for Empowering Young Children.* Washington, DC: NAEYC, 1989.

Everett-Turner, L. "Parent-Teacher Partnerships," *Early Childhood Education.* 19(2) (Summer 1986): 19-23.

Fisher, R. and Ury, W. *Getting to Yes: Negotiating Agreement Without Giving In.* New York: Penguin, 1981.

Galinsky, E. "Parents and Teacher-Caregivers: Sources of Tension, Sources of Support." *Young Children* 43(3) (March 1988): 4-12.

Greenberg, P. "Parents as Partners in Young Children's Development and Education: A New American Fad? Why Does it Matter?" *Young Children* 44(4) (May 1989): 61-74.

Hatfield, L.M. and Sheehan, S.P. "Parent Information Manual: A Vital Link between Home and School," *Exchange* 49 (May 1986): 29-31.

Henrick, J. "Keeping Your Cool When the Heat Is On," *Exchange* 53 (January 1987): 3-5.

Johns, N. and Harvey, C. "Engaging Parents in Solving Problems: A Strategy for Enhancing Self-Esteem," *Exchange* 58 (November 1987): 25-28.

Lloyd, S.R. "Managing Would Be Easy If...," *Exchange* 43 (May 1985): 5-8.

Myers, P. and Nance, D. *The Upset Book: A Guide for Dealing With Upset People.* Notre Dame, IN: Academic Publications, 1986.

Neugebauer, R. "Coping with the Chronic Complainer," *Exchange* 46 (November 1985): 37-39.

2. Parents Who Are in a Hurry

Parenting today is very hard. Many parents are single or are struggling financially. Even well-off parents with spouses have difficult lives trying to balance work and family obligations. Most parents feel they have put in 48 hours at the end of each day. Be understanding of their situations and why they are always in a hurry.

Some parents hurry out the door for helpful reasons. They know that their child will continue to cry or act out until they leave. Because they do not want to prolong the problem, they leave quickly out of consideration for you and the class.

Some parents want to spend as little time as possible in your class because they find it stressful. They may have misinterpreted a statement you made or are afraid to hear bad news about their child.

Preventing Problems

➤ Say a kind word to parents when they pick up their child at the end of a hard day. Avoid talking about their child's problem behaviors or other concerns at this time. Doing that more formally at a less stressful time is a wiser option. Use the phone for busy working parents.

➤ Choose your words carefully. When a parent picks up a child who is being fussy at the end of the

day and you say, "I didn't have any trouble with him today," the parent may interpret that as meaning, "I can handle your child better than you." Instead of this, say "Many children are fussy at the end of the day. What can I do to help?" (Galinsky 88).

➤ Offer a cup of coffee, tea, or juice to parents when they arrive to pick up their child. Set up an area in your room or, if your room is not large enough, somewhere nearby where parents can sit for a minute and relax. Provide comfortable seat-

ing, something to drink, and some magazines. Be aware that by doing this you give parents the clear message that their presence is welcomed.

➤ Provide many convenient ways for parents to communicate with you. Give them your home phone number as busy parents often have to take care of things after working hours. However, put clear limits on when the parent can call you, such as, only between 7:30 and 9:30 p.m.

➤ Set up the situation so parents have to spend only a little time at the beginning and at the end of the day dealing with any additional stress. Make signing children in and out easy and convenient for parents and organize the children's cubbies so that they are easy to find and get to. Make sure children have gathered their belongings, art work, and messages together and placed them in their cubbies before parents arrive. Have children wash their faces and comb their hair before the end of the day. Most parents associate this with being well cared for. Your thoughtfulness will also save parents time and stress if they need to go to the store or to a doctor's office directly from school.

Dealing with Existing Problems

➤ Tell the parent about the importance of staying for a few relaxed minutes when leaving or picking up his child. Explain that this helps the child move between school and home. (Parents have to build the time into their schedule by leaving home or work a few minutes earlier.)

➤ Ask the parent who hurries to find a few minutes to talk to you so you can help him think of ways to save time and reduce stress. (This will give you information about the reason for the hurrying and insights into how to help. It will also make you very appreciated by most parents.)

➤ Help the parent by brainstorming solutions together for easing the rush and stress. Set a plan

of action to implement the one or two best solutions. Meet again to evaluate the results; to revise the plan, if it is not working; or to tackle a new problem if it is. Be assured that the best plans involve you, the parent, and the child in making some changes or adjustments.

Resources

Galinsky, E. "Parents and Teacher-Caregivers: Sources of Tension, Sources of Support." *Young Children*, 43(3) (March 1988): 4-12..

Greenberg, P. "Parents as Partners in Young Children's Development and Education: A New American Fad? Why Does it Matter?" *Young Children* 44(4) (May 1989): 61-74.

3. Parents Who Linger

Another result of stress in the lives of parents may be their need for support wherever they can find it. Many early childhood teachers are experts at giving support and parents take more then full advantage of it. This may mean that you have parents who demand your time and attention when you need to focus on the children or get home to your own family.

Another reason parents may linger is because they have trouble separating from their children. They feel guilty or remorseful about leaving them. The stress facing them at work or at home may be a further inducement not to leave too fast. They may also find the classroom to be a comfortable, enjoyable place—a pleasant break from the office or home.

Preventing Problems

➤ Have a written statement in your parent handbook with guidelines for leave-taking. In the statement, recommend that parents stay for no more than ten minutes at the start and at the end of the day, unless they are actively participating in the morning's activities. If they need to talk to teachers for longer than that, encourage them to make an appointment. Describe a helpful procedure for bringing and picking up children. (See "Dealing with Existing Problems," below, for an example.) Have a message pad posted by the door. This will allow parents to leave you notes without disturbing your work with the children.

Dealing with Existing Problems

➤ Tell the parent: "I don't want to interfere, and I enjoy your company. I'm concerned however, that the mornings might be stressful for Anna. She never knows how long it will be before you will leave. I have some ideas for helping, if you would like to hear them, and you probably have some, too." Discuss solutions together. Tell the parent that she might consider the following solution: "Set a timer and tell the child that in three minutes you will be leaving. When the timer goes off, tell her when you will come back, give one kiss and a hug, say goodbye once, and then leave promptly."

➤ If the problem happens at the end of the day, try the following ideas:

• Tell the child to gather together her belongings. Stand near the door and say to her and to her parent: "I'll see you tomorrow. Have a good night."

• Tell the parent you would love to chat longer but must attend to the children and be ready to leave by a specified time. Set a time to meet with the parent when the appointment would be more convenient for you.

• Tell the parent you will call her later that evening.

• Have the parent write you a note.

• Ask the parent to help you close up and leave.

➤ Involve the parent who lingers in an activity that is helpful to you (preparing some art materials, cleaning, or giving one on one assistance to certain children). Ask her to tell you exactly how long she will be staying. Make sure she is familiar with your policies and procedures. Request a regular schedule from her if she will be involved in the classroom. Remember that consistency and routines are vital to feelings of security in young children.

➤ Note that some parents may want to get too involved, interfering in your plans and your approach to teaching and caring. Be aware that they may be doing their children a disservice by not allowing them the space to become independent. Set clear limits about what the parent can and cannot do. Assign her some tasks that will keep her involved with many different children and some that do not involve children at all.

Resources

Harvey, C. and Johns, N. "Parents Need Limits Too: A Challenge for Child Care Staff," *Exchange* 46 (November 1985): 7-9.

4. Telling Parents about the Difficult Behavior of Their Children

Many teachers dread having to confront a parent with information about their child's behavior. They worry that the parent may become upset, defensive, blame the teacher, or perhaps react too negatively towards their child. However, it is worse not to keep parents informed about their children. This chapter explains ways to talk to parents that minimize strong negative reactions.

If you work in a full day program, be sure to avoid the all-too-typical routine of informing a parent at 5:45 how "awful" her child has been during the day. At this time everyone is short tempered, tired, hungry, irrational. There is no time or space to deal with the concerns properly. Use the suggestions which follow as a guide to alternatives.

Preventing Problems

➤ Throughout the year, share a great deal of positive information about their children with parents. Do this daily if possible. Win the trust of parents through helpful, positive, and supportive communications. Show empathy and understanding, and be responsive to their concerns. (If you do this, the parents will treat your concerns seriously and respectfully.)

➤ On an ongoing basis, keep parents informed about how their children are doing. Meet with them when you first see signs of a problem. Don't spring any big surprises. Teachers often avoid doing this because it is difficult, stressful, and many times they can remedy the problem themselves or the child adjusts or matures. However, you must inform parents early, in case the problem does not improve or gets worse. They also may be able to give you vital insights into the concern or know of simple solutions. This can save you weeks of stress. When you meet early on, share your strategies for dealing with the problem and present a positive outlook for solving it.

➤ Don't talk to parents about problems when you are in a hurry or will have distractions. Set up a time when you will both have ample time to fully work through the concern. Meet in a place that is relaxing as there will naturally be stress. Arrange the seating so that you are near to each other, not across from each other. (This gives the message that you are working together on a problem.) Set a specific starting and ending time.

Dealing with Existing Problems

➤ When you set up a meeting to talk with parents about a concern tell them, "I've noticed that Mark is hitting other children. Let's set up a time to talk about helping him." Avoid saying, "I want to talk to you about your child," because this phrase causes great anxiety and stress for parents.

➤ Set an agenda with parents before you start. Consider the following agenda:
1. Teacher shares facts and observations.
2. Teacher shares her current strategies for dealing with the problem at school.
3. Parents share their thoughts and concerns

and possible reasons for the behavior.

4. Teacher shares any additional insights.

5. Teacher and parents brainstorm solutions and strategies together for school and home.

6. Teacher and parents develop a plan of action for the best solutions.

7. Teacher and parents set a date to meet again to evaluate the effectiveness of the plan.

➤ Start the conference by talking about the child's strengths and good points. End the conference on a positive note by reaffirming those strengths.

➤ In your meeting, present objective information. "Mark hit a child at 9:00 when he wanted the toy the child was playing with. After I talked with Mark about other ways to get a turn, he hit the child again at 9:10. At 9:45, he hit a child on the playground who accidently bumped into him. At 10:30 he punched the child sitting next to him at snack. I did not see a reason for this."

➤ Consider parents to be the experts on their children. Take their suggestions seriously and listen to their ideas.

➤ Follow your agenda and end on time. Note that if the conference lasts too long, parents will be reluctant to meet again. Keep written notes of what you have agreed to do.

➤ If parents refuse to meet with you, write to them about your concerns and keep a copy of your letter. Consider that some people take written remarks more seriously. (You will also have a record that you made the parents aware of your concerns.)

Resources

Bjorklund, G. and Burger, C. "Making Conferences Work for Parents, Teachers, and Children." *Young Children* 42(2) (January 1987): 26-31.

Carter, M. "Face-to-Face Communication: Understanding and Strengthening the Partnership." *Exchange* 60 (March 1988): 21-25.

Cataldo, C.Z. *Parent Education for Early Childhood: Childrearing Concepts and Program Content for the Student and Practicing Professional.* New York: Teachers College Press, 1987.

Everett-Turner, L. "Parent-Teacher Partnerships." *Early Childhood Education* 19(2) (Summer 1986): 19-23.

Galinsky, E. "Parents and Teacher-Caregivers: Sources of Tension, Sources of Support." *Young Children* 43(3) (March 1988): 4-12.

Gonzalez-Mena, J. "Mrs. Godzilla Takes on the Child Development Experts." *Exchange* 57 (September 1987): 25-26

Johns, N. and Harvey, C. "Engaging Parents in Solving Problems: A Strategy for Enhancing Self-Esteem," *Exchange* 58 (November 1987): 25-28.

Koulouras, K.; Porter, M.L.; and Senter, S.A. "Making the Most of Parent Conferences." *Exchange* 50 (July 1986): 3-6.

Morgan, E.L. "Talking with Parents When Concerns Come Up." *Young Children* 44(2) (January 1989): 52-56.

Stone, J.G. *Teacher-Parent Relationships.* Washington, DC: NAEYC, 1987.

5. Parents Who Are Late

This is a very common and persistant concern for many teachers. It is very annoying to wait for a parent, not knowing when she might finally show up. The child almost always feels worried, hurt, and abandoned. This chapter includes ways to greatly reduce the problem.

Preventing Problems

➤ State in your parent handbook your policy on lateness and why parents need to bring in and pick up their children on time.

➤ Post a large sign in a conspicuous place stating the opening and closing hours and the consequences for being late.

➤ Discuss with your supervisor the need to levy fines or raise them for late pick-ups. Be aware that for some parents a few extra dollars for being late is worth the cost. Note, however, that programs that charge a dollar for every minute a parent is late, usually have few problems with lateness.

(Even free, government-funded programs can charge child care fees after their regular hours.) Remember that, without some consequences, the problem is not likely to go away. Late fees should go directly to the person who is providing the service—the income is taxable. Reduce late fees slightly the first few times parents call to say they will be late due to unavoidable circumstances. (This rewards responsible behavior.)

➤ Thank parents who are always on time. Follow up your verbal thanks with a letter or a certificate of appreciation.

Dealing with Existing Problems

➤ Meet with parents who are late to pick up their children. Discuss together ways to solve the problem. Let them know how much their tardiness disrupts your life and the extent of the problem it causes you. Take time to let them know that lateness is a problem of great concern to you. (Often, this will turn things around.)

➤ Meet with your supervisor and discuss your concerns. Make sure she clearly understands the depth of your unhappiness about staying late. Come prepared with several solutions in mind.

➤ Convince your supervisor to raise fees for being late as discussed above.

➤ Request to have your shift changed, if possible, so that you are not on the final shift.

➤ Request that your supervisor or another person stay late with any children who have not been picked up on time or that the task be rotated between different staff people. Because maintaining positive relations with parents is so important, you should not have to be the only one to confront late parents.

➤ For chronic late pick-up offenders, request that your supervisor put a number limit on how many more times they can be late and still be served by the program. You should not have to tolerate the intrusion into your life caused by chronically late parents. Do this, however, only as a last resort, because this family may be among the neediest in your program for stable, quality education and care for their children. At the time of enrollment tell all parents of this potential consequence for lateness. Put it in writing.

➤ If the problem is that the parents bring their children in late, discuss with them the impact this has on the children. Tell them what the children miss, how the adjustment to the day is more difficult, and how it may reduce the formation of friendships. Offer your help in devising solutions to the problem.

Resources

"Prickly Problems: #1—The Late Parent." *Exchange* 59 (January 1988): 16.

6. Parents Who Want You to Teach Reading

All parents want their children to excel and be successful. For some, this desire means reading before first grade. However, knowing how to read does not necessarily mean a child is interested in or enjoys reading. Children who learn to read early are not always better or more avid readers than other children when they are older. Pushing children to read before they are ready may make them feel negative about books and reading. It promotes reading as a skill to "perform," rather than as a process to enjoy. Creating an atmosphere in your classroom that promotes a love of books and helps children understand the purpose of written language is the best way to teach young children to "read."

Preventing Problems

➤ Assure parents that reading *is* being taught. Young children in your class are learning to read by being exposed to good literature and a great deal of print and books, by being given many opportunities to write (however they are able), by being encouraged to recognize their own names and the names of the other children, by dictating stories that are written down by adults and then read to them or by them, by seeing the pictures they draw labeled, and by listening to new words being used. Explain that this is teaching reading to preschoolers in an appropriate way—it is not just prereading or reading readiness.

➤ Develop a written statement about this issue to give to parents who are looking at your program or who are new to the program. Make this part of a parent handbook (either for your class or for the whole program). Post the statement in the classroom. Ask new parents what their opinions are on teaching reading to determine if your philosophy and theirs mesh.

➤ Save examples of children's work, such as stories they have dictated to you, signs they have made, their attempts at writing, pictures they have made that are labeled, and similar items, to show to parents as examples of reading and writing development in your class.

Develop a Sensible Plan for Teaching Reading and Writing

Use all or some of the following ideas and information to develop an approach to reading and writing development for your preschoolers. Explain your approach to parents.

Read Aloud Often

➤ Reading stories to children that they enjoy is one of the best ways to ensure that they will become readers in the future (Cohen 1968). Do this often (at least once a day in half-day programs and twice in full-day programs) and let parents know you are doing it.

➤ Select books carefully. Choose those that will hold the children's interest and will not be too difficult to follow. Use original versions of classic children's literature and avoid watered-down updates. If the children start to get restless, stop reading. Continue the book at a later time or choose a more interesting book to read. Read with enthusiasm and expression in your voice.

Silent Reading

➤ Set aside a short time when everyone, including the adults, is quietly looking at or reading books. Afterwards, meet in small groups and have each child who wishes, tell everyone his favorite part or picture. (This develops a respect for the process of reading and a sense that books are enjoyable.) Post information about this part of the day on your schedule so that parents are aware that it takes place.

Avoid Worksheets

➤ Note that children who learn reading and writing skills from workbooks do *not* become better readers than children who learn those skills from hearing stories, dictating stories, doing art, writing stories, having fun browsing through books, and seeing print and hearing it read in many different places and forms. (Reutzel et al 1989) Examples of print in various forms include signs and labels in the room and outside on the street, names in cubbies and on charts, simple graphs, and classroom shelves labeled with pictures and writing. Remember that worksheets force children to be too passive and to learn rote skills. As you know, children learn more when they actively participate in the real activity and handle actual books and reading materials. Make parents aware of this.

Individualize

Most children are interested and ready to read between six and seven years of age. The children in your class who are younger than this and yet are ready and interested in reading will have many opportunities to do so through the methods discussed in this chapter.

Promote Language Development

Consider that good language skills and a good vocabulary are closely tied to developing good reading and writing skills. Show parents that you demonstrate good speaking skills, encourage children to use language as much and as well as they are able, and expose them to many new words and phrases.

➤ Establish a sharing time when children who wish to, get to formally speak to the rest of the children and the children respond by asking questions and sharing insights.

➤ Use mealtimes as a time for children to use language to get food passed, milk poured, and so on.

➤ Teach many songs and read stories that contain new words. Explain the meaning of the words to the children.

➤ Set up board games and dramatic play areas where the children will want to talk to each other in order to work out roles, ideas, and rules.

Create a "Literate" Classroom

➤ Note that a print-rich classroom will make obvious to parents when they look around your room that learning to read is encouraged and highly valued. Create this kind of classroom by including the following:

• Signs that have pictures and words on them.

• Displays of children's writing on the walls and bulletin boards.

• A cozy book corner with soft pillows and many books displayed attractively.

• Marking pens and blank sheets of paper available in the block area, dramatic play area, and art area.

• Alphabet games, letter puzzles, magnetic letters, sandpaper letters, cookie cutter letters, and so on available on open shelves.

• Labels on items in the room, such as the word *window* printed on a strip of paper and taped to the window.

• Children's names written and posted for jobs to do, on birthday charts, to identify cubbies, and many other ways.

• A dramatic play area set up as an office, hospital, post office, library, or similar place so that children can emulate the reading and writing that adults do in those places.

• Shelves and toy containers labeled with pictures, symbols and/or words that children match when putting things away.

• Sets of "key words" (words that have emotional importance to children, such as *mommy*, *daddy*, friends' names, names of favorite toys, things that

are scary) that children who are starting to sight read have in their vocabulary.

Resources

Adult Books and Articles

Ashton-Warner, Sylvia. *Teacher*. New York: Simon & Schuster, 1963.

Bettelheim, Bruno, and Zelan, Karen. *On Learning To Read*. New York: Vintage Books, 1981.

Cohen, Dorothy H. "The Effect of Literature on Vocabulary and Reading Achievement." *Elementary English* (February 1968):

Ferreiro, Emilia and Teberosky, Ana. *Literacy Before Schooling*. Exeter, NH: Heinemann, 1982.

Innes, M. "Early Reading, Early Writing." *Early Childhood Education* 20(1) (Winter 1986-1987): 28-32.

Ploghoff, Milton H. "Do Reading Readiness Workbooks Promote Readiness?" *Elementary English* (October 1959).

Reutzel, D.R.; Oda, L.K.; and Moore, B.H. "Developing Print Awareness: The Effect of Three Instructional Approaches on Kindergarteners' Print Awareness, Reading Readiness, and Word Reading," *Journal of Reading Behavior* 21(3) (September 1989): 197-217.

Schickedanz, Judith A. *More Than the ABC's: The Early Stages of Reading and Writing*. Washington, DC: NAEYC, 1986.

Trelease, Jim. *The Read-Aloud Handbook*. New York: Penguin Books, 1982.

Willert, M.K. and Kamii, C. "Reading in Kindergarten: Direct vs. Indirect Teaching." *Young Children* 40(4) (May 1985): 3-9.

Films/Videos

Foundations of Reading and Writing. Campus Film Distributors Corp., 24 Depot Square, Tuckahoe, NY 10707. (914-961-1900).

Dump the Dittos. Total Learning Consultants, 7670 SW 142nd St., Miami, FL 33518. (305-238-1829).

7. Parents Who May Be Abusive to Their Children

Each state has laws on reporting child abuse. Know these state laws. Contact the agency in your state that deals with child abuse (often called Child Protective Services, Children's Services Division, Bureau of Family Services, or a similar name), and they will tell you the laws and mail you written information about the laws.

In many states, you must report any suspected child abuse. Not doing so is illegal. In turn, you are usually protected from any accusations of wrongdoing if you are mistaken.

If You're Not Sure

Children get many cuts and bruises, so deciding if abuse is happening can be difficult. However, be confident that making a mistake and over-reporting abuse is better than taking a chance on missing abuse. At the very least, keep a detailed written record of the cuts and bruises as described below under *Write Down the Things You Notice*.

Note that many cuts, bruises, or burns over a period of time can be evidence of abuse or neglect.

Reporting abuse can be very positive and something to feel good about, as you may be the person who starts the process that will help a family change for the better.

Suspected Physical Abuse

Report the following signs if you observe any of them:

> The child has...
> - visible bruises or injuries in places unlikely to be hurt from a fall (the eye, buttocks, genitals, neck, torso, thigh, backs of legs and arms).
> - bruises in a pattern (belt marks, hand prints).
> - frequent burns or burns in unusual places or shapes (cigarette, iron).
> - bite marks.
> - numerous bruises in various stages of healing.

> The child or parent has...
> - an explanation that seems unlikely to have caused that injury.
>
> The child offers...
> - a statement freely given that the injury was the result of being hurt or neglected by a parent, adult, or older child.

Suspected Neglect

Report severe neglect because it can be just as disastrous as physical abuse to a child.

Indicators of neglect are seen in a child who is often and consistently:
- hungry
- tired and listless
- dressed inappropriately for the weather

- smelling bad
- wearing very dirty clothes
- needing medical attention that does not get taken care of
- failing to grow and gain weight
- left alone at home or in the care of a sibling under 12 years old.

Suspected Emotional Abuse

Realize that emotional abuse can be very devastating to a child and can result in negative and antisocial behaviors that last a lifetime. Some states are able to handle reports of emotional abuse and have procedures and trained staff to investigate. Other states focus more on abuse where there is physical evidence—particularly if protective service funds are in short supply.

An emotionally abused child is one who is often and consistently:
- belittled and berated
- rejected
- cursed at
- punished cruelly, such as being locked in a closet
- psychologically tortured (in extreme cases)

Evidence of emotional abuse is a number of these behaviors seen often and over a long period of time (several months). Note that the evidence is more compelling if you have also witnessed the child being treated cruelly by an adult.

The symptoms seen in the classroom behavior of an emotionally abused child include:
The child...
- displays extremes of emotions (overly happy, depressed, shy) that are often expressed at inappropriate times or in odd ways, such as laughing when hurt.
- physically hurts herself.
- isolates herself from others.
- displays strange or intense habits such as hair pulling, rocking, or head banging.
- destroys property
- sets fires.
- displays extreme fears or unusual fears.
- is cruel to other children or animals.
- is obsessed with minute details.
- steals.
- lies.
- bites (four years old and older).

Suspected Sexual Abuse

Because about one in four children will have some kind of unwanted sexual encounter with an adult before the age of eighteen (Mrazek 1980), breaking the pattern of sexual abuse is important. Preschool teachers have a vital role in doing this as approximately one-third of sexually abused children are five years old or younger (Ray-Keil 1988). Teach children, in a concrete and nonthreatening way, about how to avoid sexual abuse and about the importance of getting help. Many good books and curriculums are available to help you do this and some are listed at the end of this chapter.

Signs that a child in your class may be abused sexually include the following:

The child...

- experiences difficulty in sitting or walking due to soreness in the anal area.
- wears stained or bloody underwear.
- experiences soreness, pain, or itching in the genitals.

- has frequent yeast infections or urinary tract infections.
- displays sexually provocative behavior and adultlike knowledge of sexuality.
- displays extreme fear of men or precocious seductiveness towards men.
- does drawings which depict adults with erect penises or other sexual scenes.

Write Down the Things You Notice

Write down the nature of the bruise, where it is on the body, and the time and date you noticed it. Include any comments made by the child and/or parent. If you suspect neglect, sexual abuse, or emotional abuse, write down any signs, symptoms, and comments. Keep your report in a safe place. This is important because several days may pass before a caseworker investigates. Also, one incident may not be considered a cause for concern by the caseworker, but a number of incidents over time may build a case for possible abuse. In many states, a written report of abuse is required.

Let your supervisor know and let her follow up, make phone calls, and take responsibility. If she refuses, it may be your legal (as well as moral) duty to do the reporting yourself. Remember that not doing so may put a child in grave danger.

Never Discuss Your Suspicions with Parents

Because you care about your families, you may feel like asking the parents about the bruises or even informing them first that you will have to report the abuse. Be aware that this is not a good idea. Abusive parents may take their child and leave. You will probably not be able to find them, nor will the caseworker. The parents may also be able to talk you out of reporting, which you may later regret. Your first responsibility is to protect the child.

Warning parents about your suspicions and offering your help will most likely not change long established patterns of behavior—unless you can offer a comprehensive counseling service with staff trained in abuse and neglect. Abusive parents often do not start to get help until they are involved in the legal system.

If a Parent Asks for Your Help

If a parent is afraid she will be abusive or wants help with an abuse problem, refer her to your local Parents Anonymous organization if there is one. Suggest a counseling agency, social service agency, or the state child abuse agency as alternative choices. Keep the telephone numbers of Parents Anonymous and the other agencies handy in case such a request comes up. You may want to offer to be present when the parent makes the call to be supportive. Remember that admitting a weakness and beginning to change is a big, scary step for anyone.

Resources

Adult Books and Articles

Bailey, Patti. *Sexual Abuse Prevention Curricula: Where to Begin a Resource Guide 1986*. Oregon Chapter NCPCA, 1912 SW Sixth, Room 120, Portland, OR 97201. (Cost is $5.00 including shipping.)

Broadhurst, Diane D. *The Educator's Role in the Prevention and Treatment of Child Abuse and Neglect*. U.S. Department of Health and Human Services, 1984. (Single copies are available for free from: Superintendent of Documents, U.S. Government Printing Office/Consigned Branch, Washington, DC 20402.)

Ensminger, Jo, et al. *Dealing with Sexual Child Abuse*. Chicago, IL: National Committee for Prevention of Child Abuse, 1978.

Fraser, Brian G. *The Educator and Child Abuse*. Chicago, IL: National Committee for Prevention of Child Abuse, 1977.

Garbarino, James and Garbarino, Anne C. *Emotional Maltreatment of Children*. Chicago, IL: National Committee for Prevention of Child Abuse, 1980.

Gilbert, Neil, et al. *Child Sexual Abuse Prevention: Evaluation of Educational Materials*. Berkeley, CA: Family Welfare Research Group, School of Social Welfare, 1988.

Koblinsky, S. and Behana, N. "Child Sexual Abuse: The Educator's Role in Prevention, Detection, and Intervention." *Young Children*. 39(6) (September 1984): 3-15.

MacFarlane, Kee; Waterman, Jill; et al. *Sexual Abuse of Young Children*. New York: Guilford Press, 1986.

Mrazek, P.B. "Sexual Abuse of Children." *Journal of Child Psychology and Psychiatry and Allied Disciplines* 21 (1980): 91- 95.

Ray-Keil, Alice. "Prevention for Preschoolers: Good, Bad, or Confusing?" *Prevention Notes*. Committee for Children, Seattle, (Spring 1988):

Tower, Cynthia Crosson. *Child Abuse and Neglect: A Teacher's Handbook for Detection, Reporting, and Classroom Management*. Washington, DC: National Education Association, 1984.

Wurman, S. "Child Abuse—Can Educators Be a Part of the Solution?" *Early Childhood Education* 20(1) (Winter 1986-1987): 33-39.

Support Groups

Parents Anonymous. 22330 Hawthorn Boulevard, Suite 208, Torrance, CA 90505. (1-800-421-0353). In California only: (1-800-352-0386).

Sex Abuse Prevention Curricula

Feelings and Your Body. Shelley McFaddin, Coalition for Child Advocacy, PO Box 159, Bellingham, WA 98227.

Personal Safety: Head Start. Marlys Olson, Child Sexual Abuse Prevention Program, Tacoma School District, PO Box 1357, Tacoma, WA 98401.

Preschool Curriculum. Children's Self-Help Project, San Francisco Child Abuse Council, 170 Fell Street, Room 34, San Francisco, CA 94102.

Red Flag, Green Flag Program. Rape and Abuse Crisis Center, PO Box 1655, Fargo, ND 58107.

Talking about Touching with Preschoolers II. Committee for Children, 172 20th Ave., Seattle, WA 98122.

Part VII
Working with Other Staff

1. Difficult Bosses

2. Problems Working with Assistants or Volunteers

3. Concerns about Co-workers

1. Difficult Bosses

Fortunately, there are more supportive and reasonable bosses in the early childhood field than there are difficult bosses. Perhaps this is because most people drawn to the field are nurturing, caring people. However, like any profession, there are a great number of supervisors who do not manage other adults well.

Many supervisors in our field have proven their worth as teachers and moved up into supervisory positions with little knowledge or training in personnel management. Like the staff they supervise, they typically are overworked, underpaid, and stretched to capacity. They may really desire to be more flexible or responsive with their staff, but the leaky roof just has to take priority over a teacher's concern about a child.

This does not necessarily mean that you should just accept a poor relationship between you and your boss or accept difficult working conditions. There are many things you can do, as suggested in this chapter.

Preventing Problems

➤ Know the management style you work under best. You may prefer to be basically left alone and given a great deal of autonomy, or you may prefer to get a great deal of direction from a supervisor.

➤ During your initial interview when applying for a new position, ask your potential supervisor questions that will reveal her style of managing. If her style is very different from what you prefer, determine if you can accept the discrepancy before taking the position.

➤ In the interview, ask your supervisor about her short-term and long-term goals for the organization. (This will help you determine how well your goals fit with hers.) Make sure your teaching style and your values will be accepted and supported by your boss before accepting the position.

➤ During your first weeks on the job, discretely ask your new co-workers about the strengths, weaknesses, and idiosyncrasies of your boss. Use

that information to stay on the good side of your boss.

➤ Make your supervisor aware of the wonderful things you are doing in your classroom. Give her samples of your children's art work for her office. Offer her some of the good food your children make in a cooking project. If you do special projects for holidays, ask one of the children to volunteer to make something for your supervisor. Most children enjoy this and especially enjoy presenting it to her.

➤ Remember that bosses need strokes as much as anyone. When your boss does something you appreciate, let her know.

➤ Request regular individual meetings with her to discuss concerns and problems before they become crises. If there are no problems to discuss use the time to get and give positive feedback.

Dealing with Existing Problems

➤ Talk to your co-workers who seem to get along well with your boss to determine how they do this. You are sure to get some good ideas. Whenever you have a complaint or concern, request to meet with your supervisor at a time that will be good for both

of you. Ask for undivided attention and request that phone calls be held. Come into the meeting with at least two reasonable ideas for solving the concern.

➤ Do not circumvent your boss and go to her

supervisor or to the board of directors unless this is absolutely necessary (she violates personnel policies or does something illegal). If you must talk to her supervisors, be absolutely certain your allegations are correct, and have proof to offer.

➤ Accept the fact that you probably will not change your boss, so work on ways that you can change your own behavior or your reactions. For example, if your boss demands more paperwork than you think is necessary and discussions with your boss have not solved the problem, find ways to do the work quickly and efficiently. Don't waste time and energy complaining or being angry about the foibles of your boss.

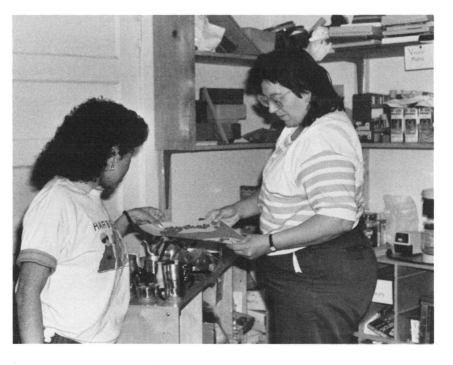

When You Have a New Boss

➤ If there is a change in supervisors, ask to meet individually with the new supervisor to discuss how you can best work together. At this time, clarify your approach to teaching young children and determine her expectations and goals.

The Dictatorial Boss

➤ A boss who is overly controlling, demanding, and unapproachable is probably insecure about the organization and her ability to manage it. She may also believe that her management style will get the best performance out of people. Get to know her on a personal level and offer empathy, understanding, and help. If you do this, she will most likely feel more positive towards you and treat you more kindly.

➤ Speak up for your rights. A dictatorial boss will come to expect compliant and weak behavior from you after a while. When you change your behavior patterns and take control of the interactions between you and your boss, she will also change her behaviors. Seek nurturance and support from friends or co-workers and stop expecting it from your supervisor.

The Ineffectual Boss

➤ Your boss may seem ineffectual because she has more to do than she can possibly handle. Offer to take responsibility for a task that you would like to do and that will give you some additional job experience. For example, volunteer to organize "Week of the Young Child" events, find a trainer for the music workshop, or take responsibility for keeping up the parent bulletin board.

➤ Your boss may be ineffectual because she is not capable of handling the job responsibilities or because she is preoccupied with personal problems. Offer your support and assistance, but take on no more than you can handle. Remember that you may help just by being a good listener.

➤ Discretely keep a written, dated log of specific, observable behaviors that show your supervisor's inability to do her job as it affects you. For example, you might note the following: "6/24—Did not show up for staff meeting. Later, at 2:00 P.M., she said that she forgot." Enlist other co-workers who are concerned to also keep a log. Write at home and keep your log there. If her supervisor or board decides to ask for her resignation, your log will be an important document to support that request. You can also choose to take your log to your supervisor's manager or to the board but be prepared for the probable consequence that you will be fired. If several other staff members join you in the process, your concerns may be taken more seriously and your chance of being fired will decrease.

If All Else Fails

➤ If you have given a great deal of time and effort to getting along with your boss but still find the situation difficult, make a decision to stay or to leave. If you choose to stay, accept the limitations of your boss and find a way to be at peace with your life at work. If your choice is to leave, determine what other employment options you have and begin to discretely seek those out. Remember that you have a right to work in an environment that helps you to be effective in your job. You and the children you teach deserve the best.

Resources

Bernstein, A.J., and Rozen, S.C. *Dinosaur Brains: Dealing with All Those Impossible People at Work.* New York: John Wiley & Sons, 1989.

Lloyd, S.R. "Managing Would Be Easy If. . .." *Exchange* 43, (May 1985): 5-8.

Hochheiser, R.M. *How to Work for a Jerk: Your Success Is the Best Revenge.* New York: Vintage, 1987.

Smith, M.J. *When I Say No, I Feel Guilty.* New York: Bantam, 1975.

2. Problems Working with Assistants or Volunteers

To successfully manage other people, you must keep in mind their level of knowledge and skill, and you accept your responsibility to the people you manage. The suggestions in this chapter will help you give them the knowledge, tools, and support to perform well.

Preventing Problems

➤ Give a thorough orientation to any new people who will be working with you. The time this takes will be worthwhile because ultimately you will have to deal with fewer problems, misunderstandings, or disciplinary meetings.

➤ During the orientation, review your approaches to and reasons for the way you teach, discipline, set your daily schedule, store materials and supplies, work with parents, handle transitions, and deal with crises. Clarify roles and tasks by specifying who will do what and when. Make your expectations and personal priorities known: "Coming on time or a few minutes early is very important to me. Mornings are hectic, and there is so much to be done."

➤ Have some written backup to your orientation. In addition to a staff handbook that outlines general policies and procedures in your program and the job description for the new employee or volunteer, provide written information specific to your class and your procedures.

➤ Give the new employee a copy of the evaluation form that will be used to evaluate her job performance. Make sure that the form is specific and detailed and that it includes such items as the following: talking positively with children, smil-

ing at children, doing tasks willingly as assigned, coming to work regularly, coming to work on time, maintaining confidentiality, being friendly to parents, learning more about child development, and so on.

➤ Request from your supervisor that you be involved in hiring or placing new staff or volunteers. You should be the supervisor of any employees who work under you. This means doing their performance evaluations, recommending or not recommending an end to probation, and being able to terminate them—with final approval of your supervisor. If you do not have these rights but do have the responsibility of making sure your assistant does a good job, you are in an untenable situation. If you have neither the rights nor the responsibility, you will find that working well with your assistant, especially if you have concerns, will be difficult and you will waste time. You will have to continually go to her actual supervisor with your concerns. Talk to your supervisor about restructuring lines of command so that you can have both the rights and the responsibility. Help her to see how this chain of command will benefit her by reducing her workload and stress.

➤ Avoid establishing close personal friendships with any person you supervise. Also avoid having a personal friend hired as your assistant. If there is a problem, friendship makes dealing effectively with the situation difficult. Meet regularly and individually with the people you work with. Use the time to discuss problems, successes, or ideas.

➤ Read books and magazines, attend workshops, and talk to experienced people about good supervisory skills. Most teachers have no training in this area, yet being an effective supervisor can be a big factor in your satisfaction with your job.

➤ Be positive with the people who work with you. Thank them often for what they do. Keep a stack of thank-you cards to use. Remember that a written appreciation, which can be kept and looked at over and over again, has a more lasting impact than a verbal thank-you. Ask your staff what you can do differently to make their jobs easier or more pleasant.

Dealing with Existing Problems

➤ Whether the problem you have with your assistant or volunteer is that she is inefficient and lazy, interferes with what you do, acts inappropriately with the children, doesn't do the tasks assigned to her, or anything else, the best approach to dealing with the problem is basically the same. If there is a serious violation that endangers the safety or well-being of the children or other staff, dismiss her immediately. (Your personnel policies and staff handbook should specify this.) Use the following procedures for less serious offenses:

1. Set up a meeting with her at a time when you both can be relaxed, not have interruptions, and are not rushed for time. Say, "I'm frustrated about not getting the help I need, especially in the morning. Let's set up a time to discuss ways to help with my problem." This is an example of an "I-message." It focuses on how the behavior impacts you rather than on what is wrong with the other person. Because she will not feel threatened or accused, the "I-message" promotes dialogue and two-way communication.

2. Start and end the meeting with positive statements about what the assistant or volunteer does well.

3. Meet together and brainstorm solutions to the problem. Continue to use "I-messages." Make a plan of action for one or two of the best solutions. Write down who will do what and when. (This plan may involve some training, adjustments in the environment, changes in assigned tasks, clarification of roles, or helpful reminders.) Set another time to meet to evaluate how well the plan worked.

4. Give her a great deal of feedback during the time that the plan is in effect. Tell her specifically what she is doing well and what she is not doing well. Bring in someone from outside the classroom who does not supervise her, such as another teacher or board member, to help her.

5. If the problem is not fixed after two meetings and several weeks, write down exactly what she does wrong. Keep these careful, objective notes over a period of time. After meeting with your supervisor to discuss your plan, review the notes with her and place her on probation for two weeks. Tell her that she will be dismissed if the situation does not improve. Ask her what supports she needs to improve. Follow through on the consequences, if necessary. Don't accept a little improvement. Remember that you and the children need and deserve to be with people who will do things well.

6. If the situation does improve, let her know clearly that you appreciate her efforts. Tell her specifically how what she does helps you and put your comments in writing: "Thank you for coming on time and doing your tasks. Mornings are now easy. Everyone is more relaxed and the rest of the day seems to go better too." Let her know that you expect things to stay this way. Move on to dealing with other problems, if there are any.

Resources

Bernstein, A.J., and Rozen, S.C. *Dinosaur Brains: Dealing with All Those Impossible People at Work*. New York: John Wiley & Sons, 1989.

Blanchard, K., and Johnson, S. *The One Minute Manager*. New York: Berkeley, 1987.

Broadwell, M.M. *Supervising Today: A Guide for Positive Leadership*. 2d Ed. New York: John Wiley & Sons, 1986.

Caruso, J.J, and Fawcett, M.T. *Supervision in Early Childhood Education: A Developmental Perspective*. New York: Teachers College Press, 1986.

Child Care Information Exchange. Exchange, PO Box 2890, Redmond, WA 98073. (206-883-9394). (This magazine, published six times a year, is aimed at directors but contains excellent information for teachers who supervise others.)

Jones, E., and Lakin, M.B. "Reflection and Dialogue: Ways to Grow Staff." *Exchange* 48 (Mar 1986): 3-6.

Laney, W.L. *How to Be a Boss in a Hurry: A Primer for New Managers*. Indianapolis: Bobbs-Merrill, 1982.

Lloyd, S.R. "Managing Would Be Easy If. . .." *Exchange* 43, (May 1985): 5-8.

O'Sullivan, B. *Staff Orientation in Early Childhood Programs*. Saint Paul, MN: Toys 'n Things Press, 1987.

Smith, M.J. *When I Say No, I Feel Guilty*. New York: Bantam, 1975.

Viscott, D. "How to Give Constructive Criticism." *Exchange* 49, (May 1986): 25-27.

3. Concerns about Co-workers

You may have co-workers who make your job difficult or who lower the quality of the program because of their poor teaching skills. This puts you in a very tough spot because they typically are your peers and you don't supervise them. But you have a right and a moral duty to express your concerns, as long as you do it tactfully. Antagonizing your co-workers will only be counterproductive. As most people do the best they can with what they know, correcting the problems often means getting more information to your co-workers. This chapter will offer you ways to do this without making your co-workers feel defensive.

Preventing Problems

➤ Establish positive relations with your co-workers. Treat them with respect. Be helpful to them by sharing your materials and ideas without acting superior. Ask for their assistance and ideas without demeaning yourself. Set up a system where each person on staff does a training session in an area in which she feels particularly strong.

➤ When returning from a conference, share what you have learned with other staff members and ask them to share what they have learned. Help organize and participate in staff meetings, training sessions, and social events with other staff members.

➤ Promote a staff retreat where there is a relaxing atmosphere and ample time to solve problems, learn new skills, clarify and agree on a philosophy and program objectives, set exciting goals, eat good food, and have fun. Create a study group to read and discuss new ideas and solutions to shared problems.

➤ Actively work towards continual improvement of communications and relations between you and your co-workers:

• Invite specialists to do team building workshops with staff.

• Think of new and better ways to communicate (mail boxes, active listening skills, a memo system, a phone tree, a sharing time before each staff meeting).

• Streamline communications (consolidate forms).

➤ Work with your supervisor on developing personnel policies and staff evaluations that include such personal capacities as the following: being friendly with other staff, supporting the growth of other staff, working as a team, sharing resources, and so on. (This makes it clear that getting along with co-workers is a vital part of the job.)

Dealing with Existing Problems

Common complaints and concerns teachers have about their co-workers are that they are lazy, incompetent, untrained, too strict, divisive, arrogant, competitive, and devious and that they make more money and can't control their children. Note that these complaints fall into three catagories: problems that affect you directly, problems that affect the program, and problems that reveal differences in teaching styles.

Problems with Co-workers that Affect You Directly

➤ Co-workers who horde supplies or belittle you in front of others create problems that directly affect you, your ability to do your job, and your happiness with your work. When this happens, confront the person directly. Although this is difficult, avoiding this step may create more problems in the end. Say, "I would like to meet with you. I feel hurt by remarks you made, and I would like your help in solving my problem." Stating your feelings in this way is called using "I-messages."

➤ Meet at a time and place conducive to relaxation, privacy, and no interruptions. Sit side by side, not across from each other. Continue to use "I-messages." Explain how her actions made you feel and ask what her intention was. Be very objective: "I felt put down when you said, 'That's not a good idea.' Did I hear you wrong or am I misunderstanding you?" After her response, specifically ask for what you want and state the consequences: "I want you to make supportive statements or say nothing about me in front of other staff. If you put me down again, I will make a formal complaint to our supervisor."

➤ If you get a denial, no cooperation, or no improvement in behaviors, follow through on your stated consequence. Keep written records documenting objectively what the person did and when. Talk with other staff members to determine if they have similar concerns. If so, ask them to keep written records, too.

➤ Use all legal and appropriate channels to stop the problem. Keep written documentation of all your meetings and the responses you received. If your supervisor clearly intends to do nothing about the concern, go to her superiors (board of directors, and so on) and/or to a lawyer, if appropriate. A lawyer can help you determine if your rights are being violated because of sexual harassment, racial bias, or other reason. Be prepared for almost certain negative consequences from your supervisor and others if you do this.

➤ If all else fails, decide whether you can live with this troublesome co-worker or not. Either find ways to be happy in your job or start looking for a better situation.

Problems with Co-workers that Affect the Program

Certain concerns you have about others may involve how they interact with children or parents. These concerns do not affect you directly. However, you feel compelled to do something, because you care about children, families, and the reputation of your program.

➤ Offer your assistance in a supportive way: "I noticed you had some difficulty with the children in the gym. I used to have the same problem. Would you like some ideas that might help?"

➤ If the concerns continue, meet with your supervisor and ask her to observe. Make no accusations and do not try to get the other person in trouble. State objective facts about what you saw and why you are concerned: "Two children in Helen's class were sword fighting in the gym this morning with pointy sticks. She told them to stop, but when they continued, she took no further action. I was very concerned for their safety, so I gave them some foam swords to use instead. It was difficult for my class to wait in the hallway while I did that. I think it might be helpful to Helen if you observed her and gave her some feedback."

➤ If the supervisor does not act to improve the situation, take notes of what you observe and bring them to her supervisor or to appropriate authorities if there are direct health, safety, or well-being concerns. Get additional written evidence of problems from other concerned staff members.

Differences in Teaching Styles and Other Problems

You may have a very different approach toward teaching young children than other staff in your program. Perhaps other teachers use direct teaching methods, worksheets, few choices for children, harsh discipline, rewards and punishment, or long periods of teaching the whole group at once.

➤ Suggest to your supervisor that the program develop and adopt a unifed philosophy on teaching young children and some guidelines for carrying out that philosophy. Recommend that a group of teachers work together with your supervisor to develop the philosophy and guidelines that will be approved by the whole staff. Volunteer to be a part of the group. Suggest that the program examine the NAEYC guidelines for developmentally appro-

priate practices (Bredekamp 1987) as one source for developing the philosophy.

➤ If other concerns you have do not threaten the health, safety, or well-being of the children, then you may have to either accept your co-workers or find work in a program that has a greater emphasis on quality.

➤ Remember that disparities between teachers in their abilities, energy levels, and motivation will exist in almost all programs. You can reduce these disparities by being helpful and supportive to others and by creating excitement and enthusiasm through the suggestions in *Preventing Problems* in this chapter.

Resources

Bernstein, A.J., and Rozen, S.C. *Dinosaur Brains: Dealing with All Those Impossible People at Work.* New York: John Wiley & Sons,1989.

Baron, *Understanding Human Relations: A Practical Guide to People at Work.* Needham Heights, MA: Allyn & Bacon,1985.

Bredekamp, S., ed. *Developmentally Appropriate Practice in Early Childhood Programs Serving Children From Birth through Age 8.* Washington, DC: NAEYC,1987.

Harvey C., and Johns, N. "Criteria for Developing Strong Caregiving Teams." *Exchange* 63 (October 1988): 33-35.

Jones, E., and Lakin, M.B. "Reflection and Dialogue: Ways to Grow Staff." *Exchange* 48 (March 1986): 3-6.

Jorde-Bloom, P. *A Great Place to Work: Improving Conditions for Staff in Young Children's Programs.* Washington, DC: NAEYC, 1988.

Lloyd, S.R. "Managing Would Be Easy If . . . " *Exchange* 43, (May 1985): 5-8.

Neugebauer, R. "When Friction Flares—Dealing with Staff Conflict." *Exchange* 65, (February 1989): 3-6.

Scallan, P.N. "Teachers Coaching Teachers: Development from Within." *Exchange* 58, (November 1987): 3-6.

Scallan, P.N. "How to Implement a Coaching Program in Your Center." *Exchange* 59, (January 1988): 35-37.

Part VIII
Your Own Needs

1. Not Enough Time

2. Burned Out/Stressed Out

3. Underpaid

4. In Over Your Head

1. Not Enough Time

Although this is a particularly difficult problem for people who work in full-day programs, almost everyone working in early childhood classrooms feels short of time. Often, this is because of a lack of funds to pay people adequately for the time they need to plan and organize.

Dealing with Existing Problems

Short on Planning Time

➤ If you never have enough time, you may not be asking for the time you need to plan and get organized. In order to improve your situation, assert your needs to your family, co-workers, or supervisor. Remember that planning and organizing are essential to doing your job well and staying in control.

➤ Plan classroom activities at least two weeks in advance to allow time to gather supplies, arrange field trips, and so on.

➤ Use an effective planning tool to reduce the time and effort needed for planning. Trying to work with a generic form may result in inadequate planning. Find or develop a lesson plan form that works for you. The form should reflect your classroom schedule, priorities, and goals.

Time Seems to Slip Away

➤ To manage your time well, set personal goals for yourself and for your teaching. If you set a goal of obtaining a college degree, the time you spend working towards that goal will be time well spent. Goals for your teaching might include encouraging the children to be more independent or involving them more actively in music activities. Not having goals will make you feel frustrated—like time is slipping away from you.

➤ Choose one realistic goal to work towards and achieve it. You will feel successful and in control.

Too Many Committees and Meetings

➤ Preschool teachers often try to be all things to all people. For your own mental health, limit your activities and commitments to what you can realistically handle and to only those which are very important to you. Learn to say no.

Rushed and Hassled

➤ If possible, go to work about an hour early to organize yourself and the day's activities and to do some planning. Remember that most people work better and are more efficient in the morning and that feeling ready and prepared when children start arriving makes the whole day go well. Note that once you are involved with the children, getting any time for yourself is difficult.

Disorganized

➤ Keep a list of things to do. Prioritize your list each day by highlighting the items that have to be accomplished that day. Each day, highlight at least one item that moves you towards a goal. Keep the list with you at all times so you can jot down a note when you need to.

➤ Use a calendar or appointment book to write down future meetings and deadlines. Refer to it daily.

Procrastinating

➤ Break down large tasks into small steps and accomplish them one day at a time. For example, to make more games for your classroom can be a big, time-consuming job, but if you plan to make one game a week, the task will be manageable. Design the game one day, make the board the next day, make the pieces and directions another day, and laminate the game on another. In a month, you will have four new games.

Too Much to Do

➤ Delegate some tasks and responsibilities to co-workers, assistants, or supervisors. For example, if you are a lead teacher and have an assistant, she may enjoy the challenge of planning and carrying out all music activities, especially if she has some talent in that area. You will be doing her a favor, while reducing your workload.

➤ Be careful not to delegate all the things you dislike doing. If you dislike them, your assistant problably will, too. Negotiate task assignments to make sure that you both have enjoyable tasks that are opportunities for growth.

2. Burned Out/Stressed Out

The entire field of education is underfunded, but in early childhood education, the problem is severe. It is ironic that young children who need the most funding, because smaller class sizes and more teachers per pupil are required, receive the least. At least forty-one percent of preschool teachers leave their jobs each year. Teachers of young children everywhere feel overworked and underpaid, so your feeling burned out is no surprise. Long hours, tremendous responsibilities, and the high level of skill needed to do the work combined with low salaries, little respect from society for the work, and small budgets for supplies will almost guarantee burnout.

Preventing Problems

Get Involved

➤ Get involved politically to advocate for more funds from your agency, local government, or the federal government to help reduce your feeling of hopelessness. You will be actively doing something about the problem. This is also a good way to meet people with whom you will have much in common. Political work can be stressful too, however, and may contribute to burnout, if you take on more than you have time for or if you hope to accomplish more than is realistic.

Find a Support Group

➤ Being involved in associations that sponsor workshops, conferences, and networking meetings can help by giving you support for your feelings and frustrations. Be assured that many teachers share common concerns and have similar problems. Much can be gained by sharing them and discussing solutions that have worked. Your involvement in promoting professionalism through these associations can bring a great deal of satisfaction. (To locate your nearest chapter of the National Association for the Education of Young

Children, call 1-800-424-2460 or in Washington, DC, 202-232-8777.)

Learn Something/Teach Something

➤ Attend workshops and classes to give you fresh new ideas, as well as to validate your current abilities. Visit teachers in other programs to learn new ideas and to connect with peers. Request time to do this from your supervisor as part of your training. (The expense to your program of paying a substitute for the day is well worth the return in increased quality.)

➤ Offer to give a class or workshop yourself to fellow staff members, at a conference or through a local college. You probably have a particular area of expertise or a special skill that others will love to learn. If you do not, cultivate an area of expertise that is particularly interesting to you. For example, become the local expert on creative dramatics for children by reading all you can about it, talking to experts, attending classes, and trying out many ideas with your class.

(For more information about early childhood education associations and advocacy groups, read the chapter, "Being an Advocate for Families, Children, the Profession, and Yourself" on pages 182 to 186.)

Let Your Environment Nurture You

➤ Set up a classroom that reflects your taste and aesthetic values, that is fun to be in, that is pleasant to look at, and that has warm and soothing colors. This will be a classroom you will want to return to everyday. It is worth the extra time and effort to carefully set up your classroom and to make periodic changes, which make you feel comfortable being there.

➤ Provide yourself with a space that you can call your own even if it is just a shelf. This is your private area. You can set it up as neatly or as sloppily as you like and it can contain your important materials and books. (One teacher keeps a jar of hot peppers in her area as a daily treat in the afternoons.) A small file cabinet, just for your own use, which contains activity ideas, notes, and articles from magazines, will make your job easier.

➤ Keep one comfortable adult-sized chair in the room. Constant sitting on small, hard children's chairs causes stress. Although being on the same level with the children is important, an occasional stint on your chair, if only during nap time or to read to a child, will be good for your health.

Take a Break

➤ Get out of the classroom and take a lunch break everyday. Take a brisk walk, jog, exercise, go window-shopping, or read a good novel. Give yourself a mental vacation and get a change of scenery in the middle of each day. Remember that this is vital to maintaining good mental health and preventing burnout.

Take Care of Your Health

➤ Start an exercise group with your co-workers. Eat healthy foods and sleep as much as you need. Stay home when you are sick. If your energy level is good, you will be better able to meet the challenges of the day.

➤ A hurt or aching back is an occupational hazard for teachers of young children. Working with a bad back will increase your stress tremendously. Avoid back problems by doing the following:

- When standing for long periods, bend your knees slightly, keep your legs apart (directly under the shoulders), have one foot slightly in front of the other, and distribute your weight evenly over both legs.

- When sitting for long periods, put your feet on a low box so that your knees are slightly higher than your hips. To avoid leaning forward in your chair or sitting on the edge, push the chair close to the table or desk.

- Reach up to get something from a high place by standing on a step designed for that purpose. Keep your knees bent slightly.

- When standing at a sink to wash your hands, bend your knees and rest them against the cabinet below the sink. If the space below the sink is open, put a low box there and put one foot up while washing.

- Push, rather than pull, heavy items.

- When lifting a child, get down in a squat position with the knee of one leg on the floor, and put your other leg forward, bent at the knee with the foot flat on the floor. Lift with your legs and keep the child close to your body. Or, bend your knees so that you are in a slight squat position and have the child jump up into your arms (from a standing, not running, position) when you both count to three.

Don't Work Alone

Do you have an assistant? In programs for young children there should be at least two capable adults in every classroom. Guiding children, maintaining order, and individualizing are almost impossible with only one adult, but of most importance are safety concerns. If there is an emergency to take care of, someone needs to be with the hurt child while another person is in charge of the rest of the children. Tracking down a supervisor or another adult at this time may leave children unsupervised.

➤ Working with other adults also helps keep you from burning out. You will have someone with whom to discuss ideas and problems. If at all possible, avoid working in programs where there is only one person in a classroom for children under six years of age. If avoiding this situation is not possible, work on ways of getting an assistant. Consider the following ideas: parent volunteers, community volunteers (RSVP, Foster Grandparents, Green Thumb), and student helpers. Or, assist the program director to restructure the budget to include another position.

Get Control

The lack of control over numerous aspects of your job can be a huge source of stress. All adults need to feel that they can try out their ideas, take chances, learn from mistakes, and make changes. Programs using preplanned curriculums with daily activities spelled out take that sense of control away from the teacher. This is also true where teachers have to accept whatever materials and equipment are supplied to them.

➤ If you are in a situation where either of these is true, work cooperatively with the powers that be to get some changes made. Request a small monthly budget with which you can purchase supplies. (This is a reasonable request and might be a place to start to gain more control.) Note that a flexible curriculum that has relevance to your particular group of children is a vital part of a quality preschool. If two children in your class have mothers who are about to give birth, you need to be able to do a unit on babies. Your supervisor should be able to see this as an issue of improving the quality of the program. If she cannot or if she does not have control over the decision, consider implementing your ideas anyway. Many teachers finish the required curriculum quickly and minimally and then use the extra time to implement their own activities. As many early childhood programs do give teachers a great deal of control over their classrooms, consider taking your skills and talents elsewhere.

Limit Yourself

➤ Know your own limitations. Preschool teachers are generally very giving, caring, generous people, but sometimes they have trouble saying no. Involving yourself in the role of therapist for a troubled family or spending your hours after work helping a needy family find resources are noble things to do, but not required. You can easily burn out by taking on more than you can cope with or have skills for. You will then be less able to be a good teacher. Being a good teacher is the first obligation to yourself, your children, and their families.

➤ Remember that overly involving yourself in the lives of your families and children may not ultimately be helpful to them because they can develop a dependency on you and never learn to solve problems for themselves.

Set Goals

➤ Everyone needs to feel like she is going somewhere, heading in a direction. Set goals as a way to achieve that feeling. You will be much less likely to burn out. You may want to be a head teacher, education coordinator, director, owner, teacher of older children, a consultant, a senator, or a better preschool teacher. Whatever the goal, have one, write down the steps needed to achieve it (get an advanced degree, read one professional book each month, and so on), and begin working towards it. Everyday do something that will bring you closer to your goal, even if all you have time for is reading one page of a book.

Experiment

➤ Take some risks by trying out new and different ideas with your class. Evaluate the results and discuss them with co-workers to determine what worked, what can be improved, or what needs to be scrapped completely. For example, try a completely new curriculum approach, change your schedule, create an "automobile service station" dramatic play area, or create a theme around television— visit a TV studio, teach critical viewing skills, create a TV show in the classroom, discuss alternatives to watching TV.

Have Fun

➤ Making your job more fun may be the single most important thing you can do to prevent burnout. Some of the many ways you can do this are:

- Have regular parties with other staff.

- Use humor (not sarcasm) with your children.

- Share the funny things your children say and do with parents and other staff.

- Sing funny songs.

- Get silly. Paint your face (use a cold cream base and add coloring), have a pajama party, make footprint pictures, finger-paint a huge mural, have a fancy dress-up day and set up an "expensive restaurant" dramatic play, have a backwards day when you reverse your schedule and routines.

➤ There isn't a better job in the world for having a fabulously fun time than teaching young children. Just think, you could be working in an office all day!

Resources

Aronson, S.S. "Health Update: Health Concerns for Caregivers." *Exchange* 54 (March 1987): 33-37.

Aronson, S.S. "Health Update: Coping with the Physical Requirements of Caregiving." *Exchange* 55 (May 1987): 39-40.

Greenberg, H. *Coping with Job Stress*. New York: Prentice Hall, 1980.

Health in Day Care: A Manual for Day Care Providers, Washington, DC: Georgetown University Child Development Center from a grant from ACYF and MCH, 1986.

Jorde Bloom, Paula. *Avoiding Burnout: Strategies for Managing Time, Space, and People in Early Childhood Education*. Washington, DC: Acropolis Books, 1982.

Modigliani, Kathy. "Twelve Reasons for the Low Wages in Child Care." *Young Children* 43(3) (March 1988): 14-15.

Townley, K.F.; Thornburg, K.R.; and Wise, G.W. "Burnout: Causes, Consequences, and Cures." *Exchange* 48 (March 1986): 31-34.

Whitebook, Marcy, et al. *Raising Salaries: Strategies That Work*. Berkeley: Child Care Employee Project, 1988.

Willer, Barbara A. *The Growing Crisis in Child Care: Quality, Compensation, and Affordability in Early Childhood Programs*. Washington, DC: NAEYC, 1987.

3. Underpaid

As described in the chapter "Burned Out / Stressed Out," being underpaid is a chronic condition of working in the field of early childhood education. In a report of 1985 data, child care workers were found to be the second lowest paid profession for the level of education they have. Clergy were first (National Committee on Pay Equity 1987).

> *Accept the fact that wages are low, have been low for many years, and will most likely continue to be low. This does not mean that you should be apathetic. Without many people becoming actively involved in lobbying for better wages conditions will definitely never improve. This does mean coming to terms with living on less, for now, and finding satisfaction from the work you do. This is important for your own mental health. (For more information about ways to be involved in improving salaries, see "Burned Out / Stressed Out" on pages 169 to 174, and "Being an Advocate for Families, Children, the Profession, and Yourself" on pages 182 to 186.)*

Dealing with Existing Problems

➤ Make a list of the positive things about your job. Include the things that most satisfy you. The list might include the following:

- I learn a lot about myself from the children.
- I get joy from seeing happy children.
- I know the children love, trust, and respect me.
- I get strokes from satisfied parents.
- I am doing a great service to society by keeping children safe and happy and by helping them learn and grow.
- I am helping secure a bright future for society by helping to bring up well-adjusted children.
- I am good at what I'm doing.
- I have fun at my job.
- I have the respect of my boss, co-workers, and parents.

➤ Keep the list where you can read it every morning or when you are feeling depressed about your low wages.

➤ Many early childhood educators need to cut expenses by sharing housing; clipping coupons; using public transportation or car pooling; shopping for sales; and frequenting discount stores, flea markets, and garage sales.

➤ Perhaps there are other sources of income you can find to supplement your current income without burning yourself out. Writing or consulting about what you know, starting a small business out of your home, or obtaining a part-time sales job are some possibilities.

Better Paying Jobs in Early Childhood Education

➤ If staying in the field and earning more money are both important to you, set some career goals for yourself.

➤ Opening your own program may be a goal for you. The experience and expertise you gain as a preschool teacher will be a great asset as an owner. Although few people make very much money as child care/nursery school owners, the potential is there. You often need to own several sites (expanding after you have been successful), before you can earn substantially more than working for someone else. However, running your own business based on your own ideas and methods can be tremendously rewarding.

➤ There are some well paying jobs in the field, but they often require a master's degree or more, specialized training, and years of experience. These include the following: early childhood education instructor, trainer, consultant, writer, editor, publisher, center director, education coordinator, program administrator, researcher, state certifier of child care centers, and salesperson of preschool supplies and equipment. There may be a job here that you wish to aspire to, although even these jobs usually do not pay as well as similar jobs in other fields.

➤ Preschool teaching can also lead you into higher paying jobs in closely related fields, although some specialized training will most likely be necessary. Preschool teaching requires a wide variety of skills, and these provide good training for related careers. These include the following: social worker, business owner, principal, human resource spe-cialist, family life instructor, parenting instructor, recreation director, extension agent, journalist, politician, therapist (also psychologist and counselor), children's book writer (also editor and publisher), community education director, child development specialist, health educator, public relations director, pediatric nurse, and pediatrician.

Grants

➤ You may want to get involved in helping your program write grants proposals. Many programs have been able to increase salaries and expand job opportunities by obtaining grants for setting up new programs or for expanding existing programs. Obtain grants from the federal government, your state or local government, foundations, businesses, and agencies.

➤ Develop projects with other organizations in your community, such as mental health programs, parent education agencies, child nutrition programs, or programs for children with handicaps. Agencies that give grants usually prefer projects in which two or more agencies collaborate to help children and families. When you collaborate, more expertise is available, services are consolidated, and dollars can be stretched.

Resources

Carney, Lilah Christina. "Postscript: Reassessing the Teacher's Status in This Society." In *Joys and Risks In Teaching Young Children*, edited by Elizabeth Jones. Pasadena, CA: Pacific Oaks, 1978.

Modigliani, Kathy. "Twelve Reasons for the Low Wages in Child Care." *Young Children* 43(3) (March 1988): 14-15.

Seaver, Judith, et al. *Careers with Young Children*. Washington, DC: NAEYC, 1979.

Whitebook, Marcy, et al. *Raising Salaries: Strategies That Work*. Berkeley: Child Care Employee Project, 1988.

Wolf, Dennise, ed. "Being Teachers." *Beginnings* 3(1) (Spring 1986).

4. In Over Your Head

If you work with young children and have less experience or training than you need to do the job well, you are not alone. Many people started out that way and learned on the job. Experienced teachers often look back on their first year or two on the job and wonder how they and the children ever survived. Many teachers have found the same problem happening when they switch positions to work with a different group of families or in a different setting (such as moving from a half-day toddler program for children of middle-class families to a full-day four-year-old program for low income families), even with many years of experience.

Dealing with Existing Problems

➤ Don't muddle through by pretending that you know what you are doing. Accept that you will make mistakes. People who know their limitations and actively work at overcoming them get far more respect than people who make similar mistakes but act like they are skilled.

➤ Ask for help from co-workers who are competent. They will most likely be flattered by your request and be glad to offer suggestions and direct assistance. Other teachers in your own program are apt to know practical ways of dealing with problems specific to your situation.

➤ Ask for more training from your supervisor. She will probably be very willing to help you. Supervisors sometimes put training needs on the bottom of their priority list (coping with numerous crises comes first) but are responsive when asked directly.

➤ Read books and magazine/journal articles. Specialty publishers, libraries, and bookstores are carrying more and better books about early childhood education. (See "Being an Advocate for Families, Children, the Profession and Yourself," on pages 182 to 186, for a list of magazines and journals.)

➤ Delegate some of your work to other co-workers or supervisors. Ask others to take on some tasks that are particularly difficult for you while you learn ways to do them better. (This will free up some time and energy to train yourself on other aspects of your job.)

➤ Develop a network of support people who can help you solve problems and who can answer questions. Include among these people local health professionals, early childhood education instructors, trainers, consultants, and experienced teachers. Although most of these people charge for their services, they often are willing to help occasionally for a short time for no charge or for a small favor in return from you.

➤ Have confidence in your ability to learn and to improve. Take the pressure off by giving yourself two years to gain the skills and knowledge you need to be a good teacher by attending classes, workshops, reading, asking people with expertise, and so on.

Part IX
Promoting Yourself as a Professional

1. Protecting Yourself from Being Accused of Abuse

2. Making Tough Ethical Decisions

3. Being an Advocate for Families, Children, the Profession, and Yourself

1. Protecting Yourself from Being Accused of Abuse

Unfortunately, teachers of young children have to deal with this concern. The reality is that abuse of young children is too prevalent, that it does happen in early childhood programs (rarely), and that the concern of parents and professionals about this issue will always be there.

The good news is that the concern is not as out of proportion as it was in the early- to mid-eighties and that you can do many things to reduce the concern. Male teachers need to be particularly vigilant about doing these things, as they are more likely to be accused of abuse.

Be Pro-Active

"The best defense is a good offense." This may be an old sports cliche but it is very helpful for this situation. You can take the offensive on the issue of abuse.

➤ Ask your supervisor about the procedures used, the role of the program, and the insurance coverage available if a staff person is accused of abuse. Find out the procedures that the program would use if a parent made an accusation of abuse by a teacher. If the policies seem unfair or inadequate to protect you or other staff if falsely accused of abuse, work with your co-workers to have the policies changed. (The resources on page 176 have detailed examples of reasonable policies.)

➤ Consider obtaining your own personal insurance policy. Contact your insurance agent, independent broker, or the National Association for the Education of Young Children (NAEYC), 1-800-424-2460, about such policies.

➤ Inform parents verbally and in writing about your policies and procedures to prevent abuse in your classroom.

➤ Inform parents about the facts: A child is less likely to be abused in an early childhood program than in her own home. The number of teachers who are abusive is extremely small. (Finkelhor 1988).

➤ Tell parents about your professional background, including work history and education. Request that your supervisor inform parents that

references are thoroughly checked on any staff member who is hired.

➤ Teach children to protect themselves from being abused. Do this by reading books, using curriculums designed for that purpose, using puppets, and doing role plays. (See the resource list in "Parents Who May Be Abusive to Their Children" on pages 154 to 157.) Let parents know that you are doing this as well as how and when you are doing it. Hold a meeting beforehand for any interested parents to discuss all the issues surrounding abuse prevention for children.

➤ Post the phone number of your local Parent's Anonymous chapter in a prominent place.

➤ Make sure that all parents know that they are welcome to visit or participate in your classroom at any time. Explain that calling ahead is appreciated but not necessary. This open door policy assures parents that no harm can be done to their children behind their backs.)

➤ Educate yourself about the signs and symptoms of abuse. Report abuse right away. (There have been a number of cases where a teacher has been blamed for the abuse of a child that was done by someone else.)

➤ Make an official accident report of any injury a child has to the genital or anal area. Note that bruises caused by playground injuries can be misconstrued as abuse.

➤ Insist on having another person working with

you at all times. Insist that your volunteer or assistant teacher never works alone with the group of children. Join with another teacher if you find yourself alone with only a few children (typically at the beginning or end of the day). At naptime, avoid being alone if at all possible or at least keep yourself visible to other staff. This will protect you and other staff from false accusations of abuse, as there will always be a witness, and will prevent anyone who works with you from committing an abusive act.

➤ As the majority of abusive incidents in child care programs happen in the toileting area (Finkelhor 1988), make sure that this area is open and visible, that it cannot be locked, that adults do not go in there if this is not necessary, and that children stay out of adult bathrooms.

➤ Do not take children away from the school or center setting unless for a prearranged, approved field trip with permission from each parent. Do not take a child to an isolated, private area of the building.

➤ Work hard toward positive, open, clear, and trusting communications with all your parents.

If You Are Falsely Accused

For those who have been falsely accused of abuse, the situation was highly traumatic, emotionally wrenching, and continues to stay with them. Many of them have left teaching and feel very bitter. Because the experience is so awful, implementing the prevention strategies discussed above is extremely important.

If you are accused of child abuse, your actions will be greatly limited by what you are told to do by state authorities and your supervisor. During an investigation, you may be asked to take a leave with pay, be given office work, or have restrictions placed on you while at work. You can't be fired or forced to take an unpaid leave unless you are actually convicted of a crime or a supervisor witnessed the abuse.

➤ Get a lawyer. You will need one in almost all cases. Some programs have insurance to help you pay for this, but many do not.

➤ Avoid discussing the situation with anyone or gathering evidence in your defense without the advise of a lawyer experienced in these matters. If you go about defending yourself in the wrong way, you could hurt your case.

➤ Demand the confidentiality from staff and supervisors to which you are entitled. (Gossip will make matters worse.) Keep yourself private. Do not talk to the press, police, or parents directly. Do not attempt to publicly defend yourself. Discuss the situation only with those in authority who are experienced and knowledgeable about these matters (state children's protective service) or to people who can be helpful and supportive.

➤ Seek the advice and support of someone who has been through a similar situation. Deal with the isolation by seeking support from friends, relatives, and a professional counselor experienced with abuse cases. If other parents call you to give you support, suggest that they form a support group with other parents and start a legal defense fund.

➤ Ask for clarification of policies and procedures and know your rights every step of the way. Your lawyer or state agency doing the investigation will be able to tell what those rights are. Find out exactly what you are being accused of, by whom, and based on what evidence.

➤ Write down, while still fresh in your memory, exactly what you were doing and who was there during the time that you are accused of abuse. Also write down everything you can remember about your interactions with the parents and the child and their interactions with each other.

➤ Avoid taking out any resentments you have against your supervisor, board of directors, or co-workers. Don't quit your job or burn any bridges. Be assured that the best way to heal from this is to stay around long enough to get your reputation back.

➤ Once you are cleared, ask for the support you need from your supervisors and co-workers to begin the healing process. You and your supervisor should meet with all the parents to explain what happened, to answer questions, to ease anxiety, and to discuss what will be said to the children.

➤ Speak to the state authorities after you have been cleared to find out any missing information you were not allowed to know during the investigation.

Resources

"Abuse and Neglect: The Positive Role of Child Care." *Beginnings* 2(3) (Fall 1985): Issue contains numerous articles on the topic.

Finkelhor, D., et al. *Sexual Abuse in Day Care: A National Study*. Durham, NH: University of New Hampshire, 1988.

Stephens. K. "The First National Study of Sexual Abuse in Child Care: Findings and Recommendations." *Child Care Information Exchange* 60 (March 1988): 9-12.

Strickland, J., and Reynolds, S. "The New Untouchables: Risk Management for Child Abuse in Child Care— Before Establishing Procedures." *Child Care Information Exchange* 63 (October 1988): 19-21.

Strickland, J., and Reynolds, S. "The New Untouchables: Risk Management for Child Abuse in Child Care— Policies and Procedures." *Child Care Information Exchange* 64 (December 1988): 33-36.

Strickland, J., and Reynolds, S. "The New Untouchables: Risk Management for Child Abuse in Child Care— Additional Strategies for Supervisors and Working with Parents." *Child Care Information Exchange* 65 (February 1989): 37-39.

Strickland, J., and Reynolds, S. "The New Untouchables: Risk Management for Child Abuse in Child Care— New Laws and Trends." *Child Care Information Exchange* 66 (April 1989): 51-55.

Wilson, C., and Steppe, S.C. *Investigating Sexual Abuse in Day Care*. Washington, DC: Child Welfare League of America, 1986.

2. Making Tough Ethical Decisions

A major hallmark of a professional is the ability to confront an ethical dilemma and make a good decision about what to do based on a sound code of ethics. The National Association for the Education of Young Children has developed such a code (Feeney and Kipnis 1989).

Early childhood teachers face tough ethical decisions almost daily. Some examples are the following: Do you force a child to stay on her cot during naptime even though she is clearly not tired? If so, for how long? Do you physically restrain a child who is hurting another child, and if so how much force can you use? Do you follow a parent's wishes that her child not take a nap because she doesn't fall asleep at home until 11:00 P.M., even though she is very tired at nap time? Do you follow a mother's request that the child's father not pick up the child, because he has been abusive, until a restraining order can be obtained? Do you follow a father's request that the child not be seen by his estranged wife because she has threatened to kidnap the child? Do you allow a child to use a bathroom inside the building alone or accompany her, leaving the children who are playing outside by themselves? Do you report your own program to state authorities if the supervisor tells you to do something that violates licensing laws?

Dealing with Ethical Dilemmas

The following recommendations are for your consideration when dealing with ethical dilemmas. They are meant as helpful guidelines. Ultimately you have to do what you believe is right.

➤ Remember that your children's health, safety, and well-being are your main priorities. Choose a child's well-being over the wishes of a parent or a supervisor or the smooth running of your class-room. Above all, do no harm to the child.

➤ Carefully determine the best way to put children first without hurting yourself. Note that licensing standards are established to protect the health and well-being of children and therefore any violation has to be reported. You can do this, however, without giving your name, so your supervisor cannot retaliate. Consider that your own

health, well-being, and job security are important considerations in making an ethical decision. Anything that jeopardizes these is not a good choice. Not only will you suffer but your children will be harmed because you will be less effective in your job.

➤ Work out a compromise or alternative solution whenever possible, if it will not harm the child. Note that a third or fourth option often can be found, although these typically involve more work. For example, if a parent asks you to keep her child awake during naptime, discuss the possibility of allowing the child to sleep for half of the naptime while the parent enforces a regular, reasonable bed-time at home. Gradually increase the amount of time the child naps while the parent gradually makes the bedtime earlier. If this kind of compromise cannot be worked out, the bottom line is that you cannot keep the child awake because this is harmful to her. When refusing, explain clearly and graciously to parents your reasons, based on your professional knowledge.

➤ Follow the letter of the law, unless the child will be harmed by it. Recall that people with high ethical standards, many of whom have come to be our heros (Gandhi, Martin Luther King, Jr.), have sometimes had to break unjust laws because they believed the laws themselves hurt people. If possible, however, do not let yourself be put in this position, especially when acting on behalf of your organization or your school. If a parent cannot legally ask you to stop her spouse from picking up their child, then you should not keep the spouse from the child. Instead, ask the parent to keep the child home until a restraining order is obtained or agree that you will call her if the spouse shows up (but you will not stop the spouse). Do not allow yourself to be put into a lose-lose dilemma of breaking the law or harming the child. No one has the right to force that on you.

➤ Choose the course that will cause the least harm to the fewest numbers of children. One solution to the dilemma of the child who has to use the bathroom, is to gather all the children together and go inside with all of them for a few minutes. Several children probably need to use the bathroom, anyway. Although this is harmful to the children who are outside because it shortens their gross-motor time and disrupts their play, it is less harmful than the potential dangers of leaving any young child unsupervised.

➤ Before making a decision, gather as much information as you can about a situation. Often a solution is easy once you obtain a key piece of information.

➤ Continue to monitor the results of your decision. Many times situations change or new information is obtained. Few decisions are irreversible. A sign of a person with high ethics is someone who can change her mind, or even a passionately held belief, when faced with new evidence.

➤ Work on developing policies and procedures that will eliminate ethical dilemmas. Being alone with a group of children will put you in dilemmas over and over again. Work with your supervisor on solving the problem. Perhaps an inexpensive intercom can be purchased. (See "Don't Work Alone" on page 171 in "Burned Out/Stressed Out" for more ideas.)

➤ When making an ethical decision, be careful not to impose your own values or biases on others. Carefully consider the family's beliefs and values before making your decision, but do not let their values be the only criteria. (There are cases in every state of families whose beliefs preclude giving medical services to their children yet the state may intervene if the child is in danger.)

➤ Remember that every decision has repercussions. What seems like a good choice now may not ultimately be good for a family. For example, you may decide to help a family out of an immediate crisis, but the long-term result may be that they become dependent on you to bail them out of other crises. In this case, assist the family in finding ways to help themselves.

Resources

Feeney, S. "Ethical Studies for NAEYC Reader Response." *Young Children* 42(4) (May 1987): 24-25.

Feeney, S.; Caldwell, B.M.; and Kipnis, K. "Ethics Case Study: The Aggressive Child." *Young Children* 43(2) (January 1988): 48-51.

Feeney, S.; Katz, L.; and Kipnis, K. "Ethics Case Studies: The Working Mother." *Young Children* 43(1) (November 1987):16-19.

Feeney, S., and Kipnis, K. "Public Policy Report: Professional Ethics in Early Childhood Education." *Young Children* 40(3) (March1985): 54-58.

Feeney, S., and Kipnis, K. "Code of Ethical Conduct and Statement of Commitment." *Young Children* 45(1) (November 1989): 24-29.

Feeney, S.; Riley, S.S.; and Kipnis, K. "Ethics Case Studies: The Divorced Parents." *Young Children* 43(3) (March 1988): 48-51.

Feeney, S., and Sysko, L. "Professional Ethics in Early Childhood Education: Survey Results." *Young Children* 42(1) (November 1986): 15-20.

Katz, L.G., and Ward, E.H. *Ethical Behavior in Early Childhood Education.* Washington, DC: NAEYC, 1978.

Kipnis, K. "How to Discuss Professional Ethics." *Young Children* 42(4) (March 1985): 26-30.

3. Being an Advocate for Families, Children, the Profession, and Yourself

The results of conducting yourself and promoting yourself as a professional will not only benefit the families and children you serve, but ultimately yourself. Without public perception of early childhood teachers as professionals, better salaries and benefits, more respect, better working conditions, and more funds to help parents pay for services may not happen. Professionalism is mostly based on public perception and public perception can be swayed. You, as an individual, can have a great impact on helping families and promoting the cause of quality care and education for young children. Everything you do really does make a difference.

Building a Professional Image

➤ Dress appropriately but well. Wearing a business suit to work with young children makes no sense, but wearing neat, clean, fashionable and comfortable clothes does. Keep a change of clothes and a bottle of stain remover with you. Wear shoes with rubber soles for comfort and for running with children, but do not wear torn, dirty sneakers.

Keep a good pair of shoes on hand for meetings or for parent conferences.

➤ Join professional groups, clubs, political groups, and civic and/or religious organizations. (These should not only include those within the profession but groups such as Kiwanis, American Association of University Women, Junior League, Red

Cross, Lions, National Association of Jewish Women, Democratic or Republican Club, National Organization for Women, and so on.) Note that many of these groups consider issues related to educating and caring for young children an important part of their work. They will benefit from your expertise and you will benefit by being recognized as an active, interested community member.

➤ Educate yourself about current political issues related to the field. Get involved in helping to pass beneficial state and federal legislation. Don't feel that you have to be an expert or a great public speaker or that you have to invest a huge amount of time. There is a great deal of work to do and any help, from stuffing envelopes to gathering signatures on a petition, would be a great contribution.

➤ Know what the opposition is and why it is there. Many people would like to keep early childhood teachers from becoming more professional because they are worried that the cost of care would increase. Work together with parents to fight for more state and federal funds to help them pay for the more expensive care their children deserve and the better salary you deserve.

➤ Know the results of a few key studies that support the work that you do. For example, the Perry Preschool Study showed that for every dollar invested in a good preschool program for children from low-income families, four to six dollars were returned later in reduced costs for juvenile crime, unemployment, welfare, and special education services (Berrueta-Clement 1984). Another study found that good quality child care and preschool benefits children, even when they start attending as young babies (Field et al. 1988). Other studies revealed that giving children choices and helping them learn through play benefits them more than direct teaching methods (Schweinhart et al 1986).

➤ Learn what constitutes good management practices for people who operate or supervise early childhood programs. (This book contains many ideas.) Offer suggestions to your supervisor or work with other staff to lobby for improvements. Be assured that this will make life easier for you, allow you to be a more effective teacher, and provide a higher quality program to children and families.

➤ Refer to yourself as a child development specialist, an educator, a teacher, or a teacher-caregiver. (Unfortunately, teacher has a more professional connotation than caregiver or provider.) Correct anyone who uses terms such as *babysitter*.

➤ Follow a set of principles of what constitutes the best practices in early childhood education. Be able to articulate those principles clearly and explain how you put them into practice. For example:

• "The work of Jean Piaget showed that young children learn and grow best when they are touching and actively interacting with real things and caring people around them. Therefore, I provide many hands-on activities, opportunities to converse, and integrate subject areas."

• "Parents are the primary educators of their children. Therefore, I involve parents as much as possible, make myself available to them, communicate often, ask for their opinions, and act supportively."

➤ Follow a code of ethics as described in the previous chapter.

➤ Learn the jargon used in the field. For good or bad, all professional groups have their own jargon. (See the Glossary of Common Terms and Jargon, pages 187 to 190.)

➤ Continue your own education by working toward a higher degree or credential, taking classes, workshops, reading, and attending conferences. Subscribe to or use library copies of magazines and journals in the field to keep current.

➤ Be helpful to others in the field. Be a mentor to a new teacher, offer to help a co-worker solve a problem, share favorite songs of your children.

➤ Build bridges between yourself and colleagues who work in other types of programs (Montessori, public school, private day care, Head Start, and so on). Focus on all the things you have in common rather than on the few differences between your programs.

Professional Organizations and Agencies

Academy—See National Academy of Early Childhood Programs.

Administration for Children, Youth, and Families (ACYF). PO Box 1182, Washington, DC 20013. (202-245-0572). The federal agency that administers Head Start and other federal programs.

Association for the Care of Children's Health (ACCH). 3615 Wisconsin Avenue NW, Washington, DC 20016. (202-244-1801). Seeks to humanize health care for children and families.

Association for Childhood Education International (ACEI). 1141 Georgia Ave, Suite 200, Wheaton, MD 20902.

Association for Supervision and Curriculum Development (ASCD). 125 North West Street, Alexandria, VA 22314-2798.

Black Child Development Institute—See National Black Child Development Institute.

Center Accreditation Program (CAP)—See National Academy of Early Childhood Programs.

Child Care Action Campaign. 99 Hudson Street, Suite 1233, New York, NY 10013. (212-334-9595). Educates and lobbies for better and more affordable child care.

Child Care Employee Project. PO Box 5603, Berkeley, CA 94705. (415-653-9889). Main organization advocating for the rights and needs of child care workers.

Child Care Law Center. 625 Market Street, San Francisco, CA 94105. (415-495-5498). Advice and assistance on legal matters related to child care.

Child Development Associate (CDA)—See Council for Early Childhood Professional Recognition.

Child Welfare League of America (CWLA). 440 First Street NW, Washington, DC 20001-2085. (202-638-2952). Educates and lobbies for the rights and needs of children.

Children's Defense Fund (CDF). 122 C Street NW, Washington DC 20001. (202-628-8787). The organization that leads national efforts for increasing government support for children and families.

Council for Early Childhood Professional Recognition. 1718 Connecticut Avenue NW, Washington DC 20009. (1-800-424-4310 or 202-265-9090). Administers the Child Development Associate credential (CDA), a national certificate certifying basic competence in working with young children.

Council for Exceptional Children (CEC). Division for Early Childhood (DEC), 1920 Association Drive, Reston, VA 22091.

Council on Interracial Books for Children (CIBC). 1841 Broadway, Room 500, New York, NY 10023. (212-757-5339). Promotes children's books and other learning materials that are free of bias.

ERIC/EECE (Educational Resources Information Center/Elementary and Early Childhood Education. University of Illinois at Urbana-Champaign, 805 West Pennsylvania Avenue, Urbana, IL 61801. (217-333-1386).

Families and Work Institute. 330 Seventh Avenue, New York, NY 10001. (212-465-2044). Researches and educates about child care issues, particularly as they relate to the role of employers.

High / Scope Educational Research Foundation. 600 North River Street, Ypsilanti, MI 48198-2898. Researches and trains on the effectiveness of early childhood education and on its own curriculum approach.

National Academy of Early Childhood Programs. 1834 Connecticut Avenue NW, Washington, DC 20009. (202-232-8777 or 1-800-424-2460). Administers a national voluntary accreditation system for centers or schools, sometimes referred to as CAP (Center Accreditation Program).

National Association for Campus Child Care. 2114 East Kenwood Boulevard, Milwaukee, WI 53201.

National Association for the Education of Young Children (NAEYC). 1834 Connecticut Avenue NW, Washington, DC 20009-5786. (202-232-8777 or 1-800-424-2460). The lead professional organization and largest single organization in the field. To receive information about political issues and advocacy efforts ask for Barbara Willer.

National Black Child Development Institute (NBCDI). 1463 Rhode Island Avenue, Washington, DC 20005. (202-387-1281). Organization dedicated to improving the quality of life for black children, youth and families.

National Center for Clinical Infant Programs. 733 Fifteenth Street NW, Suite 912, Washington, DC 20005-2112. (202-347-0308).

National Commission on Children. 1111 18th Street NW, Suite 810, Washington, DC 20036. (202-254-3800).

National Head Start Association (NHSA). 1309 King Street, Alexandria, VA 22314. (703-739-0875). For information about political issues and advocacy efforts ask for Don Bolce.

Society for Research in Child Development. 5720 South Woodlawn Avenue, Chicago, IL 60637.

World Organization for Early Childhood Education (OMEP). U.S. National Committee, School of Education, Indiana State University, Terre Haute, IN 47809.

Magazines and Journals

The American Journal of Orthopsychiatry. AOA Publications Office, 49 Sheridan Avenue, Albany, NY 12201-1413.

Building Blocks. 38W567 Brindlewood, Elgin, IL 60123. (1-800-233-2448 or in Illinois 312-742-1031).

Child & Youth Care Quarterly. Human Sciences Press, 233 Spring Street, New York, NY 10013-1578. (212-620-8000).

Child Care Employee News. Child Care Employee Project, PO Box 5603, Berkeley, CA 94705. (415-653-9889.)

Child Care Information Exchange. Exchange, PO Box 2890, Redmond, WA 98073. (206-883-9394).

Child Development. University of Chicago Press, Journal Division, PO 37005, Chicago, IL 60637.

Child Study Journal. Bacon Hall 306, SUNY College at Buffalo, 1300 Elmwood Avenue, Buffalo NY 14222.

Child Welfare. Journal of the Child Welfare League of America, Inc., 440 First Street NW, Washington, DC 20001-2085.

Childhood Education. Journal of the Association for Childhood Education International, 1141 Georgia Avenue, Suite 200, Wheaton, MD 20902.

Children Today. Department of Health and Human Services, Room 348-F, 200 Independence Avenue SW, Washington, DC 2020.

Day Care and Early Education. Human Science Press, 72 Fifth Avenue, New York, NY 10011.

Developmental Psychology. American Psychological Association, 1400 North Uhle Street, Arlington, VA 22201.

Early Childhood Education. Alberta Teacher's Association, 11010 142nd Street, Edmonton, Alberta, Canada TSN 2R1.

Early Childhood News. Peter Li, Inc., 2451 East River Road, Dayton, OH 45439. (513-294-5785).

Early Childhood Research Quarterly. Ablex Publishing, 355 Chestnut Street, Norwood, NJ 07648.

Early Childhood Teacher. Edgell Communications, PO Box 6410, Duluth, MN 55806-9893.

Educational Leadership. Journal of the Association for Supervision and Curriculum Development, 125 North West Street, Alexandria, VA 22314-2798.

ERIC / EECE Newsletter. University of Illinois at Urbana-Champaign, 805 West Pennsylvania Avenue, Urbana, IL 61801. (217-333-1386).

Exchange—See Child Care Information Exchange.

Extensions: Newsletter of the High / Scope Curriculum. High/Scope Press, Department 10, 600 North River Street, Ypsilanti, MI 48198. (313-485-2000).

First Teacher. PO Box 6781, Syracuse, NY 13217-7915.

High / Scope Resource: A Magazine for Educators. High/Scope Press, Department 10, 600 North River Street, Ypsilanti, MI 48198. (313-485-2000).

Human Development. S. Karger Publishers, 79 Fifth Avenue, New York, NY 10003.

Infants and Young Children: An Interdisciplinary Journal of Special Care Practices. Aspen Publications, 7201 McKinney Circle, Fredrick, MD 21701.

Instructor's ECE Teacher. PO Box 6099, Duluth, MN 55806.

Journal of the Division for Early Childhood. Council for Exceptional Children, Division for Early Childhood, 1920 Association Drive, Reston, VA 22091.

Merrill-Palmer Quarterly. Journal of Developmental Psychology, Wayne State University Press, 5959 Woodward, Detroit, MI 48202.

Pre-K Today. Scholastic Inc., 730 Broadway, New York, NY 10003.

Topics in Early Childhood Special Education. Pro-Ed, 5341 Industrial Oaks Boulevard, Austin TX 78735.

Young Children. NAEYC, 1834 Connecticut Avenue NW, Washington, DC 20009-5786. (202-232-8777 or 1-800-424-2460).

Resources

Bergen, J.J. "The Professional Role of the Teacher." *Early Childhood Education.* 22(1) (Winter 1988-1989): 6-8.

Berrueta-Clement, J., et al. *Changed Lives: The Effects of the Perry Preschool Program on Youths through Age 19.* Ypsilanti, MI: High/Scope Press, 1984.

Bredekamp, S., ed. *Developmentally Appropriate Practice in Early Childhood Programs Serving Children From Birth Through Age 8.* Washington, DC: NAEYC, 1987.

Caldwell, B. "Advocacy Is Everybody's Business." *Exchange* 54 (March 1987): 29-32.

Dresden, J., and Myers, B.K. "Early Childhood Professionals: Toward Self-Definition." *Young Children* 44(2) (January 1989): 62-66.

Field, T., et al. "Infant Day Care Facilitates Preschool Social Behavior." *Early Childhood Research Quarterly* 3(4) (December 1988): 341-359.

Forman, G.E., and Kuschner, D.S. *The Child's Construction of Knowledge: Piaget for Teaching Children.* New York: Teachers College Press, 1983.

Goffin, S.G.. "Putting Our Advocacy Efforts into a New Context." *Young Children* 43(3) (March 1988): 52-56.

Greenman, J. "Living in the Real World: 'Is Everybody Singing Our Song? Child Care and Early Education.'" *Exchange* 65 (February 1989): 25-27.

Katz, L.G. "The Professional Early Childhood Teacher." *Young Children* 39(5) (July 1984): 3-10.

Lombardi, J. "Now More Than Ever . . . It is Time to Become an Advocate for Better Child Care." *Young Children* 43(5) (July 1988): 41-43.

"NAEYC Position Statement on Nomenclature, Salaries, Benefits, and the Status of the Early Childhood Profession." *Young Children* 40(1) (Nov. 1984): 52.

National Association of State Boards of Education (NASBE). *Right From the Start: The Report of the NASBE Task Force on Early Childhood Education.* Alexandria, VA: NASBE, 1988.

Peterson, R., and Felton-Collins, V. *The Piaget Handbook for Teachers and Parents: Children in the Age of Discovery, Preschool-3rd Grade.* New York: Teachers College Press, 1986.

Pettygrove, W.; Whitebook, M.; and Weir, M. "Beyond Babysitting: Changing the Treatment and Image of Child Caregivers." *Young Children.* 39(5) (July 1984): 14-21.

Radomsky, M.A.. "Professionalization of Early Child Educators: How Far Have We Progressed?" *Young Children* 41(5) (July 1986): 20-23.

Schweinhart, L.J.; Weikart, D.P.; and Larner, M.B. "Consequences of Three Preschool Curriculum Models through Age 15." *Early Childhood Research Quarterly* 1(1) (March 1986): 15-45.

Spodek, B.; Saracho, O.; and Peters D., eds. *Professionalism and the Early Childhood Practitioner.* New York: Teachers College Press, 1988.

Watts, D.W. "Extraterrestrial Children and Techno-Professional Society: Why 'Learning Through Play' Has Not Caught On." *Early Childhood Education* 21(1) (Winter 1987-1988): 26-31.

Weikart, D.P. "Hard Choices in Early Childhood Care and Education: A View to the Future." *Young Children* 44(3) (March 1989): 25-30.

Zigler, E.F.; Kagan, S.L.; and Klugman, E., eds. *Children, Families, and Government: Perspectives on American Social Policy.* Cambridge, England: Cambridge University Press, 1983.

Glossary of Common Terms and Jargon

ABC — Act for Better Child Care: The Federal child care legislation to help parents pay for care and to increase the quality and availability of care. (This bill has not been signed into law at the time of publication.)

Academy of Early Childhood Programs: See *National Academy of Early Childhood Programs.*

Accommodation: Term used by Jean Piaget to describe how children learn by altering old concepts to include new information. For example, a child alters his idea of "dog" to include small, short-haired creatures after seeing a Chihuahua for the first time. This is the second part of the *adaptation* process. *Assimilation* is the first part.

Active Listening: A variety of techniques to be able to listen well, elicit information from others, and communicate effectively. Includes using "I-messages," restating what the person says, making eye contact, and asking clarifying questions.

ACYF: Administration for Children Youth and Families.

Adaptation: Term used by Jean Piaget to describe how children learn by *assimilating* new information and *accommodating* their previous knowledge to incorporate this new information.

ADD: Attention Deficit Disorder.

ADD-H: Attention Deficit Disorder with Hyperactivity.

Administration for Children, Youth and Families (ACYF): Federal agency that administers Head Start and other federal programs related to children and families.

Affect: The emotional part of a person — values, feelings, interests, motivations.

Affective Development: See *Affect.*

Areas of Development: Includes social, emotional, cognitive, self-help, language, small-motor, and large-motor skills.

Assessment: Testing or evaluating children. Assessments can be formal (psychometric, standardized tests like the Wechsler Intelligence Scale for Children) or informal (checklists of children's development like the Portage Guide Checklist).

Screening tests, developmental assessments, readiness tests, diagnostic tests are all types of assessment used for different purposes.

Assimilation: Term used by Jean Piaget to describe how children learn by taking in new information and sensations. For example, a child sees a Chihuahua and hears an adult say "doggie." This is the first part of the *adaptation* process. *Accommodation* is the second part.

Associative Play: Children playing together but in an unorganized way, without a central purpose.

Attention Deficit Disorder (ADD): The inability of a child to concentrate or pay attention to something so that the child's behavior causes problems in learning or getting along with others. It must happen consistently and in all situations to be labeled ADD.

Behavior Modification: Changing a person's behavior through rewards, punishment, or some system of reinforcement.

Behaviorism: Branch of psychology that ascribes the cause of all human behavior to how other people and the environment reinforce it or do not reinforce it.

CAP: Center Accreditation Project. See *National Academy of Early Childhood Programs.*

CDA: See *Child Development Associate.*

CDF: See *Children's Defense Fund.*

Center Accreditation Project: See *National Academy of Early Childhood Programs.*

Child Development Associate: A national certificate certifying basic competence in working with young children. Administered by The Council for Early Childhood Professional Recognition.

Children's Defense Fund: Organization that educates and lobbies for better lives for children and families.

Classification: Grouping items by like characteristics. For example, sorting all red objects into a box.

Cognition: The process of thinking or coming to an understanding of something.

Cognitive Development: See *Cognition.*

Communicative Competence: The ability to make one's message clearly known to others by any means (words, sign language, writing, and so on).

Conservation: The principle that amounts of things stay the same even when they are moved or reshaped. Most preschool age children cannot conserve. They believe, for example, that after a liquid is poured from a short, wide glass into a tall, thin glass, the latter contains more liquid than the original container did.

Constructive Play: Play in which the child builds or creates something.

Constructivism: Term used by Jean Piaget to describe the process by which children learn. They construct their own knowledge of the world and how it works by interacting with real things and people. For example, a child invents or constructs for himself the idea of "half" by dividing up his playdough in equal amounts to give some to his friend.

Cooperative Play: Children playing together with a common purpose.

Daily Schedule: The order of the routines and activities of the day and how long they last.

DAP: See *Developmentally Appropriate Practice*.

Developmental Delay: Any handicap or disability that results in the child's skills and learning ability maturing more slowly than his peers.

Developmental Milestones: Major points in a child's life by which his growth is measured. Examples include sitting up, crawling, walking, first word, first primary tooth, first primary tooth falling out, and so on.

Developmental Psychology or **Developmental Education**: The branch of psychology or education that ascribes human behavior to the interaction between the growth/maturing process and the environment.

Developmentally Appropriate Practice: Guidelines by which teachers do activities, interact, and create environments that meet the needs of young children according to their age level and their individual strengths, weaknesses and interests. These guidelines are described in the following publication: *Developmentally Appropriate Practice in Early Childhood Programs Serving Children From Birth Through Age 8 Expanded Edition*, edited by S. Brekekamp. Washington, DC: NAEYC, 1987.

Dramatic Play: Situations in which children interact while taking on roles. Some examples are children playing a family on a camping trip, firefighters putting a house fire out, or superheroes fighting "bad guys."

ECE: Early Childhood Education.

Egocentric: Term used by Piaget to describe the inability of young children to see the world through another's eyes, and the belief that events and actions are caused by or directed at them.

Emergent Skills: Abilities that are in the process of developing in children. Emergent literacy refers to a child's early attempts to write and read.

Empathy: The ability to understand and relate to how another person feels or thinks.

Empowerment: To give someone the ability to have control over a situation, themselves, or their lives. Children are empowered when they are given choices and encouraged to make meaningful decisions.

ERIC: Education Resources Information Center.

Expressive Language: The ability to use words or sounds to communicate.

Eye-Hand Coordination: The ability to use the hand and the eye together to complete a task, such as putting a peg in a hole or hammering a nail.

Fine Motor: See *Small Motor*.

Free Choice: The part of the program day when the children choose from a wide variety of activities and materials and make decisions about how to participate and for how long.

Functional Play: Repetitive, practice play in which the child performs the same action over and over.

Goals: Statements of what adults hope to help children gain, accomplish or achieve. For a very shy, withdrawn child, an example of a long term goal (one year or more) would be the following: "The child will play cooperatively with other children." An example of a short term goal (a few months or less) would be: "The child will engage in associative play with one other child." The length of a goal depends on a child's ability level. Goal statements are typically followed by objectives.

Gross Motor: See *Large Motor*.

Guidance: Helping children to develop self-control.

Head Start: Largest preschool program in the United States. Funded by the federal government to serve low-income and needy children and families. The type of program (half-day or full-day, three days per week or five days per week) varies according to the need in each community. It is characterized by its comprehensive services, which include medical care, nutrition, and social services, and by its emphasis on parent control and involvement.

Hot-Housing: Pushing children to grow and learn faster than is appropriate for their ages or abilities.

Hyperactive: Behavior characterized by a very high activity level and the inability to remain still for even a short period of time. This behavior occurs consistently over time and in all situations.

"I-Messages": Communicating by starting a sentence with "I…" This tells how the speaker is feeling or thinking, as opposed to beginning with "You…," which tends to interrogate, accuse, or blame.

IEP: See *Individualized Educational Plan*.

IFSP: See *Individualized Family Services Plan*.

Individualized Educational Plan: Required by law for all children receiving special services, this plan details the child's current abilities, sets educational goals and objectives, lists the services the child will receive, and tells where the child will spend his time. A team of people including the teacher, specialists, and the parents develop the plan. Parents must approve and sign the plan before it can be implemented. It must be reviewed and updated periodically.

Individualized Family Services Plan: Required by PL 99-457 for children from birth to age three with special needs, this plan is similar to an individualized educational plan, but it includes supporting the needs of the family to aid the child.

Individualizing: Meeting the needs of each child by altering activities, interactions, the schedule, and the environment to optimize each child's learning and well-being.

Integration: Serving typical and disabled children in the same classroom and ensuring the full participation of children with handicaps in all activities.

Kinesthetic: Sensation or learning achieved through touching, feeling, or moving any part of the body. Petting real animals, feeling three-dimensional figures of animals, or moving the way various animals move are kinesthetic ways to become familiar with animals.

Lanham Act: Federal funding of child care during World War II. Produced widespread, quality, affordable or free child care but ended when the war ended in 1945.

Large Motor: Skills related to using the head, arms, legs, and feet. Running and climbing are large-motor skills. Also called *Gross Motor*.

Literacy: Skills related to reading and writing.

Mainstreaming: Process of integrating children with disabilities into classrooms that mostly contain typical children, either part or full time.

Manipulatives: Toys or activities that involve using the hand and the eye to work them. Legos™ and Tinkertoys™ are manipulatives.

Modalities: Various senses by which children learn. These include visual, auditory, tactile, olfactory (smell), and taste. Most children learn best by using several modalities.

Modeling: Demonstrating a behavior or action by showing how it is done. Adults who use polite words model good manners for children.

Mondale-Brademus Bill: A 2.5 billion dollar comprehensive child care legislation that was approved by congress but vetoed by President Nixon in 1972.

NAEYC: See *National Association for the Education of Young Children*.

National Academy of Early Childhood Programs: The agency that administers a voluntary certification of centers and schools for young children called the Center Accreditation Project (CAP). Also called "The Academy."

National Association for the Education of Young Children: The major professional membership organization for teachers and professionals who work with young children.

Object Constancy: The principle that objects stay the same even when they are moved, turned, or felt rather than seen.

Object Permanence: The principle that objects still exist even when hidden from view.

Objectives: Statements of what children will do to meet a goal. Usually they are specific, measurable, observable, and follow a sequence. Objectives for the goal "The child will engage in associative play with another child" are the following: 1) the child will play near another child for ten minutes each day; 2) the child will play with the same materials and near another child for ten minutes each day; and 3) the child will play with the same materials and with another child for five minutes each day. Objectives are typically followed by teaching strategies for implementing the objectives.

Parallel Play: Children playing alongside each other, usually with the same materials, but playing independently.

Perceptual Motor: The ability to move the body in tune with what the eye sees, and the ability to know the position of the body without visual cues. Walking through a room without bumping into furniture is an example.

Piaget, Jean: Swiss developmental psychologist who developed the constructivist theory of how intelligence develops in children. Most of his research was done by observing his own children.

PL 94-142: Federal legislation enacted in 1975 that mandates states to provide free and appropriate services to handicapped children from ages five to twenty-one in classrooms that are least restrictive. "PL" means "public law." The numbers indicate that this was the 142nd law passed by the Ninety-fourth Congress.

PL 99-457: Federal legislation enacted in 1986 that extends the provisions of PL 94-142 to children from age three. It also provides funding for states to plan and implement services for children from birth through age two.

Preoperational: Term used by Piaget to describe the ages from about two-and-one-half to eight. Children in this stage think concretely, are egocentric, and learn by actively interacting with real things.

Pro-Social Behavior or **Skills**: The ability to interact with others in positive, pleasing ways; the ability to make and maintain friendships.

Punishment: A negative consequence for a negative behavior, such as sitting in a time-out chair for hitting another child.

Receptive Language: The ability to understand what is said by another person.

Red-Shirting: Starting a child in school at an older age than he is eligible to start at, so that he will experience academic success.

Reinforcement: Providing verbal or tangible rewards or punishment to change behavior.

Representational Play: See *Symbolic Play*.

Screening: Determining (usually with a test) a child's general areas of strength an weakness. Typically a child who is weak in one or more areas of development is referred for further testing.

Self-Concept: The sense of who one is and how a person sees himself. This includes a person's view of his own roles (sibling, son, friend), abilities, interests, values, beliefs, and more. Children with good self-concepts have a realistic sense of their own strengths and weaknesses. They feel comfortable with who they are and with what they like and dislike.

Self-Esteem: The feelings of one's worthiness. It is one part of self-concept. Children with good self-esteem generally feel competent, worthwhile, able, confident, and positive about themselves.

Self-Help Skills: The ability to take care of one's own basic needs such as toileting, dressing, washing, and eating.

Sensorimotor Stage: Term used by Piaget to describe the first stage of life. It is characterized by learning through all the senses without language. For example, infants typically put things in their mouths to learn through taste what the object is.

Seriation: Ordering items based on their size, weight, thickness, quantity, or similar quality.

Small Motor: The ability to use the hands and fingers, and to manipulate objects. Stringing beads is a small-motor task.

Spatial Relations: The sense of how things relate to each other in terms of their position in space. For example: on, below, above, behind, to the left, and so on.

Social Skills: The ability or lack of ability to interact and form and maintain relationships with others.

Symbolic Play: Play in which the child substitutes pretend items for the real thing, such as using a block to represent a glass of milk.

Temporal Relations: The sense of how things relate in time, such as knowing that a past event happened yesterday, last week, last month, or last year.

Tactile: The sense of touch.

Transitioning: Helping a child make a positive move from preschool to kindergarten or from any grade to the next.

Verbal Skills: The ability to speak and to be understood.

Other Redleaf Press Publications

Basic Guide to Family Day Care Record Keeping — Clear instructions on keeping necessary family day care business records.

Business Receipt Book — Receipts specifically for family child care payments improve your record keeping; 50 sets per book.

Busy Fingers, Growing Minds — Over 200 original and traditional finger plays, with enriching activities for all parts of a curriculum.

Calendar-Keeper — Activities, family day care record keeping, recipes and more. Updated annually. Most popular publication in the field.

Calendario-Archivo — The *Calendar-Keeper* is now in Spanish!

Child Care Resource & Referral Counselors & Trainers Manual — Both a ready reference for the busy phone counselor and a training guide for resource and referral agencies.

Developing Roots & Wings: A Trainer's Guide to Affirming Culture In Early Childhood Programs — The training guide for Roots & Wings, with 11 complete sessions and over 170 training activities.

The Dynamic Infant — Combines an overview of child development with innovative movement and sensory experiences for infants and toddlers.

Family Day Care Tax Workbook — Updated every year, latest step-by-step information on forms, depreciation, etc.

Heart to Heart Caregiving: A Sourcebook of Family Day Care Activities, Projects and Practical Provider Support — Excellent ideas and guidance written by an experienced provider.

Kids Encyclopedia of Things to Make and Do — Nearly 2,000 art and craft projects for children aged 4-10.

The (No Leftovers!) Child Care Cookbook — Over 80 child-tested recipes and 20 menus suitable for family child care providers and center programs. CACFP creditable.

Open the Door, Let's Explore — Full of fun, inexpensive neighborhood walks and field trips designed to help young children.

Pathways to Play — Help children improve their play skills with a skill checklist and planned activities.

Roots & Wings: Affirming Culture in Early Childhood Programs — A new approach to multicultural education that helps shape positive atttitudes toward cultural differences.

Sharing in the Caring — Packets with family day care parent brochure, contracts and hints.

Snail Trails and Tadpole Tails — A fun nature curriculum with five easy-to-do, hands on units that explore the lifecycle of these intriguing creatures: snails, worms, frogs, praying mantises and worms.

Staff Orientation in Early Childhood Programs — Complete manual for orienting new staff on all program areas.

Teachables From Trashables — Step-by-step guide to making over 50 fun toys from recycled household junk.

Teachables II — Similar to *Teachables From Trashables*; with another 75-plus toys.

Those Mean Nasty Dirty Downright Disgusting but... Invisible Germs — A delightful story that reinforces for children the benefits of frequent hand washing.

Trusting Toddlers: Planning for Two- to Three-Year-Olds in Child Care Centers — Exerienced professionals address issues and problems unique to toddler caregiving.

CALL FOR CATALOG OR ORDERING INFORMATION 1-800-423-8309